A
SLENDER
THREAD

D1089204

A SLENDER THREAD

A Novel of World War II

JOHN RHODES

ROUNDEL
HOUSE

While this is a work of fiction, I have described certain historical characters and given them imaginary dialogue. I hope I have done so respectfully. I have also used real locations when applicable. All other people, places, and names are fictitious, and any similarities to real people, places, and names are coincidental and unintended.

Copyright © 2022 John Rhodes
All rights reserved.

No part of this book may be reproduced, or stored in a retrieval system, or transmitted in any form or by any means, electronic, mechanical, photocopying, recording, or otherwise, without express written permission of the publisher.

Published by Roundel House, Wilmington, North Carolina
johnrhodesbooks.com

Edited and designed by Girl Friday Productions
www.girlfridayproductions.com

Cover design: Anna Curtis
Project management: Sara Spees Addicott
Editorial: Bethany Davis
Image credits: cover © Shutterstock/Hawkeye68, Shutterstock/Laborant, Shutterstock/Verina Marina Valerevna, Shutterstock/Hudyma Natallia, Shutterstock/Everett

ISBN (paperback): 978-1-7353736-2-1
ISBN (e-book): 978-1-7353736-3-8
ISBN (audiobook): 978-1-7353736-4-5
Library of Congress Control Number: 2021925402

With thanks to Chris, Les, Perry, and Bunnie
and
in memory of the brave people of Malta

*"What **a slender thread** the greatest of things can hang by."*
—Winston Churchill, 1940

Letter from King George VI to the Governor of Malta, and the Governor's reply:

The Governor
Malta

To honour her brave people I award the George Cross to the Island Fortress of Malta to bear witness to a heroism and devotion that will long be famous in history.
George R.I.
April 15th 1942

By God's help Malta will not weaken but will endure until victory is won.
Lieutenant-General Sir William Dobbie

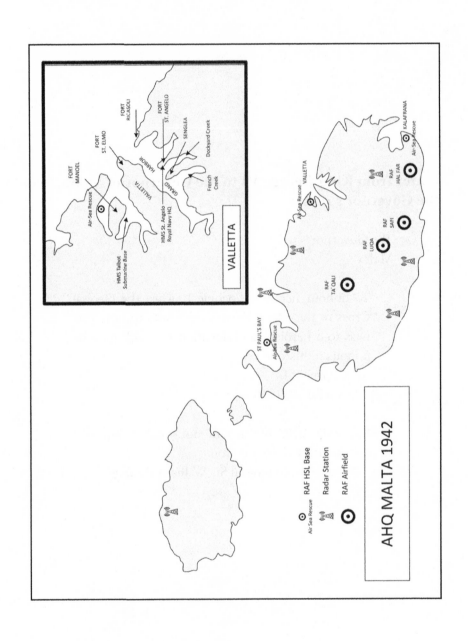

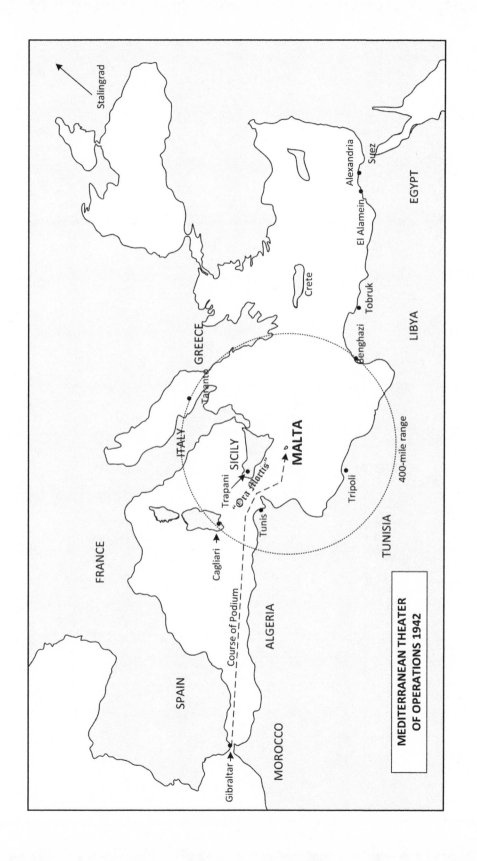

MEDITERRANEAN THEATER
OF OPERATIONS 1942

PART ONE

Counterpunch

ONE

Eleanor Shaux woke an hour before dawn. She stretched and kicked off the covers. Johnnie grunted without waking. He always slept on his back, with his arms and legs wide apart, like Leonardo da Vinci's famous sketch of a man drawn in a circle. Pity, she thought: they had to be at Luqa by 0530 at the latest.

The bathroom plumbing produced a trickle of rusty water. The water company's pump house must have been bombed again, or maybe it was yet another broken water main beneath a broken street. It was always something: Malta had been bombed every single day for the past six weeks—in fact, almost every day for the past two years—and now, in the middle of 1942, reliable running water and electric lighting were dim memories from the peacetime past. She wondered how long it would take for her teeth to turn brown, although, on the bright side, she'd heard iron was good for the blood.

Johnnie appeared. She saw he had his preoperational face, his thoughts turned inward as he prepared himself for the day ahead. He was, she knew, stiffening his sinews, summoning up his blood, and disguising his fair nature, as Shakespeare said, for the fight to come.

They dressed quickly, saying nothing, for there was nothing to say. In these straitened times, official Royal Air Force dress codes had been all but abandoned. The naval convoys struggling to reach Malta through repeated bombing and torpedo attacks had no room for non-essentials like regulation uniforms. Everyone wore an assortment of denim garments in various shades of khaki—the RAF and the navy as well as the army. Women, thank God, were actually allowed to wear trousers. And, miracle of miracles, women were even allowed to wear forage caps, which allowed them to look like women instead of like women pretending to be men.

There was time for one fierce embrace, a sort of urgent unspoken prayer for mutual survival, and then they clattered down the stairs of the married officers' quarters and into the first faint glimmerings of the Mediterranean predawn.

Charlie, their big black Bouvier des Flandres, led the way, erupting down the stairs and bounding into the back seat of their tiny RAF Austin 7 PD car. Keith Park, their boss, swore that the dog was larger than the car, but somehow Charlie managed to squeeze into the narrow space behind the seats. Only his lolling pink tongue and his white silk scarf were visible in the darkness, a canine version of the Cheshire cat's grin.

Eleanor clambered into the driver's seat, and Johnnie cranked the starter handle. The engine started with an explosive backfire followed by a staccato racket that belied its diminutive size and woke everyone within a hundred yards. Johnnie jumped in, and Eleanor, crashing the gears with abandon, propelled them forward like a race car; it was amazing what high-octane aero fuel could do in a 700cc motorcar engine. The headlights, inadequate at the best of times, were half covered in black tape to dim their beams as a precaution against stray bombers, and Eleanor could scarcely see the narrow streets of Valletta, Malta's capital. Thank God the crowded buildings on either side were whitewashed. Piles of fallen masonry from bombed-out buildings overflowed into the streets, and she drove like a slalom skier coming down a steep hillside. The car had no rearview mirror, but they could rely on Charlie to keep watch.

Eleanor had a sudden memory of her father, a wounded survivor of the First World War, dominated and diminished by her mother. He had taught her to drive. She remembered him becoming animated and excited as she wove and lurched her way down a steep English country lane, slipping and sliding through drifts of autumn leaves, pulling and pushing at the gear stick as she tried vainly to engage a gear. Her mother had complained that the car, a Humber, was "far too big for a girl to handle," and the whole project was immodest besides: young ladies could not drive and keep their knees together at the same time.

"Lean on it, Ellie. You'll find a gear!" her father had burst out, his reedy voice rising above the harsh grinding of the gearbox. "They're all in there somewhere!"

Finally she had managed to get the car in gear—the wrong one, but who cared?—and they had both crowed in triumph. She had never seen him so exuberant.

Eleanor reached the guardhouse at the main entrance to RAF Luqa, the island of Malta's principal airfield. It was a large field pockmarked by dozens, if not hundreds, of bomb craters. The guards recognized the car as it approached—no other Austin 7 in the entire world sounded quite like it—and raised the barrier. Eleanor swept through and jerked to a halt at the ruins of the main station building.

They parted silently, with her giving just the slightest touch on his arm that said everything. Eleanor descended the dank stairs leading down to the bomb shelters, while Johnnie climbed in behind the wheel and set off for the dispersal area on the far side of the field.

The sky was growing brighter in the east, and he could just make out a random scattering of little hummocks of aircraft hiding beneath camouflage netting. The smaller humps were Spitfire Mark IXs.[1] The bigger humps, farther off and still almost invisible in the scrub, were Bristol Beauforts, twin-engine torpedo bombers. The army was building blast-proof limestone revetments over at Ta' Qali to protect the aircraft there, but they hadn't reached Luqa yet.

The largest hummock—well, a full-fledged hillock—was the dispersal hut. He stopped in front of it. Charlie burst forth from behind the seats and galloped off in search of enemy weasels and other agents of the Axis powers. The ground crew pulled camouflage netting over the car. A young airman silently handed Shaux a mug of hot tea glutinous with sugar. He sat down in an armchair with broken springs facing due east, awaiting the dawn, and lit a cigarette. He had stopped smoking, he recalled, except when he hadn't.

---

1. Spitfire versions were denoted by "Marks," and each successive Mark was given a number in the form of a Roman numeral. Thus, "Mark V" means "Mark 5," "Mark IX" means "Mark 9," etc.

* * *

Eleanor sat down at the tiny desk jammed into a corner of the operations bunker and made a futile attempt to wipe her desktop. Every time Luqa was bombed—which was pretty much every day, sometimes twice a day—vibrations from the explosions shook the bunker like shock waves from an earthquake, and dust and debris drifted down from the ceiling. Everything gradually turned brownish-gray and acquired a gritty texture—including, infuriatingly, her hair.

An orderly appeared with a mug of tea and an armful of papers and files.

"Good morning, ma'am," she said. "Here are this morning's dispatches. Oh, and Air-Vice Marshal Park would like you to join him as soon as possible."

Eleanor took the mug and set off for Park's office, zigzagging her way through a serpentine series of tunnels that were like the catacombs of ancient Rome. There were deep shadows everywhere, punctuated at intervals by the harsh light of unshaded lightbulbs. Rooms and offices appeared at random, and other passageways led away into the gloom. The whole layout was haphazard, carved out of the dirt and rock as occasion demanded. It was easy to get lost, and Eleanor sometimes wondered if the mythical Minotaur—half man, half bull—would suddenly spring, snarling, from around some stygian corner.

They were building a fine new bombproof control center under the Barrakka Gardens, near the Lascaris Battery, she had been assured, in some old Roman catacombs, but they said it would not be ready for some months. RAF months, she knew from bitter experience, could be very long months indeed.

Park was one of her favorite men. He was a New Zealander who had fought with great distinction as a fighter pilot in the First World War. At the beginning of this war, two years ago in April 1940, he had been placed in command of 11 Group, Fighter Command, just in time for Hitler to launch his sudden attacks—blitzkriegs—westward into Holland, Belgium, and France. In a rapid succession of disasters, the Dutch, Belgians, and Danes were overwhelmed and surrendered; the defending British and French forces were crushed; the British Expeditionary Force just managed to escape from Dunkirk, brought home in large part by civilian volunteers; and the French army, the largest in the world, collapsed. Then, in an accelerating crescendo of seemingly unstoppable power, the German Luftwaffe air force launched massive bombing attacks on England in what Churchill named the "Battle of Britain."

But, against all odds, the Luftwaffe had been stopped. Park had organized his limited supply of defending Spitfire and Hurricane fighter squadrons and sent them into battle. For five weeks, in August and September 1940, the conflict had raged over southern England. Heavily outnumbered but not outfought, Park's forces had turned back the raiders.

That was when she had first met Park. He had plucked her from tedious clerical duties in the Air Ministry and set her up in 11 Group HQ, where she had developed the zero-sum mathematical model of the battle that would become known as Red Tape.

Park had defeated the Luftwaffe, but his rivals in Fighter Command defeated Park: he was dismissed from the glamour of the victorious 11 Group and sent into obscurity. Now he was back in action, appointed Air Officer Commanding Air Headquarters Malta—AOC AHQ Malta, as the RAF called it—just a few weeks ago. Once again, the enemy forces were overwhelming and the odds against success were long.

As Eleanor reached his open door, she could see Park sitting at his desk, his thin face lit by a bright desk lamp amid the surrounding gloom. He looked up and waved her in with a smile. He had a visitor, she saw, sitting with his back to her, a civilian in a gray worsted suit. He's ridiculously overdressed for this climate, the poor man, she thought as she entered.

"This gentleman claims he knows you, Eleanor," Park said with a smile, gesturing towards his guest. The man turned, and Eleanor saw it was Harry Hopkins, President Roosevelt's personal emissary and perhaps the second most powerful man in America and therefore in the world.

"I'm delighted to see you, sir," she said, meaning every word. She had worked with Hopkins in the months leading up to Pearl Harbor, months in which the United States was not at war but was sympathetic to Britain's resistance to Hitler's Germany.

"As am I," Hopkins said as they shook hands. Eleanor found a place to half sit on a side table piled high with gritty manila folders. Hopkins looked drawn and exhausted, she thought; he kept a grueling schedule and suffered from the debilitating aftereffects of stomach cancer. She had come to understand that he was driven by willpower, the power of a tenacious mind over a wasting body—just as his boss, President Roosevelt, was driven.

What on earth was he doing here in the middle of the Mediterranean?

* * *

Charlie loped back to the dispersal hut. Shaux loved the way he looked—that big shaggy head and that powerfully athletic body, his coat cut close to keep him cool in the Mediterranean summer. Shaux and Eleanor had debated bringing a black dog to a hot climate, but he would have been bereft if they'd left him behind. As a consequence, Charlie's life experiences had been dramatically expanded to include an aircraft carrier across the Med, encounters with gibbering rhesus monkeys in Gibraltar and snarling camels in Egypt, long flights in Catalina flying boats, and now self-organized canine security patrols against the local Maltese weasels. Shaux sometimes wondered if Charlie felt it was beneath his dignity to hunt mere weasels, but they were the largest wild carnivores Malta had to offer, so it was weasels or nothing.

One of the ugly facts about Malta's privation and suffering was that almost all pets and working animals had disappeared, and there were very few dogs left on Malta. Charlie was fed entirely from Shaux and Eleanor's rations—supplemented by voluntary contributions from the ground crews' rations—so he wasn't eating at anyone's expense. In addition to protecting Luqa from weasels, he also worked with Royal Engineers crews searching for people buried beneath the rubble of bombed-out buildings.

There was no need to fear that Charlie might disappear mysteriously. He was very popular, not only for his search-and-rescue work but also because he vaguely resembled a giant version of the so-called Black Maltese dog breed, a cross between a Maltese and a shih tzu.

Just as the Greek gods had descended from the gigantic Titans, so they said, the little Black Maltese had descended from a sort of primordial Titanic Charlie. They called him "Kelby," which, Shaux understood, was a combination of the Maltese word for "dog" and the name "Charlie."

Charlie stopped and stared at Shaux, leaning slightly forward, using all his senses—including the unquestionable canine sixth sense. Apparently satisfied that Shaux was in no imminent danger of a medical crisis, Charlie disappeared inside the hut in search of water and perhaps a modest snack.

Shaux accepted another mug of tea from the young airman as the eastern sky turned violet and gold. Shaux did not believe in God, but he freely acknowledged that two of the best arguments in favor of a divine creation were the colors of the dawn and sunset skies. The Druids, or whoever they had been, had been entirely justified in building Stonehenge, at immense labor and difficulty, just to face east and watch the dawn.

Apart from the minor inconvenience of being shot at by Messerschmitt 109s or Macchi C.202 Folgore—"Thunderbolt"—fighters on most days, and the constant life-threatening bombing, life was very pleasant, almost as if he and Eleanor were on an extended summer holiday. She was rid of the excruciating tensions of being a senior intelligence officer for Churchill in the quicksand of Whitehall and Washington and was back working for Park, a man they both respected deeply. She was his chief of staff—COSAOC as she was known in RAF-ese. He wondered if she missed the corridors of power, but she scoffed at the very idea.

Park had organized his squadrons into wings, with Shaux commanding three fighter squadrons. It was, in truth, something of a sinecure: the squadron commanders were all exceptionally able and needed no supervision. Shaux's position entitled him to shuffle paperwork around a desk; frankly he'd much rather be flying a real Spitfire than a mahogany one.

He and Eleanor were both, he supposed, wounded warriors. She was still recovering from being caught in the Japanese attack on Pearl Harbor last year, in which she had been injured, and he'd had an unpleasant time escaping from captivity in France.

Just like Charlie, Eleanor had cut her hair short. The Women's Auxiliary Air Force—WAAF—hierarchy would have been appalled, had they known, because WAAFs were supposed to sweat miserably beneath long hair tied up into buns. But Eleanor was the most senior WAAF for a thousand miles in any direction, and rank, as they said, had its privileges. Shaux delighted in her new look, a sort of waif-like street urchin cut, a *gamin*, as the French would say, or, rather, *une gamine*, if there was such a term.

Shaux himself, after a brief and unhappy interlude flying Westland Whirlwind fighters over France last year, desperately trying to avoid Luftwaffe Focke-Wulf 190s, and a short spell as a guest of the Luftwaffe followed by a similarly short spell skulking about in the shadows as an escaped prisoner of war, was now reunited with his beloved Spitfires.

Well, he had loved Spitfires in the Battle of Britain, but now, it was fair to say, he respected them. For just as the most civilized of men are coarsened and brutalized by war, so, too, are their weapons. The elegant early Spitfire Marks I and II with which Shaux had fallen in love during the Battle of Britain—works of art as much as weapons of war—had given way to the much more powerful but more prosaic Mark V, a machine designed not just to soar like an eagle but to fight like a bulldog. But German engineers and designers were as skillful as their British counterparts and had created the fearsome Fw 190, a ruthlessly efficient killing machine that chewed up Mark Vs and Hawker Hurricanes and spat them out.

In response, shocked that their iconic Spitfires had been outmatched, the British had leapfrogged over the carefully planned evolution of the Spitfire through Marks VI, VII, and VIII and thrown together the Mark IX, a Mark V airframe with a new, very powerful, Merlin 61 engine.

The Mark IX still looked like a Spitfire, Shaux thought, as he idly watched the ground crew working on the nearest—still with the long, sleek nose and the elegant elliptical wings, but it was an industrialized, hybrid sort of Spitfire, with bulked-up muscles and calloused hands, built for the express purpose of outperforming and outshooting 190s.

The key to the Mark IX's performance was its 1,300-horsepower Packard V-1650-7 Merlin, built under license from Rolls-Royce by Packard factory women in Detroit in America, a 27-liter V-12 engine with a two-stage two-speed supercharger—a supercharged supercharger—giving the Spitfire superior performance all the way up to thirty thousand feet. The Mark IX could outclimb and outturn any Axis fighter.

But that superior performance came at a cost, and, in Shaux's eyes, that cost was a series of lumps and bumps.

On one side of the Spitfire's nose, for example, below the exhaust manifolds, was a hump that accommodated a Coffman engine starter. Shaux preferred the Coffman over an electric starter, because it was lighter and faster. It was very satisfying to fire the cartridge and get the Merlin to spin immediately, rather than slowly cranking with an electrical starter, but he still regretted the hump. There was also a bulge beneath the cockpit for an additional fuel tank that created an absurd amount of drag, slowing the aircraft down and making it feel spongy. Even the elegant wings had bumps—blisters, they were called—to accommodate an odd but vicious armament of belt-fed 20-millimeter Hispano cannons and big 50-millimeter Browning machine guns.

Shaux stood and stretched and searched the skies. No aircraft. He ambled off towards the southern end of the airfield, with Charlie for company. If there was a sudden air raid, they could always shelter in one of the hundreds of bomb craters. The problem with putting an airfield on a small island, he thought, is that airfields require a large amount of flat space, and there wasn't much space—let alone flat space—on Malta.

Therefore, in addition to Luqa as the main field, there were three smaller fields, one after the other, connected by bumpy taxiways built by the army. His favorite was Hal Far, on the southern tip of Malta, which was also used by the Royal Navy's Fleet Air Arm—FAA—who called it "HMS Falcon." The station offices and buildings overlooked the Med. He was in the process of hatching a scheme whereby one of the buildings, just above a tiny beach, facing south, a little apart from the others, should be converted to RAF married officers' quarters; by coincidence they were the only married RAF officers on the island and would therefore have the place, and the beach, entirely to themselves. The building lay outside the airfield's security perimeter, but they had Charlie for protection, and he would more than suffice, come marauding weasel, come invading German *Fallschirmjäger* paratrooper.

TWO

An antique steam launch with a hemispherical brass-bound boiler ferried six motor torpedo boat crews from the destroyer HMS *Lovell* across the oily wavelets of Valletta's Grand Harbour to the navy dockyard. There they were met by a regulating petty officer who told them to hurry up and wait and then disappeared into the nearest building. The men piled their kit bags into untidy heaps and retreated to whatever shade they could find where they waited, sleeping or chatting or smoking or playing cards.

The RPO reported the arrival of the MTB crews to the dockyard deputy superintendent (Shore Establishment), Paymaster-Commander Archibald Thompson, and then retreated rapidly before Thompson could involve him further.

Thompson was an elderly man who'd had an undistinguished career in the navy before retiring in 1935. He had been brought out of retirement and sent to Malta to fulfill various administrative functions, but he lacked the energy and intelligence to deal with the complexities of the modern service and the exigencies of coping with a state of siege.

Thompson had an autocratic air, enhanced by his habit of staring down his nose at his subordinates and barking orders rather than giving them. His habitual state of mind, a slight befuddlement combined with a strong sense of irritation, was caused primarily by his character but augmented, to some extent, by gin—one of the few remaining substances still readily available on the war-torn island.

He had served in Dreadnought-class battleships in the first war and had been present at the Battle of Jutland, the titanic encounter between the Royal Navy and the kaiser's Imperial German Navy in 1916. That, as far as he was concerned, was the pinnacle of both the long, storied history of the navy and of his own career. The rest of his life, like his marriage, had been a downhill slope filled with disappointments and frustrations. Since his retirement he had lived with his wife and mother-in-law in a bungalow that backed onto a golf course he could not afford.

He stared at the roster and formed the intention of distributing the MTB crews out to the destroyer flotilla on a piecemeal, as-needed basis. The crews comprised mostly unskilled hostilities-only volunteers and conscripts scraped from the grimy streets of industrial towns—simply bodies to fill in vacancies for menial duties. Rather than dealing directly with the fate of the crews, however, which would have required thought, decisions, and an outlay of energy, Thompson did what he usually did. He delegated the task to the nearest available underling, in this case Women's Royal Naval Service—Wrens—Third Officer Dryden.

Penelope Dryden stood at attention before Thompson while he shuffled papers on his untidy desk. The room was already oppressively hot despite the early hour. The office faced east, and through the open window Penelope could see the dazzling waters of Dockyard Creek, with the Grand Harbour beyond. There was no breeze, and the ceiling fan shuddered but did not turn.

"Look, Miss . . . er, Miss . . . ," Thompson began.

"Dryden, sir."

"Er, quite so. It seems the carrier *Nonsuch* had six MTB crews on board, but the boats themselves and their officers all went down in *Tattersall Castle* during EF-4. No survivors. Well, the crews in *Nonsuch* survived, obviously, otherwise they wouldn't be here: different ship entirely." He frowned impatiently as if the confusion were hers. "They were transferred from *Nonsuch* to *Lovell*, and *Lovell* arrived from Alexandria last night. Be that as it may, the crews need to be remustered as necessary." He paused and stared up at her. "Is that quite clear?"

"Yes, sir," she said, because from experience she knew that saying no would create a longer answer leading to even less clarity. EF-4—Eastbound Fast convoy number four from Gibraltar, one of the relief convoys carrying vital supplies—had been badly mauled as it attempted to reach Malta a month ago; *Tattersall Castle*, she recalled, had been a big freighter that had been bombed and sank with all hands. Why Alexandria, at the other end of the Mediterranean? She'd ask someone else for the details later.

"We'll distribute them out to the Force K destroyers as needed. I want it done immediately, today."

"Force K is in Gibraltar, sir."

"I know that, damn it! When they return, of course. In the meantime, they'll have to be mustered as supernumerary—the men, not the destroyers. There's about seventy of them, I think—men, that is to say."

He shuffled more papers, as if to imply that lists of ships' musters and vacancies, and of the MTB crews, lay among them. His hands left damp marks on the paperwork.

There were several barges and lighters around the harbor armed with a haphazard variety of antiaircraft guns—whatever the navy could scrape together to repel the endless air raids. Penelope was the supply and mustering officer for fleet auxiliaries, as these were known. These antiaircraft "ack-ack" auxiliaries were at the very bottom of the navy's pecking order, far below glamorous fighting ships like destroyers, below even ferries and tugs, and supplying and manning auxiliaries was therefore very much a task of scavenging for leftovers. But Penelope knew every single marine tradesman on Malta—they had been her father's suppliers—and she had strong influence over the junior officer in the dockyard superintendent's office who assigned ratings to their duties, and between the two sources she managed to keep the auxiliaries stocked, supplied, and manned.

"The ack-ack lighter crews are shorthanded, sir. They could—"

"Oh no, I doubt it! I doubt it very much!"

It was typical of Thompson to have a strong opinion about something of which he knew nothing.

"Be that as it may, I haven't time for quartermastering." He gestured at his desk in justification. "I'll order the crews to report to you until further notice. Billeting, messing, and so forth. And for God's sake keep 'em occupied and out of trouble. The superintendent won't put up with any of that."

He seemed to find the piece of paper for which he had been looking and peered at it.

"The senior rating is a temporary acting petty officer named Baker . . ." He paused and stared at another paper. "Well, perhaps not." He glanced up at her. "In any event, any questions, Miss, er . . . ?"

"No, sir." Questions would be futile.

"Then, Miss . . . er, that will be all."

"Aye-aye, sir." What else could she say?

* * *

"Mr. Hopkins is making a tour of the MTO to assess the situation for the president," Park said, answering Eleanor's unspoken question. "For obvious reasons, he isn't here at all."

Eleanor nodded. Hopkins's travels were almost always highly secret. The United States must be planning something for the Mediterranean theater of operations, she thought. She prayed it would involve sending lots of supplies to Malta, and not some silly invasion of Morocco, as they had been considering last year.

"He's been gracious enough to ask me my opinion of the air war," Park added. She knew Park well enough to know that he had formed an immediate respect for Hopkins.

"Air-Vice Marshal Park has been very helpful," Hopkins said, and she saw the respect was mutual. "I'd welcome your thoughts as well. How would you assess the situation, Eleanor?" Hopkins always came straight to the point. It was one of several characteristics she admired in him.

"Grim," she said, and, as if on cue, the muffled sound of air raid warning sirens began to moan above their heads. "However, I think there's a good chance we won't lose."

One of Eleanor's strategic insights, one characteristic that had made Red Tape so powerful in predicting the course of the war, was that she proposed that the first military priority, the most important objective, should be not to lose, rather than to win.

Hopkins and Park both smiled. Everyone else talked about winning; she alone talked about not losing. Most senior military and government people condescended that this was a difference without a distinction—but she had developed an inference engine to distinguish precisely between the two, a stochastic mathematical model expressed in a unique subset of calculus to measure the probabilities involved—and she had an extraordinary record of being right.

"I've only been here in the Med for a few months, sir, first in Egypt with the AOC and now here in Malta, and I'm no longer in the strategic intelligence loop, but . . ."

"Please continue," Hopkins said. He was one of the very few men, along with Park, who did not judge her as a precocious young woman, a sort of child prodigy, in a man's world. Her critics seemed to feel it was improper, somehow indecent, for a girl to have mastered military strategy, which was man's work. Her success had muted their muttering but not their disapproval; they still believed the proper place to meet her should be in a hotel cocktail lounge rather than at the conference table in a strategic planning meeting.

"Well, sir, the Med is the gateway to Africa, to the Middle East, and, via the Suez Canal, to India and Asia."

Park had a map on the wall behind his desk, and she stood and pointed at it.

"In practical terms, the enemy either directly controls or dominates almost all the coastal countries around the Mediterranean. Just look at the map: in the western Med, Vichy France and its African territories and Spain are theoretically neutral but pro-Axis in practice. The central Med is controlled by Italy and Italian Libya. Then, to the east, Germany and Italy have overrun Greece and occupied Crete. The Med is now more or less an Axis lake."

She shook her head.

"We British are hanging on, just hanging on, to part of one country in one corner at the far end—Egypt. And we still have two little islands: Gibraltar and Malta. That's all we have: Gib at the western end and Egypt at the other, twenty-three hundred miles apart. And one tiny island sitting slap dab in the middle, at the crossroads—Malta."

She shrugged.

"If we lose Malta, we lose the Med. If we lose the Med, we lose the Suez Canal and our access to the Red Sea and the Indian Ocean. If we lose that, we lose the war."

Hopkins grunted.

"Generalleutnant Erwin Rommel is leading the Afrika Korps and the Italian Tenth Army eastward to the gates of Alexandria in Egypt," she continued. "He is the best tactician in the German army, and possibly the best battlefield general in the world—it's between him and General Zhukov, in my opinion; Rommel made mincemeat of the French army during the Battle of France. He moved so fast that even his own High Command didn't know where he was."

Again she shook her head, this time in reluctant admiration for the man they had started calling the Desert Fox, a man who always seemed to be able to anticipate and outmaneuver his enemy's next moves.

"Now the British Eighth Army in Egypt is hanging on by its fingernails; Rommel is halfway across Egypt and pushing General Auchinleck backwards like a schoolyard bully."

For a moment it was almost as if she had her old job back, analyzing geopolitical strategy at the highest levels. Almost—until she remembered how much she had hated it.

"Everything depends on whether the German Afrika Korps or the British Eighth Army is better supplied, because the better-supplied army will win. They both need tanks and aircraft and ammunition, of course, but they also need food, fuel, fresh water, spare parts, everything. They're fighting in the desert under very harsh conditions."

She reached into her pocket automatically to light a cigarette until she remembered that she had given up smoking.

"We are depending on British supply convoys from Gibraltar getting all the way across the length of the Mediterranean to Egypt via Malta, over two thousand miles. The only other route is all round the Cape of Good Hope, all round the whole of Africa, which is far safer but very, very long.

"Geography is on Rommel's side. He is dependent on Axis convoys coming down the much shorter north-to-south route from Italy and Sicily, passing us in Malta, and on to Libya. He's just pushed us out of

Tobruk, as you know, giving him another Libyan port for supply. The balance is in his favor."

She sketched the convoy routes on the map with her fingers and then stabbed at the point at which they crossed.

"And here, exactly at the center of both supply routes, east-west and north-south, Allied and Axis, just where they cross—in the eye of the storm, as it were—here is Malta. If Malta falls, the Eighth Army will lose, and Africa and Arabia will lie at Rommel's feet."

Hopkins was staring at the map, lost in thought. Now she really did feel she had her old job back. A packet of cigarettes lay open on Park's desk. Just one, she thought, reaching forward.

"There are currently two places in the entire world that will determine who wins and who loses this war," she continued. She wondered if she sounded a bit too histrionic, but Hopkins knew her well enough to make his own judgment of that. "One is in southern Russia, as the Germans approach Stalingrad. If Hitler can win there, all Russia will be his, all the way to Vladivostok, and he will have a gateway to the Pacific."

Hopkins remained silent, eyes on the map. Eleanor pointed to Malta again.

"The other place is here, this little island of Malta. Whoever holds Malta will hold the Mediterranean, the Middle East, and Africa. We, the United States and Britain, can do absolutely nothing about Stalingrad—except pray, I suppose. But here, on the other hand, this island is ours to hold, if we can."

"Can Malta hold?" Hopkins asked.

"They're bombing the convoys, they're bombing the harbor, they're bombing the airfields—" Park began.

The room shook as a bomb exploded somewhere nearby, releasing a drift of dust and grit, and the lights flickered.

"As I was saying," Park said with a thin smile.

THREE

Penelope Dryden escaped Thompson's office. A bomb exploded some-where to the west, probably near the airfield at Luqa, although the skies seemed clear of enemy bombers and the All Clear had sounded. It was not unusual for bombs to hit without exploding, only to detonate hours or even days later.

She walked to the dockyard superintendent's office and sought out the duty officer.

"There're some MTB crews that need to be mustered to the ack-ack auxiliaries and quartered," she told.

"Who said—" the DO began, but she beat him to the punch.

"Commander Thompson assigned them to me to remuster. There's space in *Silkworm* to quarter them, I believe?"

HMS *Silkworm* was an antique relic of gunboat diplomacy kept alive by the navy to serve as a submarine supply tender and used as temporary floating accommodation for sailors in transit.

"Well, I suppose—"

"Then that's settled."

She guessed from his expression that he was devoting almost all his energy to imagining her naked and, as a consequence, had almost no remaining energy left to question her.

She turned on her heel and left him gaping. She found the RPO who, after a similar exchange, summoned the MTB crews. They stood in three dispirited lines before her, vaguely at attention, their eyes squinting in the harsh early sunlight, unshaven and unkempt, still in their square rig class 1 uniforms, their canvas kit bags piled beside them. Within minutes she had distributed them among the short-handed ack-ack batteries.

"Is that clear, Baker?" she asked their senior rating.

The petty officer repeated her orders verbatim, exactly as she had given them, his eyes screwed up against the harsh sunshine but otherwise expressionless.

"Very well, Baker. Carry on."

"Aye-aye, ma'am," he said. "And, ma'am, begging your pardon, it's Miller, not Baker, ma'am."

It somehow stung without reason or proportion. His manner was correct, but he seemed to suggest he had long ceased to have high expectations of officers, the kinds of officers who could not be bothered to get men's names right, and she was just the latest in a long line of such disappointments. It was on the tip of her tongue to explain it wasn't her error, it was Thompson's, but that would have involved acknowledging the error.

He saluted as she was hesitating, and she felt, as she returned his salute, that she had been dismissed.

* * *

She walked along the waterfront as far as Fort St. Angelo, where she lit a cigarette and let the breeze ruffle through her hair, gazing out across the waters of the Grand Harbour towards Fort St. Elmo. Valletta, with its magnificent natural harbor, was one of the oldest cities in the world, stretching back long before the Romans, the Greeks, and even the Phoenicians, to the dawn of history. The earliest ruins dated to Neolithic times, thousands of years before the Bronze Age, long, long before the pyramids and temples of the Egyptian pharaohs, before even the great stone circle of Stonehenge in England.

Malta had never been an independent country, not once in the thousands of years of recorded history. But, if it couldn't be free, it seemed to Penelope that it was just and appropriate that Malta should be a British colony; after all, Malta was a great port and Britain ruled the greatest seafaring empire in history. Besides, who wanted to be ruled by Il Duce Mussolini, for God's sake?

Penelope was born and raised in Malta, and this view had always delighted her. Before the war, the harbor had been busy with coasters plying the trade routes between Italy and North Africa, larger merchantmen and passenger liners following the global trade routes through Suez and on to India and Asia in one direction, and Gibraltar and northern Europe in the other. It had seemed to Penelope, as she was growing up, that Malta stood at the crossroads of the world.

But now the skyline was marred by yawning gaps where fine buildings had once stood. Now the fury of the Axis air forces had been turned upon the crossroads of the Mediterranean. The German Luftwaffe and the Italian Regia Aeronautica were attempting to bomb the city—her city—back to the Stone Age. Every attack included several enemy aircraft, sometimes dozens. The crowded streets of Valletta had been reduced to pathways between piles of rubble. The bustling harbor was now marred with wrecks; the few ships in sight seemed to be skulking about as their nervous crews searched the skies for Stuka dive-bombers. The winds never quite seemed to be able to blow away the smoke leaking from the charred carcasses of buildings and the corpses of half-sunken vessels.

She'd had an idyllic childhood. Her family had settled in Malta after the First World War. She had grown up in Valletta and then been sent to be privately educated in England and Switzerland. Her father was a wealthy shipbuilder who loved to build high-speed motor launches; his yard was nearby on French Creek in Albert Town, now requisitioned by the navy. His prized possession, *Greased Lightning*, was said to be the fastest boat between Gibraltar and Alexandria. She loved to visit her father's yard, watching the skilled craftsmen transforming inelegant planks of wood into the graceful curves of a high-speed hull, a matchless fusion of form and function. Her father was delighted by her interest and arranged for her to attend Imperial College London, where she studied hydrodynamics. She was the only girl in the class—the first girl ever to take such a class—the object of endless ogling, risqué innuendoes, and unwanted, inept advances. She purchased a pair of heavy tortoiseshell glasses with plain lenses and hid behind them.

London was the capital of the British Empire and the largest city in Europe—London's population was more than thirty times the entire population of Malta—and arguably the cultural capital of the world. Penelope hated it: London's perpetually gray skies and smoky air made her long for the pristine blue skies above Malta.

Her mother was one of Malta's leading hostesses, filling the house with the most interesting people on the island. Everybody who was anybody in Valletta, it was said, went to her salon to see and be seen. The cognoscenti relaxed on the terraces, enjoying the views across the harbor to Fort Ricasoli, with Singapore Slings to slake their thirst in summer and hot toddies to keep out the chills of winter.

And then there was Jimmy, her childhood neighbor and tennis partner. When she had left for college in 1936, he was a sweetly goofy, gangling youth. When she returned in 1939, he had grown into a dazzling young man with an easy charm, deep-blue eyes, and an utterly irresistible body.

That summer, the summer of '39, was rapturous. Her father was thrilled by her newfound expertise in hydrodynamics and set her up as the assistant designer at the yard. The curves she drew in pencil at the drafting tables took form and substance in teak and mahogany in the hands of her father's boatwrights. Her mother hosted a series of dance parties in honor of Penelope's return, parties that began in the soft twilight and filled the warm evening skies with music and laughter. And later each evening, when the dancing was done, Jimmy claimed her full and complete attention.

Then everything changed.

First, her mother ran off with an overweight, mediocre baritone from Naples, who was half her age and had groping hands and a pencil-thin mustache. Her father was deeply shocked, not so much by her betrayal—this was not her first "distraction," by any means—as by the humiliation of her choice. How could she prefer a second-rate Italian gigolo to an English gentleman? Previously her taste had run to energetic naval officers and passing colonial plenipotentiaries. But a Neapolitan nobody, for God's sake?

In truth, the baritone's first target had been Penelope, but his sweaty jowls disgusted her, and his chubby hands attempted to stray where only Jimmy's were welcome. Having failed with the daughter, the undaunted baritone transferred his attentions to the mother, who did not resist—indeed applauded—his explorations.

Then the war started. At first it seemed of little consequence—after all, the Italians were only Italians, whereas the Royal Navy, the guardian of Malta, was the greatest naval force in the history of mankind, greater even than the Phoenicians who had sailed their quinqueremes to Malta and set foot in Valletta long before the birth of Christ.

Her mother was now literally in the hands—the chubby hands—of the enemy, perhaps in danger or perhaps a traitor. The Royal Navy requisitioned her father's yard for salvage work and odds and ends. The sleek hulls she had been working on were shoved aside, and the craftsmen were obliged to build ugly lighters, barges, and floating docks for antiaircraft batteries.

Jimmy volunteered to serve in the navy and was posted to HMS *Ratcliffe*, an elderly Acorn-class destroyer that had somehow avoided being scrapped after the last war. He looked mouthwatering in his navy-blue uniform and gold braid, with his cap set at a provocatively flamboyant angle.

Next, late in 1941, her father was killed, outrageously, by Italian Z.1007 Alcione bombers. The famously incompetent Italians had managed to bomb the shipyard and kill her father! His life's work was his funeral pyre. Another air raid all but demolished her home, slicing it in two, leaving only on one side her mother's boudoir and its discreet adjoining balcony where the opera singer had achieved his conquest, and the kitchen and scullery and the servants' quarters at some distance on the other. The salon was now an open courtyard.

She felt as she had felt at school when a clique of older girls had bullied her. Mussolini's Regia Aeronautica was blowing up her island and her life, obliterating everything she knew. She had never done anything against the Regia Aeronautica; it was grossly unfair!

Finally, to cap it all, *Ratcliffe* was sunk ignominiously by a mere Italian armed trawler half its size. Weeks later, Jimmy's body was found sailing westward towards the setting sun, somewhere south of Sicily, his clawlike skeletal fingers gripping the tiller of a lifeboat. He had died long before from thirst and exposure, tortured by the ruthless sun, his perfect body burned to a crisp and his blue eyes pecked out by seabirds.

She had not seen it, but each night the vision flickered relentlessly through her dreams and tortured her.

Now she felt impotent fury. Mussolini had destroyed her family, her profession, her love, and her island. Her ambitions for the future had been built on her father's yard and Jimmy's body. Thanks to Mussolini, both were gone. She joined the WRNS as a sort of gesture of defiance against Il Duce and because, well, to be honest, life goes on, and she would be able to meet large numbers of unattached naval officers.

* * *

"Can Malta hold?" Hopkins asked.

"In order to hold Malta, I have to control the air," Park said. "The moment we lose air superiority, the Germans and Italians will invade—they call it Operation Herkules, I understand. They have their paratroopers trained and ready. We are told that Hitler and Mussolini have personally approved the plan."

"What does it take to control the air?" Hopkins asked.

"Spitfires; Spitfires and the fuel and equipment and supplies they need, and men who can fly them."

"Do you have them?"

"The navy is bringing as many as possible from Gib; the Club Runs, as they're called," Eleanor broke in. "But no, we don't have enough—we don't have enough of anything."

"So is it fair to say that the fate of Malta is fifty-fifty? Is that fair?" Hopkins asked.

"That's very fair," Park said.

"I disagree," Eleanor said. "I don't think we'll lose. I think our chances are better than ninety-ten."

"Why so optimistic, Eleanor?" Hopkins asked.

"Because we have a secret factor in our favor, sir."

"What's that?"

"Because history has a tendency to repeat itself. The Battle of Britain was fought between Air-Vice Marshal Park with 11 Group and Generalfeldmarschall Kesselring as the commander of Luftflotte II. Now, in this 'Battle of Malta,' if I can call it that, we have Air-Vice Marshal Park at AHQ Malta, and Kesselring with Luftflotte II under his command in Italy. I have no doubt in my mind, none at all, that Kesselring will lose again."

"That's very interesting. That hadn't struck me," Hopkins murmured, while Park made self-deprecating hand gestures.

"Well, I don't know about—" Park began, but Eleanor cut him off.

"As you know, sir, I believe that men shape history, not vice versa," she said to Hopkins. "Mr. Churchill has kept us going for almost three years and will never, ever give up. President Roosevelt will make sure America wins, I'm certain of it. Stalin is even more ruthless and pitiless than Hitler, and therefore Stalingrad will hold, regardless of the cost. And the AOC will beat Kesselring again."

"Well, I'm counting on it," Hopkins said. "It is essential—essential— that Malta holds."

An orderly appeared in the doorway.

"'Scuse me, sir, but there's another raid coming in."

* * *

Air raid sirens began to wail, and Penelope hurried back towards the nearest shelter. Twin 40 mm antiaircraft guns abruptly opened fire from an ack-ack lighter as she passed it, making her jump as if scalded. She began to run. The unmistakable banshee howling of Stuka dive-bombers grew louder and closer and louder yet as they screamed down from the sky. Her hat had gone. It sounded as if the Stukas were aiming directly at her. She tripped. She had probably grazed her knees and torn her stockings. The world, her ordered, beautiful Valletta, was descending into chaos.

Thank God, here was the shelter! Just as she ran down the steps she heard, even louder than the Stukas, the high-pitched whistling shriek of falling bombs as the Stukas released them. She felt herself, in a weird disembodied way, opening her mouth to scream but knowing that her scream would be futile and wasted because it would be drowned by the noise of falling bombs. An arm reached out and pulled her the last few feet into the darkness of a cellar, and she collapsed, quivering, against a damp stone wall. Bombs exploded almost over their heads, or so it seemed, huge thunderclaps of sound, and the basement shuddered and shook.

She had thought Mussolini had already taken everything, but now his Stukas had come back to take even her dignity. She wiped her nose against her sleeve—her nanny would have slapped her, but her handkerchief had disappeared, and, in any case, she had already been stripped of self-respect—and hugged her bloody knees in the darkness.

* * *

Eleanor wondered why Hopkins, usually a phlegmatic man, was so adamant that Malta must hold. Of course it must hold, but why—

The operations controller appeared in the doorway.

"Excuse me, sir, but they just declared the All Clear again. Just a sneak attack with Stukas, it seems."

"Any damage, Freddie?" Park asked.

"They sunk a couple of tend-ders in the harbor, sir, and damaged one of the destroy-yers that came in with yesterday's Club Run. That's all we know so far."

"If the raid's over, we should perhaps take the opportunity to fly you out, Mr. Hopkins," Park said. "They'll probably send another raid before they're done. I've arranged a Spitfire escort to make sure you're safe until you're beyond the Regia Aeronautica's range."

"They're at readiness, sir," the controller said. "Digby and a couple of his chaps."

"Yes, that makes sense. Thank you," Hopkins said, rising.

He turned to Eleanor.

"Incidentally, Eleanor, speaking of Spitfires, I heard your husband escaped from a POW camp? Congratulations! What a welcome relief that must be!"

They had been together at a conference in Moscow last year when Eleanor had been notified that Johnnie had been forced down over France and captured. She still didn't understand why Hopkins was so emphatic about Malta holding, but perhaps Park understood. She'd ask him later.

"Yes, thank you, sir. In fact, even better, he's here!"

FOUR

Charlie trotted off to greet someone coming towards them. Warrant Officer Jenkins had served with Shaux since 1940. During the last days of the collapse of France, with German panzer tanks racing for the English Channel, Shaux had been based in Arras, not far from Paris, and Jenkins had been his ground crew sergeant. They had flown out of France in a Defiant, Jenkins somehow crouched on Shaux's lap. The canopy was open because Jenkins's head couldn't fit inside. Jenkins had been with Shaux more or less ever since.

"We've been called to readiness, sir," Jenkins said. "A Flight only, not the rest of 505. There's some special bigwig in a Dakota who needs an escort."

"A Dakota, no less!" Shaux said. He was convinced the bigwig was, in fact, an enormous wig. Dakotas, or C-47s, as the Americans called them, were the finest of all transport aircraft, a military version of the wonderful Douglas DC3s. Churchill, he had heard, had to make do with a mere B-24 Liberator.

"Squadron Leader Digby said he'd lead A Flight. Apparently the AOC requested it."

Now Shaux was convinced that the bigwig was very big indeed. Squadron Leader Digby, Distinguished Flying Cross and two bars, was the 505 Squadron commander and, in Shaux's opinion, the best fighter pilot in the Med. Diggers had served with Shaux during the Battle of Britain when Shaux commanded 339 Squadron.

"I didn't see a Dakota, Jenks," Shaux said as they started back. "It's a bit big to hide, surely?"

"It's over at Ta' Qali, sir. They'll fly it in when they're ready."

As if on cue, a Dakota approached on final from the north, gliding in low like a hawk with its outstretched undercarriage for talons, and landed gently and precisely. Clearly the pilot was an expert: when a really good pilot touches down, it always seemed to Shaux, the ground seems to rise to meet the wheels, so there is no bump, no landing, just a silky-smooth transition from being supported by moving air to being supported by the stationary earth. He knew the physics of ground effect and downwash and the equations governing fluid dynamics, of course, but he would still swear the airfield lifted itself to meet the Dakota.

He noticed something odd about the RAF roundels painted on the fuselage and wings—yes, they were painted on top of American stars, and he could still see the points of the stars sticking out. The plot was thickening indeed.

The route back to the dispersal area led them past the ruined HQ buildings, and Shaux saw a small group emerging from the underground shelters, including Park and Eleanor and an overdressed civilian. He must be the Dakota's passenger. The Dakota completed its rollout and turned towards them, its mighty Pratt and Whitney Twin Wasp engines kicking up dust and fine particles of sand as it moved in a serpentine manner dictated by the bomb craters in the taxiways.

Shaux stood back, but Park beckoned him over. Charlie came, too—just in case he might be needed.

"Ah, Shaux, let me introduce you to Mr. Harry Hopkins from the United States. Mr. Hopkins, this is Wing Commander Shaux, Eleanor's husband."

Hopkins was a big man, taller than Shaux, but he gave the impression that he was smaller than he once had been, as if he were collapsing in upon himself. Shaux remembered Eleanor saying that he had some terrible form of cancer eating away at him. She had commented that the two most powerful men in America, Roosevelt and Hopkins, were both dying, slowly but inevitably, and might not survive to see the end of hostilities.

"And who is this?" Hopkins asked, gesturing to Charlie.

"This is Charlie, *Le Grand Charles*, of the Aviation Militaire Belge, sir, the Royal Belgian Air Force," Shaux said. He liked Hopkins immediately: doubtless he was under enormous pressure, with many weighty matters on his mind, and yet he was able to take a moment to be human, to scuffle the hair on Charlie's mighty head.

"Ah yes. A Bouvier, I think?" Hopkins asked.

"Exactly so, sir," Shaux said.

"What's this medal?" Hopkins asked, finding a brass emblem hanging from Charlie's collar.

"Oh, that's not a medal, sir. That's a Royal Engineers cap badge. He assists the Sappers searching bomb-damaged buildings for survivors trapped in the rubble."

"Very admirable."

"Indeed so, sir, and it also gives him rights of access to the Royal Engineers' mess kitchen."

Hopkins chuckled.

"Wing Commander, I have long valued your wife's advice, and I'm delighted that you escaped from Nazi hospitality. But time is of the essence. I hope we'll meet again and make a better acquaintance."

He turned back to shake hands with Park, Eleanor, and the admiral in charge of the navy's Malta squadron, and then started to climb, just slightly unsteadily, into the Dakota.

"E/A fifty miles, zero-zero-zero degrees," a loudspeaker erupted above their heads, startling everyone. "Yorker Freddie to readiness."

"Go! Go! Go!" Park yelled at Hopkins, who disappeared inside the Dakota. The Twin Wasps began to roar and the big aircraft rolled forward, its rudimentary stairs dragging behind.

* * *

Wailing sirens sounded the All Clear, and the occupants of the cellar pulled themselves together. Penelope straightened her uniform and wiped her nose once more, ingloriously. The hem of her skirt would disguise her bloody knees. God only knew what her hair looked like. She climbed the steps into the open air, but the sirens began to wail once more. Jesus *Christ*! She turned back into the dank darkness and returned to her spot by the wall.

A wave of self-pity swept over her. Jimmy was dead; his younger brother, Peter, seemed to think he had some kind of biblical right to replace him in her bed. Her father's yard—her yard, now—was filled with ugly, utilitarian hulls no better than floating hulks, and she was no better than a general factotum to the idiotic, sweating Thompson. Her mother was probably reclining on a Neapolitan chaise, engaging with the enemy. The convoys were not getting through; Malta, already on very short rations, would soon begin to starve, or so her uncle Bertie feared. The Italians would win, and she'd have to be nice to them or else. Oh God!

Peter had no such right, she was almost certain, but, in the last analysis, who cared?

* * *

Shaux began to run back across the field to the dispersal area, Charlie bounding by his side, as if this was a race. Jenkins chugged in their wake.

Shaux made his plans as he ran. "E/A" meant enemy aircraft. They were fifty miles to the north, coming towards Malta from Italy and Sicily. "Yorker Freddie," YF, was 505's squadron code. "Readiness" meant that the pilots had to be in their Spitfires with the engines running, ready to take off immediately. Diggers, 505's skipper, would be escorting the Dakota. Therefore, Shaux would lead the rest of 505 against the enemy.

If the E/As were bombers and fighters coming at, say, 250 miles per hour, they'd be here in twelve minutes; if they were fighters only, they'd be here in only ten.

It took a minute to reach the dispersal area. Nine minutes left. The ground crews were pulling the camouflage netting off the Spitfires, and 505's pilots were running to their aircrafts. A sergeant was leaning into Shaux's cockpit at an awkward angle, his one leg in the air as he went through the starting sequence. There was a bang from the Coffman starter as he fired a cartridge. The engine spun and caught with only the slightest hesitation, the exhaust manifolds on both sides of the engine burping fire and smoke. Shaux jumped onto the port wing, engulfed in acrid fumes. A corporal handed him his flying gear.

Shaux threw it all into the cockpit and struggled into his life jacket and parachute harness—he knew from bitter experience it was impossible to put them on once he was seated in the cockpit.

An automatic, ingrained search above: no enemy aircraft in sight. A mighty roar rose from the runway as the Dakota's Twin Wasps and the escorting Spitfires' Merlin engines wound up to takeoff revs.

Someone emerged from the dispersal hut and fired a Very pistol into the air: the order to take off. Shaux stepped into his cockpit, wriggled his way down, and nudged the throttle, hoping the ground crew had had the wit to remove the wheel chucks. They had. Shaux taxied to the end of the field as fast as he dared, stamping on the brakes, left or right, to steer the Spitfire around the bomb craters, and then, close to the northern fence, slewed around into the wind.

Eight minutes left. He opened the throttle, and the Spit accelerated immediately. Shaux fished around by his feet in search of his helmet and gloves. No more dodging potholes—he had to steer exactly straight during takeoff, correcting for the Merlin's powerful torque, and just hope he wouldn't hit anything, although the easiest way to break a Spitfire was to drive one of its wheels into a hole at speed. The air was full of dust and fine debris, like a mini sandstorm: the big Dakota was taking off directly ahead of him, and he was racing into its prop wash. The radiator inlet filters would be a mess. The rest of 505 was following him in random order. Out of the corner of his eye, he saw Charlie sitting beside Jenkins as he flashed past them. He couldn't see whether Park and Eleanor were still outside the HQ building, but he doubted it. They'd be hurrying to the Operations Room.

He finally found his helmet beneath the compass, hiding under the rudder bar. He stuck it more or less on his head and plugged in the R/T wires. Without the helmet on his head, he couldn't communicate. The Spitfire reached flying speed, and he eased it into the air. He turned south, right, to avoid catching up with, and potentially ramming, the Dakota. He saw it almost immediately, already below him, heading east. Someone was leaning out of its still-open doorway, trying to grapple with its dangling stairs. He hoped Hopkins had not been shaken up too badly by the rapid departure. He had seemed both tough and fragile at the same time.

Shaux adjusted the Spitfire for a maximum rate of climb. With the magical 1650-7 two-stage supercharger, the Spitfire could climb at an astonishing 3,500 feet per minute. The E/As could be here in six minutes or so. In six minutes, he could be at twenty thousand feet. Height was everything in aerial combat. If the enemy were above twenty thousand feet, then 505 would be in danger, because the latest Messerschmitt 109-Gs—if the E/As were 109s—performed best above twenty thousand feet. That was above angels two-zero in RAF code—"angels" meant height, and each thousand feet counted as one angel.

Tiny noises buzzed from his helmet, as if it contained an entrapped and enraged mosquito. He twisted the helmet on his head so that the earphones fitted against his ears, and buttoned the mask with his oxygen and microphone across his face.

"York-er leader assist Dum-bo," he heard the controller's voice, no longer sounding like a mosquito. "Yorker leader" was Digby; he assumed Hopkins's Dakota was "Dumbo."

"Dumbo escort," said Shaux's earphones in Diggers' voice, acknowledging the controller.

"York-er vector one-eight-zero to angels two-zero."

The controller wanted 505 to fly south, away from the enemy, while gaining height. Doubtless after three or four minutes, they'd be ordered back north so that they'd arrive back over Malta at twenty thousand feet, angels two-zero, ready to meet the enemy aircraft as they arrived.

"Yorker," Shaux said, assuming command of 505.

His Spitfire bumped and bounced as it climbed. Shaux was always surprised how turbulent the air was above the Med, with invisible thermals rising unevenly as the morning sun warmed the air above the sea. Where the hell was his left glove, dammit?

"York-er vector zero-zero-zero."

"Yorker."

They were climbing through angels one-zero, and the turn northward would bring them back to Malta as they reached two-zero. Shaux had seven aircraft with him; Diggers and two more of 505's Spitfires were shepherding Harry Hopkins away from danger. The Med was its deepest dark-blue-green, almost black, furrowed by endless successions of waves and sparkling where cat's-paws of wind whipped their crests into spume. Shaux shaded his direction a little eastward. He wanted to arrive back over Malta just to the east of Valletta so that he'd be lost in the glare of the sun to any enemy aircraft directly over Malta.

"Bandits overhead Vic-toria," Shaux's earphones announced.

The enemy was at the gates once more. Where in God's name was his bloody glove?

FIVE

Shaux wriggled and resettled himself in his seat. Spitfires might be the most beautiful and powerful aircraft ever built, he thought, but they required the pilot to sit on his parachute and its cumbersome webbing, which were always hard and lumpy, causing a variety of irritations and ailments, including nasty cases of numb bum.

He would meet the enemy in four minutes, five at the most; in the meantime, there was nothing to do but wait for his Spitfire to carry him higher and higher into the thinner and thinner air in which his two-stage supercharger would become increasingly effective and provide him with a greater advantage over the enemy.

People imagined that flying a Spitfire meant constant, nerve-wracking action. In fact, it meant the opposite. Most of the time, you never saw the enemy at all, and when you did, you seldom got close enough to engage. If you did get close enough to engage—to fire or to be fired upon—the action seldom lasted more than a few seconds. Shaux's estimate was that he engaged the enemy for five seconds for every couple of hours he flew—perhaps a twentieth of one percent of operational flying time.

The key was to achieve a sort of mental contradiction, to be vigilant yet relaxed at the same time. Vigilance demanded that you search the sky constantly for the tiny black dots in the glare that could sprout wings and fuselages and evolve, in just a few seconds, into enemy aircraft spitting cannon shells. But you could not remain tightly wound up, adrenalin pumping, all the time: that would quickly make you exhausted and skittish and error prone, jumping at every shadow. Therefore, you also had to be relaxed, conserving your strength and judgment and keeping a cool head so that you could survive when the moment of peril finally came.

Shaux had been flying against the enemy since the spring of 1940, when the full might of Hitler's forces burst into Western Europe. In those early days, he had locked himself into a sort of fatalistic stoicism—he was bound to die, sooner or later, he had reasoned, and there wasn't anything he could do about it. The average life expectancy of a fighter pilot in the Battle of Britain was five hours of flying time, just two or three days at the most, and therefore there was no point in wasting time and energy on anxiety.

The poem by William Butler Yeats that begins *I know that I shall meet my fate / Somewhere among the clouds above* had been a refuge, a retreat, a place to escape the stress that drove other pilots past the breaking point. Yeats's poem had taught Shaux the comfort of despair.

As he had beaten the odds and survived, as the days and weeks and months of combat had stretched into years, he had found—stumbled across—the magic balance, the ability to search with one half of his brain and relax with the other. His old mentor, Professor Harry Pound, had likened it to the state of the physicist Schrödinger's famous cat, which was both alive and dead at the same time, in a state of what a theoretical physicist would call a quantum superimposition. "Close your eyes to see more clearly," Pound had said.

Well, there was nothing to do for the next four or five minutes, Shaux thought, and therefore he would do nothing. His hands and feet rested upon the controls with just a featherweight of pressure, at one with the aircraft, a part of the mechanism. His eyes ranged the skies methodically but automatically, independent of conscious thought or direction; the roaring of his Merlin was just a background murmur, like the thunder of a distant waterfall.

Malta lay before him, gleaming in the bright morning sun, an archipelago of little islands like shiny stones on a string, lost in the vastness of the sea. Yet it was one of the most important places in the world, the key to the Mediterranean and Africa and the trade routes to Asia. He'd been here four weeks—no, probably more like six by now—and the Luftwaffe and the Regia Aeronautica had bombed Malta just about every day. They'd been bombing for two long years, ever since Mussolini joined Hitler in June 1940, as France collapsed, bombing day in and day out, as if Mussolini was intent on bombing until Malta was pounded into limestone gravel and sank beneath the waves. In fact, they'd bombed the convoy that brought Shaux to Malta, three times before he even got here.

* * *

Six weeks before, HMS *Nonsuch* had plowed through the Mediterranean towards Malta, rolling in the quartering sea in an ungainly, corkscrew fashion.

She had been built as a heavy cruiser during the First World War and then converted into an aircraft carrier in the 1920s. All her upperworks had been removed, and she had been stripped down to the main deck. Then two hangar decks had been built above the main deck, with a flight deck above, an island superstructure for her bridge and funnels on the starboard side, and platforms for antiaircraft batteries projecting over her sides. The new hangar decks, rising thirty feet above the main deck, acted as a sail and gave her a clumsy motion in moderate or heavy seas.

But she could carry forty aircraft with all their equipment and supplies in her hangars. She was fast, and she was long enough, at over five hundred feet, for modern aircraft to take off.

On this run, a fast convoy from Gibraltar to Malta, code named EF-4—"E" for "Eastbound" and "F" for "Fast"—she was ferrying sixteen desperately needed Spitfire Mark IX fighters to reinforce Malta's defenses.

Shaux paced the flight deck, grimly determined not to remember how much he hated the sea. Well, to be fair, the only time he had really come face to face with the sea was when the schooner that was carrying him back to England from Dunkirk had been dive-bombed by a Stuka, and he had spent two days in the Channel. So, he had to admit, if this was the elegant ocean liner *Queen Mary* rather than *Nonsuch*, and he and Eleanor were taking a stroll around the promenade deck before a leisurely luncheon, his opinion of the sea might have been very different.

Tomorrow morning *Nonsuch* would be close enough to Malta for the Spitfires, fitted with extra fuel tanks, to fly off. But that assumed that EF-4 would be allowed to proceed on its present course and speed without further attacks by the combined German and Italian navies and air forces.

He knew without thinking that there were no enemy aircraft in the sky at this moment because his fighter pilot's eyes never, ever stopped searching the skies.

The Spitfires were lashed down to the deck at the back of ship— on the afterdeck, he corrected himself. They looked utterly miserable, he thought, like dogs told to sit and wait in a rainstorm. They were crouching there as the salt air and the flying spume did their best to eat away at their vital parts. They'd never been on an aircraft carrier before, and he had never taken off from one. Tomorrow he would have the interesting experience of pushing the throttle of his aircraft wide open and hurtling forward down the pitching deck.

It would be an act of imminent suicide, he thought, to drive his Spitfire as fast as possible straight over *Nonsuch's* bow, fighting the Merlin's torque and any crosswinds that might try to push him over the side instead. The fact that it was very difficult to see forward in a Spitfire on the ground, because of its long nose, would make the experience even more interesting. In theory, of course, his Spitfire would reach flying speed well before it reached the bow and lift safely into the air, released from the ship and back into its natural element.

He knew the mathematics of his Spit's acceleration, the yardage it needed to achieve flying speed, and the added benefit of the *Nonsuch* sailing at full speed straight into the wind, thereby increasing his airspeed upon takeoff by twenty knots or so. That American chap Doolittle, Shaux also knew, had miraculously flown lumbering twin-engine B-25 bombers off a carrier a couple of months ago in the Pacific and actually bombed Tokyo. But, even so, the proof of the pudding is in the eating, and tomorrow he'd open the throttle and find out if he could also eat pudding, or whatever the hell that ancient adage was supposed to mean. It would be a blind leap of faith.

He flicked his cigarette over the side and descended an absurdly steep ladder to the hangar deck below. It was vast, gloomy, and noisy and seemed to be pitching more than the open deck above. The deck was jammed with cargo for the embattled British Eighth Army, for *Nonsuch* was going to bypass Malta and continue on to Alexandria in Egypt. Part of the hangar housed passengers who could not fit into *Nonsuch*'s accommodations. They were crammed into their own tented encampment, including some miserable-looking crews for six motor torpedo boats. The boats themselves, Shaux had been told, were lashed down as deck cargo on another ship in EF-4.

Shaux might hate the voyage, but at least he had a comfortable cot in the *Nonsuch* officers' quarters, the use of the officers' wardroom, and freedom to roam wherever he wished, provided he didn't get in anyone's way. The MTB crews were stuck here in this noisy, damp, drafty, depressing corner and allowed to get some fresh air up on deck only for brief intervals.

One of the MTB crew members was a young chap from Manchester. Shaux had found him one day examining a spare Merlin engine, and the chap, Leading Seaman Miller, had asked a number of very detailed and acute questions. It turned out that Miller had been a garage mechanic before the war and now maintained the Packard 4M engines that drove the MTBs. Miller had been intrigued that the mighty Merlin, generally agreed to be the finest liquid-cooled piston engine ever built, was also built by Packard under license from Rolls-Royce. Shaux had also been a mechanic when he'd first joined the RAF, a fitter, as mechanics were known, and he and Miller had struck up one of those casual acquaintanceships that you sometimes form when surrounded by strangers, with nothing else to do, like passengers on a long train journey.

"Action Stations. Action Stations," loudspeakers erupted throughout *Nonsuch*, the harsh sound ricocheting off the hangar walls. All hands, including passengers, were given duties during Action Stations, and Shaux had been assigned to a damage control party—a group of men armed with pickaxes and crowbars and an assortment of similar blunt instruments responsible for clearing away wreckage if the ship was attacked and damaged. Shaux and Miller climbed to the flight deck and squatted down just aft of the bridge structure, where a group

of a dozen men formed Starboard Flight Deck Damage Control Party
No. 2.

Nonsuch took on an urgent deep-throated thrumming vibration
that Shaux could feel through his knees as her engines worked their
way up to full power and she turned into the wind. Some corner of
Shaux's mind noted that her movements were becoming smoother, as
if she had been designed, like a cheetah, to perform best at speed.

A Sea Gladiator, an obsolescent biplane flown by the Royal Navy
Fleet Air Arm, snarled along the flight deck and laboriously hauled
itself into the sky, followed by two others. Shaux watched them grimly.
They would have difficulty surviving an encounter with the Regia
Aeronautica, he thought, and no chance at all against the Luftwaffe.
He had flown outmatched aircraft himself, the Boulton Paul Defiant
during the Battle of France and the Westland Whirlwind last year, and
he knew exactly what the Gladiator pilots must be feeling. He'd heard
the Admiralty hadn't managed to get the naval version of the Spitfire,
the Seafire, to really work, and the navy had started flying American
Grumman Martlets instead—not really competitive with Luftwaffe
109s but better than Gladiators.

He'd heard that Gladiators were the only aircraft defending Malta
early in the war—just three of them, nicknamed *Faith, Hope,* and
Charity. It seemed incredible that the air defenses of Malta had been
limited to three obsolete biplanes. If the story was true, then their
pilots must have been men of extraordinary bravery and determination, and Malta must have been in dire straits indeed.

Shaux couldn't see much as he crouched on the deck clasping his
crowbar, but he was grateful to be out in the open. Almost everyone
on the carrier was deep belowdecks, with no way of knowing what was
happening, grimly staring at the bulkheads and watertight doors and
praying they'd hold if *Nonsuch* was torpedoed or bombed or struck by
gunfire or a mine, like those thousands upon thousands of American
sailors trapped in sinking ships when the Japanese bombed Pearl
Harbor six months ago, or like HMS *Hood,* sunk by the *Bismarck,* or
the *Prince of Wales,* or the *Bismarck* herself.

Just ahead of him, actually aft of his position, he could see a
40-millimeter twin pom-pom antiaircraft gun platform, its crew staring into the sky towards the north. A petty officer with binoculars

yelled instructions, and the gun rotated off to port and its elevation rose steeply. Somewhere forward, out of Shaux's sight, what sounded like a 50-millimeter machine gun fired a long burst. Shaux guessed the gunner was inexperienced or scared or both—the longer the burst, the more the gun jumped and the less likely it was to hit the target.

The petty officer yelled, and Shaux jumped when the pom-pom guns in front of him opened fire, with very loud poms rather than bangs, towards a target he couldn't see, and he jumped again as a massive column of water, higher than *Nonsuch*'s bridge and superstructure, arose from the sea a hundred yards away from the port side. A Heinkel 111 flashed across his range of vision from right to left, its bomb doors open, and another huge waterspout erupted from the sea off the starboard side. If a bomb struck the flight deck, it was clear that it would penetrate deeply down into the hangar spaces before exploding, causing only-God-knew-what damage.

The pom-pom ceased firing, and everything else—the waves, the stiff breeze, the thrumming of the engines, the petty officer's orders, even the flapping of the signal flags and the slapping of the ropes running up to the masthead high above him—was suddenly loud. The gun crew began reloading racks of ammunition as Shaux watched with humble admiration—it must take Herculean strength to lift those racks of 2-pounder shells shoulder-high on a heaving, slippery, wet gun platform and slot them into place. Shaux doubted he could do it more than once or twice, but in a long engagement, these young sailors—just boys, really—must keep doing it, regardless of the circumstances. At least they were in the Med; just imagine what it must be like on the icy Arctic convoys through the Barents Sea to Archangel in the depths of winter.

The petty officer yelled again, and the gun swiveled and opened fire. Two more aircraft flashed overhead, three-engine bombers of a type that Shaux had read about but never seen. These must be Italian SM.79 Sparviero torpedo bombers. They looked awkward—well, frankly, ugly to Shaux's eyes—like humpbacked camels, two-engine aircraft with an extra engine stuck on the nose like an afterthought. But they were also tough, and if three Gladiators were all the FAA could put up against them, the enemy aircraft could do pretty much whatever they wanted.

The Sparvieros flew on unharmed, descending almost to wave height, headed for a big, lumbering merchantman that Shaux could just see on the horizon. The Sparvieros pulled up—Shaux assumed they'd released their torpedoes—and swung away to the north. A black cloud rose above the merchantman, and Shaux heard a sound like distant thunder.

"*Jesus*, that's the *Tattersall Castle*!" Miller swore.

"That's our bleeding boats!" someone else groaned.

"They got the *Tat*!" Miller said in a voice full of shock and mourning.

It was hard to see at this distance, but some instinct told Shaux that the ship had been mortally wounded. A second explosion bellowed across the water, and bits of something sizzled upward like rockets on Guy Fawkes Night. Red fire glared and lit the underbelly of the billowing smoke.

"They got the bleeding *Tat*!" Miller repeated, as if unwilling to believe his eyes. "Now what are we going to do?"

SIX

Eleanor watched as a WAAF sergeant moved a little marker across the map table, showing 505 closing in on a flight of bandits. The table was perhaps ten feet on each side, with a map painted on it showing Sicily to the north and Malta in the center. Tripoli appeared on the southern edge, which Eleanor always found annoying because the map made it look as if Tunisia was about as far away as Sicily, whereas in real life it was four or five times farther. She kept making a mental note to get the table repainted, or extended, or something, but the project never made its way sufficiently far up her priority list. The new map table in Lascaris would be drawn to scale, she had been promised—if they ever got the new bombproof War Rooms finished.

This map table—indeed, the whole Luqa Operations Room—was a far cry from the 11 Group Operations Room in Uxbridge on the outskirts of London. Two years ago in 1940, she and Park had stood on the balcony, watching the Battle of Britain play out on the big table below them, as the fate of Britain teetered in the balance. This room was no more than an overgrown cellar with the roof braced by steel girders and wooden beams at odd angles. The ceiling was festooned with telephone wires and electrical circuits, and dust drifted down whenever Luqa was bombed—which was often—and gave the table a gray patina. Eleanor could trace 505's path back to Malta in the little marker's faint track through the dust, like a wake, as a WAAF nudged it along.

But some things remained unchanged since the Battle of Britain, Eleanor thought. The enemy was still on the offensive, still pounding away at helpless civilian populations in the hope of military advantage. There were still many enemy bombers and escorting fighters but just a handful of Hurricanes and Spitfires to ward them off. And, as it had turned out, it was still Albert Kesselring of the Luftwaffe against Keith Park of the RAF—the heavyweight prizefighter "Smiling Albert" Kesselring versus the agile counterpuncher Park. Park had outmaneuvered Kesselring in 1940, circling and jabbing away at Kesselring's bomber force until it was but a shadow of its former self. Now, Eleanor believed, Park could and would do it again.

Johnnie was still flying, she thought—that was another thing that was unchanged. She had come to accept it as inevitable that he would be in the thick of the action, month in, month out. This, she supposed, would always be her definition of war—herself in some ramshackle underground bunker at Park's side, calculating the odds as Park deployed his forces, with Johnnie represented by a cardboard sign in a wooden holder on a painted, out-of-scale map, the real Johnnie somewhere far above them, high in the thin air and the blinding glare of the killing fields.

She was reminded of Plato's allegory of a cave, in which the cave dwellers see shadows on the wall and think they are reality. The Operations Room was the cave: the map table was Plato's wall, the markers were the shadows, and only Johnnie existed in the real world. Plato would have understood this room immediately, she thought, even though he lived four hundred years before Christ.

The markers had the words "Caffe Cordina" and "This Table Is Reserved" printed neatly on one side, a reminder of their prewar purpose. It was increasingly difficult to remember dining leisurely in restaurants that hadn't suffered bomb damage. It all seemed so long ago. Her childhood and her years at Oxford seemed like a figment of her imagination rather than a real memory.

Sometimes she wondered what she and Johnnie would do when— if—the war ever ended. Obviously, if the Nazis won, then they'd have very little choice, doing whatever they were told to do under a totalitarian regime. She wasn't sure if the Germans would treat Johnnie with respect, as an honorable fighter in a losing cause, or seek vengeance for the losses he had caused the Luftwaffe. God alone knew what the Nazis might do to her and her model.

But if England won, or, to be precise, if America won and therefore dragged England through to survival, then something approximating prewar peace and freedom would return, and she and Johnnie would be responsible for their own destiny in a world without operations rooms and map tables and wooden squadron markers and constant aerial battles. It would be a world in which it was highly likely that Johnnie would come home for supper every day, unlike the present world in which the daily odds of his return were seldom better than fifty-fifty, even though, so far, he had always come.

Johnnie, she knew, foresaw that future almost entirely in terms of erotic fantasies played out in thatched huts beneath palm trees beside secluded beaches somewhere in the tropics.

"But what would we live on?" she had protested.

"Love and coconuts."

That was fine as far as it went, but sooner or later, more prosaic considerations would come into play, like what jobs to get to earn a living and where to live; one could live *for* love, she thought, but not *on* it. Johnnie's counterargument that coconuts were highly nutritious simply didn't pass muster.

She had always assumed she'd do something academic—teaching mathematics at Oxford, perhaps, or doing a doctorate at Princeton in America. But her experiences with Red Tape, the mathematical model based on zero-sum game theory she'd pioneered to analyze the Battle of Britain, had soured her to academic pursuits. If mathematics and logic could be applied to warfare, then they could be made to serve evil purposes. Red Tape had been swallowed up by Military Intelligence and had become, in her mind, a Pandora's Box.

Churchill had once given a wonderful speech in which he said that this war would be Britain's "finest hour." But he had also said in that speech that, if Britain lost, the world would sink into the abyss of a new Dark Age. He had said that this bleak future would be made more terrible "by the lights of perverted science." She sometimes wondered if she had become a perverted scientist, an intellectual killer. She wondered if her theory of asymmetric zero-sums—a theory originating in innocent children's games, played for fun—had been warped into a calculus of death.

The Americans had asked for her to join the Manhattan Project, the secret program to create a bomb of unimaginable power based on shattering atoms into their constituent particles, thereby releasing untold bursts of energy. It was only after she had pleaded with Churchill not to send her that he had intervened and transferred her to Park instead. How was that project progressing, she wondered, as scientists set aside their search for knowledge for its own sake and searched for knowledge leading to unspeakable death and destruction instead? How long could she keep claiming to be an academic mathematician and not a creator of some new intellectual Frankenstein?

"It won't be long now," Park commented, breaking into her reverie and gesticulating to the map. "The fighters will intercept the bandits just as they reach their targets. We detected them a little late, I'm afraid, so they'll reach their targets. Better late than never. Still, I want a full investigation of why the radar chaps didn't give us more of a warning."

Eleanor shook her head to clear it and returned to the present.

"Yes, sir," she managed, scientific ethics thrust aside.

"You know, that husband of yours is the complete professional," Park continued with a chuckle. "He's a fighter pilot's fighter pilot, as it were. He's positioned 505 so that the Italians can't see them in the glare of the sun. I sometimes wonder if he consciously thinks these things out or does them automatically out of instinct."

A second WAAF pushed two markers representing enemy aircraft south across St. George's Bay.

"They're heading due south at the moment," Park commented. "They could take a shot at us in Luqa or swing over to the harbor."

"There're several new ships at the dockyard," Eleanor said. "The remnants of yesterday's convoy."

"That would be my guess," Park said, nodding. "They missed 'em coming in from Gib, so they'll try to finish them off today." He turned towards a navy petty officer seated beside the map table with his own set of telephones arrayed before him, who acted as Park's liaison with the Royal Navy. "What do you think, Chief?"

"Very likely, sir. There're two destroyers and a minesweeper, if they can get at them, as well as the merchantmen."

"Let 505 know, would you, Freddie?" Park asked.

The controller sitting beside Park spoke into a radio telephone that connected him directly to the fighters. His voice was calm and precise, projecting a sort of absolute oracular truth as he reported the enemy's current position overhead St. George's Bay. He enunciated every syllable separately, Eleanor noted, to avoid any miscommunication. She had heard him ordering dinner in the officers' mess: "I'll have me-knee-stroh-knee soup-er, please."

* * *

Xghajra slid by beneath Shaux's port wing.

"Yorker, this is Armchair. Bandits are overhead St. George's Bay heading one-niner-zero," said his earphones in the controller's carefully enunciated voice. Shaux would bet Freddie had been an announcer at a railway station in his former life: "The train-er arriving on platform fiver twenty-niner to Kings Crossss . . ."

"Armchair, this is Yorker," Shaux said into his microphone. "Overhead Fort Ricasoli in one minute."

Valletta stretched out just ahead. He could see little clouds of dark smoke bursting into existence above the Grand Harbour. Some overly enthusiastic ack-ack flak battery must have opened fire prematurely, he thought. The controller had said the enemy was still overhead St. George's Bay, at least a minute away to the north.

Shaux searched the sky around him, quadrant by quadrant, looking everywhere except St. George's Bay. A successful fighter pilot—that is to say, a fighter pilot who lives to tell the tale—looks everywhere except at the known enemy, searching for the unexpected, searching for the enemy he hasn't seen. On this occasion he could see nothing.

* * *

Park picked up a telephone.

"Tell our ack-ack not to open fire, if you please," he said. "Friendly aircraft arriving overhead."

* * *

Miller stared northward through his binoculars across the expanse of the Grand Harbour, searching for the nonexistent enemy bombers that the ack-ack battery officer had instructed him to fire at. His view was partly obscured by a haze of smoke rising from a destroyer that had limped in last night on fire and was smoldering still, listing as if exhausted by the murderous run from Gib. Three hoses from a civilian fireboat were drenching the destroyer but to no visible effect.

In Miller's opinion, the battery officer, Sublieutenant James, was a bit of a wanker. He'd been in a nervous twitter, like Miller's Aunt Gladys, since Miller arrived on board. He stood side by side with James on a converted barge moored just off Fort St. Angelo, a so-called ack-ack lighter. It had two QF 6-pounder gun platforms bolted to its deck and could be towed around the oily waters of the harbor by an ancient tug and repositioned as needed.

The 6-pounders had Molins automatic loaders, a rack of six shells in a feeder mechanism that allowed each gun to fire a burst of six rounds in six seconds. These guns weren't really suitable for air defense—they were really anti-tank weapons—but they were better than nothing, Miller thought, and the barge could put a lot of metal in the air. They might even be effective if the officer would simply wait until there was an actual enemy up there to shoot at. Unfortunately Sublieutenant James seemed to be exactly the sort of officer you'd put in command of a barge without an engine.

"Hold your fire!" a loudspeaker erupted.

The gun crews ceased firing. Sublieutenant James cleared his throat but said nothing. In the sudden silence, Miller could now hear aircraft coming from all directions, or so it seemed, as the sound reverberated back and forth across the harbor. Now he could see shapes above Valletta, black dots crawling across the azure Mediterranean sky above the destroyer's haze. He'd been in the Med long enough to know they were almost certainly Italian SM.79 Sparvieros, Sparrowhawks, ugly but tough. That RAF officer he'd met on the aircraft carrier that brought them to Malta had told him how to identify them and other enemy aircraft too. Sparvieros had sunk the *Tat* with Miller's MTBs lashed to her decks. But for Sparvieros, Miller would have been in an MTB, with beautiful high-powered engines and guns that could actually point upwards into the air, instead of in a bleeding ack-ack barge with no engines at all commanded by a complete wanker.

Miller counted five—no, six; no, eight—of the enemy, growing rapidly larger and louder as they droned towards him. Now there was another sound, with a higher pitch. Looking eastward across to Fort Ricasoli, he could see Spitfires heading in this direction. They were much smaller than the bombers and much more elegant. The Sparvieros *growled*, Miller thought, with their three nine-cylinder air-cooled engines, a sort of workman-like industrial rumbling in the back of their throats, while the Spitfires with their V-12 Merlins, now that he could hear them too, *roared.*

He wondered if one of the Spits was that very decent officer he'd met on *Nonsuch*, that wing commander. He'd had three rings on his sleeves and medal ribbons and a pilot's badge on his chest, but he'd seemed just like a regular bloke who, like Miller, loved powerful engines.

The last Miller had seen of the pilot had been when he'd taken off from *Nonsuch*. His Spitfire had stood at the very stern of the flight deck, quivering as the Merlin spun up towards its maximum takeoff revs and emitting a wonderful howling sound. The torque must have been incredible.

The officer—he'd subsequently found out his name was Shaux—had released the brakes, and the Spitfire had bounded forward. The tail came up before it was halfway down the flight deck, racing towards the bow. Miller's heart was in his mouth: the Spit seemed to be glued to the deck despite its rapidly increasing speed. It was going to go straight over the bow, down to a hideous fate of being crushed and drowned beneath the onrushing *Nonsuch*. Miller could scarcely dare to look. At the very last moment, thank God, just in the nick of time, the wheels lifted perhaps six inches off the deck, no more, and the Spit howled off; it was flying but was no higher than the bow, mere feet above the wave tops.

Then in a moment of pure exhilaration, Miller saw the Spitfire seem to gather itself, shuffle off the bounds of gravity, lift its nose to sniff the salt air, raise its wheels, and climb swiftly into the Mediterranean morning.

Miller had once gone all the way to Aintree, in Liverpool, to see the Grand National Steeplechase. It was almost forty miles from

Manchester, the farthest he'd ever been until he joined the navy, except for Blackpool. The horses had had the same motion, he thought: the gathering of strength in the muscles, the measuring of the height of the fence ahead of them and the planting of the hooves, and then the smooth surge of power as they leapt.

Miller had watched the Spitfire as he had watched the horses, rapt. In his mind's eye, he was inside the Spitfire's engine cowling, inside the engine, watching the tappets drive the valves in and out of the combustion chambers, watching the gears whirling in the supercharger, watching each piston rising and falling an astonishing sixty times a second. He knew twelve pistons were rising and falling in perfect harmony, milled metal spinning inside milled metal machined to a thou tolerance and lubricated by a hair-thin skin of hot super-slippery oil forced in under high pressure. The entire mechanism created a power strong enough to defy gravity, lifting the Spitfire higher and higher above *Nonsuch* until it disappeared into the relentless glare.

Miller hoped Shaux was all right, that he hadn't been shot down or anything, because fighter pilots were constantly in the thick of it. Miller, in sharp contrast, had been doing exactly nothing since the *Tat* was lost. *Nonsuch* had escorted the remnants of the convoy to Malta and then continued east without entering the harbor, all the way to Alexandria in Egypt, where the MTB crews had done nothing for two weeks before being transferred to a cruiser, *Lovell*, which had brought them back to Malta. This morning, that Wren officer with the blond hair and the good figure had assigned him to this badly armed ack-ack barge commanded by a wanker, and he was still doing nothing as the Spitfires approached overhead to engage the enemy. The barge rocked gently at its moorings with silent guns and wasted brass cartridge cases rolling back and forth in the scuppers, offering a rhythmic clanking sound, as if to emphasize their futility. Perhaps he should apply to transfer to the RAF and work on Merlins.

SEVEN

Shaux noted that whoever it was had ceased their useless ack-ack. He'd been shot at by friendly fire on several occasions over the last couple of years, and it seemed a particularly pointless way of dying. Now he could see the bombers approaching the heart of Valletta just as 505 was approaching Fort Ricasoli. There were several new ships at anchor in the harbor—they must be the remnants of the convoy that had arrived late yesterday afternoon from Alexandria. One of the ships, a destroyer, he guessed, was on fire, and another had her bow down in the water.

In about a minute or a little less, 505 would reach the Sparvieros as they crossed the docks and jetties that lined the southern bank of the harbor. He would be too late to prevent the Sparvieros from dropping their bomb loads, but the bombers would pay a price. They seemed to be making the mistake that Shaux had trained himself not to make— they were focused on the enemy they could see and were not looking for other dangers.

About two miles to a probable point of intersection over Senglea. Revs for 250 miles per hour, a mile every fifteen seconds. A quick glance at the temperature and pressure gauges, an automatic check before an engagement ever since he had lost an engine in the midst of a dogfight over France last year. It was an annoying habit, a complete waste of a second. Shaux, like all experienced pilots, knew exactly the condition of the engine just by listening to it—most of the engine dials were unnecessary.

"Yorker, tallyho," he said, giving Fighter Command's traditional order to attack. He dipped his port wing, turning into the length of the Grand Harbour at an angle that would bring him into position for a flank attack on the enemy, and 505 followed in his wake.

The enemy must be very determined or getting desperate, Shaux thought. Sending a handful of unprotected bombers over Valletta in broad daylight, knowing there would almost certainly be Spitfires waiting, was foolhardy to say the least. Perhaps, as sometimes happened, there had been a balls-up, and the bombers had a 109 escort, but they'd never found each other. Perhaps this was the first wave of a much bigger, well-escorted raid that was arriving prematurely. Perhaps, always a possibility, these bombers did indeed have an escort of 109s hiding in the glare of the sun, and Shaux hadn't spotted them. Perhaps the bombers were bait in a trap into which Shaux was leading 505.

Thirty seconds, with Fort Ricasoli sliding away beneath his port wing.

Perhaps there was a mutual balls-up. Radar had been very late in detecting the bombers, and this was the second wave to reach Valletta this morning. Park always wanted to meet the enemy before they reached Malta, not after they arrived and delivered their deadly loads. Perhaps this was a new strategy by the enemy—sending frequent small raids in the hope of catching the Spitfires refueling and rearming on the ground, leaving Valletta's docks and shipping open and helpless.

Perhaps . . . well, solving such puzzles was Eleanor's department. Whatever the reason, she had said that the situation in North Africa was moving towards a decisive moment, a climactic clash between the British Eighth Army and Rommel's Afrika Korps. Sometime in the next few weeks, the two armies would meet, and one of them, the better-supplied one, would prevail. Therefore, both sides had to keep their supply lines open regardless of the costs—and the costs for attacking British shipping in broad daylight in Valletta's Grand Harbour on this particular morning would be very high.

Shaux completed the left turn past Fort Ricasoli towards the length of the Grand Harbour, knowing without looking that 505 was turning with him. Digby had trained 505 to the perfection of Grenadier Guards

outside Buckingham Palace, eight aircraft in two finger-four[2] formations moving as one.

Twenty seconds.

The southern side of the Grand Harbour consisted of a series of
natural promontories separated by narrow inlets, perfect for docks
and moorings, deep enough for seagoing ships, and well protected
from the ravages of sea and wind. It was easy to see why Malta, such
a superb natural harbor set at the crossroads of the Mediterranean,
had been settled so long ago, thousands of years before the Egyptians
built the pyramids of their pharaohs or the Greeks built the temples
of their gods.

Fifteen seconds.

He could see the gaggle of aircraft, presumably Italian three-
engine Sparviero bombers, crossing above the center of Valletta and
over the Grand Harbour. The bombers were approaching the docks
and jetties on the southern shore—still little toys at this distance but
growing rapidly, moving from right to left in Shaux's perspective—as
505 closed on them.

Each Sparviero carried about a ton of ordnance, give or take, usually in a payload of eight or ten bombs. Shaux spared a brief glance
down. The bombers had their bomb doors open and a trail of destruction followed in their wake. Columns of water were erupting from the
harbor where bombs had fallen. When the bombers reached the docks,
the water columns were replaced by flashes of explosions and erup-
tions of smoke and debris: an ugly trail leading southward from the
heart of Valletta, across the harbor, through a pall of thick, oily smoke
above a cluster of burning ships and on into the docks and jetties and
warehouses on the southern shore.

* * *

Miller heard the high-pitched whine of falling bombs as he sheltered
in the lee of a 6-pounder mounting. The whining was even louder than
the raucous bellowing of the bombers as they flashed overhead. There
was absolutely nothing the ack-ack crew could do to protect itself and

---

2. A formation of four aircraft positioned like the fingertips of an outstretched hand.

absolutely no way of fighting back. He inched one eye above the bulkhead and saw bombs exploding on or around the burning destroyer—it was impossible to tell in the midst of all the bursts of smoke and plumes of water and flying debris. One bomb must have definitely struck the fireboat beside it because he saw the hoses die abruptly. Another bomb fell closer, in the middle of the harbor, halfway between the destroyer and the ack-ack barge, and yet another fell not twenty feet in front of Miller.

The blast plucked up Sublieutenant James, who had been, absurdly, standing and looking upwards through his binoculars, and dropped him into the harbor. A tidal wave of water followed and swamped the barge, and Miller found himself swimming for his life.

* * *

Ten seconds. The left profile of the leading SM.79 bomber filled Shaux's gunsight as he flicked off his safety catch. The Sparviero was painted in some sort of dark mottled camouflage. Its humpbacked shape made it an exceptionally large target. The open doors of its bomb bay hung beneath it. He could see the pilot and the dorsal gunner clearly as they stared down to see where their bombs were hitting. "Look out!" he felt like screaming at them. "I don't want to have to kill you!"

He did not hate his enemies even if they were, as now, trying to kill people with their bombs. Shaux thought of the aircrew on both sides of the conflict as helpless pieces locked in a game of chess. If a rook took a pawn, it wasn't the rook's fault but that of the player who moved it. Similarly, the responsibility for this attack on Malta lay not with these pilots but with their commanders, all the way up to Mussolini. Long ago, in the Battle of Britain, when Shaux had adopted William Butler Yeats's poem as his personal catechism, he had embraced "those that I fight I do not hate" as one of his principal articles of faith.

Five seconds. One last quick glance at the horizon; still no 109s in sight. If they were there, then Shaux was flying into their trap. Time would tell. No escape for the Sparvieros and no escape from Shaux's obligation to shoot them down. He waited until the range was less than two hundred yards and the Sparviero was filling his gunsight. He depressed the firing button on his control column and felt, as much as heard, a thump-thump-thump from the recoil of the 20-millimeter cannons crunching back against the spars in each of his Spitfire's wings. It was almost like a car bumping over deep ruts in a country lane. Immediately he could see tracer sparkling on the cowling of the Sparviero's left engine.

Thump-thump-thump. Just another short burst of a few 20-millimeter rounds. That would be enough.

He had always thought of machine guns—particularly the light .303 Brownings in earlier versions of the Spitfire—as weapons to point and spray at the enemy in the hope that a lucky shot struck something vital. A Spitfire could fire about 120 rounds in a second. The propaganda newsreels in the cinemas always showed shaky camera-gun snippets of accurate fire, lines of tracer leading to the fuzzy shape of an enemy aircraft that promptly burst into flames, as if all Spitfire pilots were expert marksmen. In real life, there was always too much going on—too many variables, too much motion, too much confusion—for accuracy. In real life, most camera-gun footage recorded pilots firing at empty sky with nary an enemy aircraft even in sight, let alone in range.

On the other hand, a 20-millimeter cannon at close range, at 200 yards and closing, left nothing to chance. It was a sharp ax in the hands of an executioner.

How could the crew of the Sparviero have failed to look for Spitfires, he wondered, as a thick stream of oily smoke sprang from the bomber's left engine? How could they have been so recklessly oblivious to such an obvious danger? They still hadn't turned their heads to see him as he flashed past them. Perhaps they were raw trainees and this was their first operation, in which case, unfortunately for them, it would also be their last. If they died, they would never have seen their executioner. He'd heard that the Italian crews called these raids the *rotta della morte*, the "route of death." No wonder!

Time always seemed to slow down when one finally met the enemy, Shaux thought for the thousandth time. Perhaps one's senses were sharpened or one's reflexes were faster. These moments were like the moments captured by a camera gun, sixteen frames in each second. Normally one couldn't see the individual frames, the frozen images, flashing by—that's what gave the illusion of movement when you saw the film on a cinema screen, of course. But up here, with the Sparviero so close that he could see the dents and dings in its fuselage, the way that the door of a hatch on the left side of the fuselage didn't quite fit correctly, and that there was black oil welling from the engine cowling he had hit, he felt he could see each individual frame of the film, one at a time, click, click, click. He saw—no, he had to be imagining it—the beginning of a look of shock on the rear gunner's face as cannon shells exploded all around him.

Then Shaux flashed over the Sparviero, and time reverted back to normal. The Sparviero became, in his mind, just another aircraft in a very, very long list of aircraft that Shaux had been obliged to damage and perhaps destroy, something to be buried and forgotten, at least theoretically, in some remote corner of his brain.

Shaux sometimes wondered if the prison warders who executed murderers, the hangmen, remembered or mourned their victims, or whether at the end of their shift they just went home as if nothing had happened.

"Did you have a good day at work, dear?" their wives might ask.

"Nothing special, love—just the usual. What's for supper?"

"Sardines on toast, dear. I'll just put the kettle on."

"Splendid!"

Shaux was always grateful that he didn't believe in God or an afterlife, because he wouldn't have to face all the enemy aircrew he had shot down. He wouldn't have to apologize for denying them their lives or the lives of the children they might have sired. He wouldn't have to try to justify his actions to them. He wouldn't have to face their mothers or their wives or girlfriends, with their eyes filled with loathing as they asked, "How could you do that to him?"

After 505 swept over the bombers—the entire engagement lasted less than five seconds—Shaux immediately led 505 into a tight U-turn over Kordin and Albert Town at the innermost end of the harbor, bringing them back around towards the Sparvieros. As he completed the turn, he could just see two or three of the surviving bombers turning eastward towards the sea in a desperate attempt at escape.

There was still no sign of 109s or any other bandits. The survivors were now two miles away from 505. The Spitfires had a 100-mile-per-hour advantage over the Sparvieros—less than two minutes to catch up to them.

"Follow me," Shaux said, nudging his throttle open.

* * *

"Yorker is in pursuit of the band-dits, heading north," the controller reported to Park. "Two minutes to catch up."

"Any damage reports yet?" Park asked the room at large.

"The destroyer that came in yesterday on fire, sir, HMS *Grand*, has been hit again," the petty officer said. "She may not be salvageable. An ack-ack lighter was swamped. No other shipping reports yet, but there's probably more damage. All the dock areas have sustained bomb damage, sir, but we don't have any details yet."

"Enemy losses?"

"That's not clear, sir," a young RAF corporal, with a telephone at each ear, responded. "But so far it looks as if they lost two probables and have two more damaged. One of them is reported as flying south towards Libya at low altitude, trailing smoke. No losses reported on our side, sir."

"Radar?"

"Nothing on the screens, sir."

Park pondered.

"This may have been just a nuisance raid just to get us up," he said. "Or perhaps their 109s and bombers got separated. Any thoughts, Eleanor?"

"Well, he's done this before, sir," she said, nodding. "He's sent in a small raid or two and then a much larger one, trying to catch us out. Perhaps this is a new strategy, sending small raids one after the other. But I don't know; perhaps these bombers simply lost their escorts, and it was all just a balls-up."

Park looked away in embarrassment and Eleanor kicked herself. Park was punctilious about not using strong language in front of women, seldom saying anything worse than "damn." But "balls-up" was such a normal expression—almost an official technical term—that it had popped out of her mouth automatically.

"Sorry, sir," she muttered.

"Where's Digby? Do we know?" Park asked the controller, obviously pretending he hadn't heard anything.

"They're returning, sir. They should land in twenty minutes. Dum-bo is safely away."

"Very well. Tell 505 to break off pursuit and return," Park said to the controller. "I don't want to risk losing anyone at sea."

Johnnie would return safely, Eleanor thought. With a bit of luck, he wouldn't fly again today. Charlie would be happy, too—he was always nervous when Johnnie flew.

"I want them refueled and rearmed and ready to go again at a moment's notice," Park continued. "They caught us out on this one, and I don't want it to happen again. My bet is that they'll return in greater numbers to have another go at what's left of that convoy. So we'll organize standing patrols to meet the next wave before they get here. And get onto the radar chaps, please, and find out why they didn't give us more warning. Are they having technical difficulties?"

The controller began speaking into his telephone.

Eleanor glanced at the clock. It was 0900 hours, still quite early, with many more hours left for the enemy to pound Malta. Out of the corner of her eye, she saw, or thought she saw, Park suppress a yawn. Poor man, she thought, he's already been at work for hours, and most of the day was still ahead of him. He'd turned fifty in June, so in peacetime he'd be getting ready for retirement; instead he was in one of the most stressful positions in the world. She'd never had a reason to question his abilities or his energy, but, even so, at fifty he was no spring chicken.

She suppressed a yawn herself. She was no spring chicken, either. She was already twenty-four, and she hadn't even started having children or having a real job. The war was stealing everybody's life, and she assumed it would continue at least another three or four years, by which time she'd be in her late twenties, still with no babies and perhaps already with a few gray hairs.

EIGHT

Miller thought he was going to drown. He had Sublieutenant James's supine body in his arms, and he was attempting a sort of backwards dog paddle. They were both weighed down by waterlogged clothing. Miller was not a strong swimmer, and he was wearing boots. He could barely keep his head above water.

He had vague and unpleasant memories of going to the Victoria Baths back in Manchester when he was eight and being thrown into the water, in accordance with the classical "sink or swim" theory. Eventually, having being dragged from the water after three or four near-drownings, he had learned a sort of desperate paddle, powered by terror. He had not been in water since.

The nearest jetty was only twenty feet away, but it might as well have been a thousand. He supposed he'd have to let go of James and save himself, but that was easier said than done.

In the midst of his struggles, he heard aero engines overhead and knew they were Merlins. If he survived, he promised himself, he would definitely apply for a transfer to the RAF and work on Merlins.

Now he found there was something under his feet, something lifting him. He kicked against it, and whatever it was pushed them upwards. Thank God! He kicked once more and saw he was being lifted by a broad raft of wooden planking, a fragment of a jetty or something that had been blown into the harbor by one of the bombs and was now refloating itself. He let it lift him, taking gulps of air, with Sublieutenant James's sodden body still in his arms.

It was clearly his destiny to work on Merlins in the RAF, but in the meantime James was very heavy and Miller lacked the strength to wriggle out from under him. The sounds of aircraft died away; suddenly it was very peaceful. Miller breathed a long sigh of relief, and James shuddered and began to vomit.

* * *

The 505 dispersal area resembled a disturbed ant nest. The returning pilots were parking their Spitfires at random intervals, and ground crews were pulling camouflage netting over them, even as armorers were clambering on the wings to replenish the ammunition drums. Fuel bowsers made their way from Spitfire to Spitfire to top up their tanks. One aircraft had its cowlings off, and three fitters were examining its Merlin—supercharger trouble, Shaux guessed, from where they were poking about.

As he finished taxiing in, Shaux could see Charlie bounding from aircraft to aircraft, looking for him. Shaux ran through his post-flight routine, switched off his Merlin—always a moment of shocking silence—opened the canopy, dragged off his sweaty helmet, and whistled. Charlie looked up and galloped towards him, almost knocking Jenkins over, and leapt onto the wing to greet him. Shaux bent down and cradled Charlie's massive head as Charlie gave him slurpy kisses.

"Of course I knew you'd come back," Shaux knew Charlie was thinking as they stared into each other's eyes. "I wasn't the least concerned, not even for a moment. Of course I knew. But, just to be on the safe side, you'd better not leave again!"

"Yorker Freddie, stand by," roared the loudspeaker, as if denying Charlie's silent request.

The dispersal area had already been full of purposeful bustle, and now it became hectic. Jenkins took charge. He jumped on the cab of a fuel bowser and yelled instructions left and right, gesticulating with his arms like a semaphore. Shaux stood back, staying out of the way, admiring the ground crews. The public believed that the pilots were the only men that really mattered in a fighter squadron, but Shaux, from long experience, gave most of the credit to the ground crews, the men who kept the Spitfires in perfect condition, fueled, armed, and supplied. For every pilot in his cockpit, there were twenty men and women who put him there and gave him a chance to win. No, wait; there were sixty pilots, give or take, and more than four thousand people working at Luqa. It was closer to seventy-to-one.

At times like these, when speed was of the essence, it was very easy to make a costly mistake—to spill fuel, or accidentally back a lorry into an aircraft, or forget a necessary tool, or misalign an ammunition belt so that the guns would jam, or upset an aircraft's aerodynamics by failing to close an access panel, or leave the cap off a tank, or any of a hundred such errors. But Jenkins had trained his men like the interlocking pieces of a machine: when the pressure was on, as now, the machine simply changed to a higher gear without any loss of precision. And they were doing all this, Shaux noted in silent appreciation, in the midst of a siege that had created severe shortages of just about everything so that improvisation and scavenging and making-do were the orders of the day. They were under the hot mid-morning Mediterranean sun and on short rations so that they were almost permanently hungry.

These were men with grit in their hair and oil under their fingernails, men who had not had a decent meal or a day off in months and who were dressed in an assortment of ill-fitting kit and housed in uncomfortable buildings with rudimentary plumbing that might be bombed into rubble at any moment, men who might be called upon to work from dawn to dusk and then until midnight under poorly lit, claustrophobic camouflage netting. They had their own language—"Gimme a wrenches, sprocket, five-eighth"—and their own esprit de corps, their own pride in the condition of the aircraft, and their own fiercely competitive determination to outperform their Axis competitors. They were "erks," "bods," armorers, riggers, fitters. Given a choice between living with these men or in the rarefied air of the officers' mess, Shaux would have chosen their company every time.

* * *

Eleanor stared at the enemy markers looming to the north, approaching across the table halfway between Sicily and Malta. The WAAF at the table seemed to be moving them forward reluctantly, as if blaming herself for the approaching danger.

"ROC speculates that it's a stronger signal than before, sir," a WAAF with a headset reported to Park, referring to the Royal Observer Corps who manned the radar systems. Eleanor thought she saw Park grimace. What use was speculation? Even after several years of development, radar technology remained inexact, to say the least.

"Perhaps your idea of successive waves to catch us off guard is right, Eleanor," Park said, staring at the map. "We'll deal with the current batch of bandits and put up a picket line as well."

Poor Johnnie, she thought. He wouldn't even have time for a cup of tea and a smoke—although, of course, he'd stopped smoking, just as she had—before going up again. She knew without thinking that he'd choose to fly, even though he didn't have to.

It was hard to decide who should get credit for inventing aerial picket lines. The idea was that a small flight of Spitfires would fly north at very high altitudes and search for incoming enemy formations, to find them beyond the range of the ground-based radars. The idea took advantage of both Digby's phenomenal eyesight and the Mark IX's excellent performance all the way up to thirty thousand feet. Airborne radar was improving by leaps and bounds, but it was still hit or miss—too often miss. The same was true of antiaircraft radar on ships. Eleanor believed that radar technology would eventually come to dominate naval and aerial warfare, but in the meantime, human eyesight was still essential.

Actually, to be fair, the original idea was probably Park's, back in the Battle of Britain—he had often sent Johnnie's old squadron, 339, to "loiter" above the south coast of England, she recalled, reporting inbound Luftwaffe raids. In those crucial days, Johnnie and Digby had spent many hours high above Dover, reporting on the Dorniers and Heinkels and their attendant 109s and 110s that flowed in like a flood tide, bringing death and destruction to rain down on southern England, and then ebbed away back to France in painfully mauled remnants.

Park had instituted a similar plan as soon as he had arrived in Malta. The idea was to detect incoming raids as they formed over Sicily, to give the waiting fighter squadrons time to take off, climb to the north, and meet the raiders before they reached Malta. It took a squadron at readiness three minutes to start up and take off and then seven minutes to climb to twenty thousand feet—to angels two-zero. By then, the raiders, flying south, would be halfway to Malta, but there would still be enough time to force them down or turn them back.

Park preferred to send two squadrons, if he had them available, in addition to the pickets: one to engage a fighter escort, if there was one, and a second to deal with the bombers. It didn't always work, and the bombers could still get through—that had already happened twice this morning—but there was no question that the severity of the raids had been declining over the past month.

The whole thing depended on having enough aircraft for Park to deploy and enough fuel and all the necessary supplies, and that, in turn, depended on the brave men who manned the convoys from Gibraltar, without whom the island could not last more than a week or two.

* * *

Charlie had heard the loudspeakers and stared at Shaux in seeming disbelief. He knew what these sudden announcements might portend.

"Not again!" he seemed to be thinking.

Shaux bent down to him. *"Je reviendrai, mon brave, je promets,"* he whispered. "I'll come back, old friend. I promise."

Charlie's head went down. Shaux believed it comforted Charlie to hear the language he had heard when he was a puppy, but it didn't seem to have worked on this occasion. He turned away and trotted off to find Jenkins—he at least could be trusted not to fly away.

* * *

Miller groaned inwardly as he heard the air raid sirens going off for the third time this morning. It was unbelievably frustrating to be subject to constant bombardment without any chance of fighting back. They were stuck with the wrong guns. Why couldn't the navy give them 20-millimeter Oerlikons so that they could actually shoot back?

Sublieutenant James had been taken to the hospital, leaving Miller unexpectedly in charge of the flak barge.

"For God's sake, don't do anything," James had rasped at Miller as he departed. "Just stay out of trouble."

Miller had come halfway round the bleeding world, or so it seemed, to fight the enemy in motor torpedo boats, but he had no bleeding boats, no bleeding guns, and he was under strict orders to do sweet bleeding nothing.

He heard a distant roar off to his left, beyond Valletta, and saw the tiny specks of Spitfires rising from the airfield out there, climbing towards the north. The navy just had to sit here and be bombed, he thought. At least the RAF was fighting back.

That's it, he thought. That's enough.

* * *

The most important thing to know about angels two-five, Shaux thought, is not that it is five miles up but that it's *cold*. He had managed to grab his leather flying jacket before they left the ground but not his usual cold weather stuff—silk gloves, silk underwear, an extra sweater, and two pairs of socks. Eleanor had laughed at him the first time she saw the outfit, calling him "the Michelin man," but he'd rather look ridiculous than feel bloody cold. Besides, he thought it was dangerous; his body was burning energy trying to keep warm and therefore fatiguing him, and he was distracted and his reactions were slower.

He had no one to blame but himself, of course. He had chosen to fly instead of sitting in a safe, warm bunker shuffling requisition forms—that was no choice at all!

They had climbed above the incoming formation of Sparvieros, leaving them to be dealt with by the rest of 505 and a squadron of Hurricanes. Now he and Digby and a couple of wingmen were flying in a lazy figure eight pattern, waiting to see if any more bandits appeared out of the glare. They had enough fuel to stay up here for an hour, Shaux thought despondently. How much colder would he get?

Last week someone from the Air Ministry had flown in to assess what the Malta fighter squadrons needed.

"We see enemy shipping quite often, and we could take a crack at them, but we have no way of attacking them effectively," Shaux had said. "Could we have wing racks for bombs or rockets?"

"Spitfires as fighter bombers?" the Air Ministry man had said, with a slight curl to his lips. "I shouldn't think so! We're developing new aircraft for that purpose."

"Typhoons?" Shaux asked. "Are they ready?"

The Air Ministry man appeared to be wondering if Shaux was an enemy agent. "I'm not at liberty to say."

"We really need more operational range," Shaux said. "We need much larger long-range tanks."

"We might consider that."

"Drop tanks under the wings, say fifty gallons apiece."

"Why so much?"

"Well, the farther our range, the better our defenses."

"But that would be double your current capacity."

"Surely that's a good thing, isn't it?"

The Air Ministry man pondered. "We'll have to see. It seems a bit excessive to me."

"Weapon pods, like the *Waffenträgers* some 109s have?" Shaux asked, changing his tack. "They could be very effective against—"

"Definitely not."

"Cockpit heaters?"

"Good God, no!" The man was aghast. "Heaters? Surely you jest? This is summer in the Mediterranean! Out of the question!"

"But . . ."

"Please don't waste my time, Wing Commander!"

Now Shaux desperately wished the Air Ministry man—who was doubtless back in a comfortable office somewhere in Whitehall, happily exchanging lengthy memoranda with his chairborne colleagues as they all flew their mahogany Spitfires—was with him on picket duty at angels two-five; he would very quickly understand why they needed heaters. American-built P51 Mustangs had heaters, Shaux knew, and were powered by the same Packard-built Merlin engines; perhaps he could find out what source of heat they used, and how they were made . . .

"Armchair, this is Vulture," Digby's voice broke into Shaux's thoughts. "Bandits, bearing zero-zero-zero, angels one-five."

"Vul-chewer," the controller responded.

"Vulture" was the call sign Digby had chosen for these picket patrols. Shaux had not liked the name, thinking of vultures as ugly, turkey-like creatures feeding on rotting flesh, harbingers of death. He'd seen them at the cinema, sitting in leafless trees, patiently waiting while the hero slowly died from thirst under the merciless sun. The hero would stagger across the desert sand dunes, eventually falling to his hands and knees and crawling painfully on. Mournful background music would reach a crescendo. Just when the hero finally collapsed and the vultures began to move in, the rescue party would arrive to save him in the nick of time. The heroine, her blouse inexplicably torn, would cradle his head and bring a water bottle to his parched lips.

"No, vultures are not ugly at all!" Diggers, an ornithologist, had objected. "Vultures are wonderful creatures, large, powerful carnivores as big as eagles but specially adapted through Darwinian evolution to be able to fly at great heights, at angels two-zero or even higher, with very little oxygen."

"Vultures have superchargers, Diggers?"

"High-efficiency oxygen-converting hemoglobin—a far superior natural solution."

That was typical of Digby, Shaux thought. He knew everything.

"Bandits are twenty-plus twin-engines and twenty-plus escorts," Digby said, as if to prove Shaux's point.

"Square Bravo Three," Digby's wingman added. Digby had divided the sea between Malta and Sicily into one hundred squares on a map, and Bravo Three—second column from the left, three rows down, about thirty miles southeast of Agrigento—was their best estimate of where they were.

"Fort-tee-plus bandits at angels one-five at Bravo Three, Vulchewer," the controller acknowledged.

Shaux imagined this information being reported to Park, who would order the necessary Hurricanes and Spitfires into the air to meet the bandits before they could do damage. The dispersal area would again be a beehive of fast but disciplined activity as the squadrons raced to take off. Charlie would be waiting patiently, watching the skies for returning aircraft. It occurred to Shaux that it was a bad idea to speak to Charlie in French; Charlie had surely worked out that French meant Shaux was leaving him.

The enemy seemed to have an inexhaustible supply of pilots and aircraft, Shaux thought. Evidently the Regia Aeronautica in Sicily and southern Italy had been reinforced by Luftwaffe units returning from Greece and Russia. They were commanded by Park's old adversary, Kesselring. Eleanor described him as a brilliant administrator but an unimaginative tactician.

This was the third or fourth wave they had sent this morning, but Park had invented the art of defensive fighter tactics, and Eleanor had turned it into a science. Unfortunately Park was hobbled by an acute shortage of everything he needed to be able to defend Malta successfully; everything depended on the convoys.

NINE

Eleanor stared at the map table. Digby's squares had been drawn on it in chalk and were constantly being rubbed away. The controller ordered Vulture to move eastwards to square Easy One, where the radar might or might not have picked up a signal. Suddenly the room seemed claustrophobic, and the incoming waves of bandits seemed like a scratched gramophone record that kept repeating itself over and over. The amateurish chalk lines were symptomatic of the endless two-year Siege of Malta, which had reduced everything to make-do and improvisation.

For the first time in a long time, she felt useless. There was, in truth, nothing she could do to help, so she turned away and escaped to the open air. The heat met her like a blow.

That morning she had told Harry Hopkins that Malta would survive. Now she was not so sure. If even a single convoy didn't get through, then the fighters might not be able to fly, the navy might not be able to sail, and the population would begin to starve. Part of her job was to review requests for provisions and supplies to be included in the convoys' bills of lading. She had calculated, with a sort of grim sadism, exactly how long Malta could last, exactly how long it would be before the children would stop being just hungry and start actually starving.

The navy was committing enormous resources to the convoys— sometimes forty or more fighting ships to guard a dozen merchantmen— but the enemy had proved remarkably skillful in attacking them by using a combination of bombers, torpedo bombers, submarines, and fast attack boats, one after the other. It might be useful to review the records of past convoys to see whether there were better ways of defending them. Of course it would be useful—she kicked herself for not thinking of it before. The navy must have records . . . she'd contact them as soon as she got back to her office.

Another convoy was in its final stages of preparation, she knew. EF-6 had left Liverpool and made the long passage to Gibraltar. After pausing there to refuel and pick up more escorts, it would head for Malta. Some combination of spies and Luftwaffe reconnaissance aircraft would probably spot EF-6—they nearly always did—and then the Axis powers would have plenty of time to organize a gauntlet of fire.

It was a big convoy, she had been told, including two tankers and a cargo ship jam-packed with Spitfires in disassembled components. The convoy had been given its own name: Operation Type. The Admiralty was rolling the dice; the desert war was reaching a crisis, with Rommel at the gates of Alexandria and the British Eighth Army without a commanding general: William "Strafer" Gott had just been killed on his way to take command.

A hundred years ago, in a half-forgotten war, some general or other had sent cavalry up a valley with enemy artillery firing down from both sides. It had been a bloodbath, memorialized in a poem that Eleanor half remembered from school, something about *into the jaws of death, into the mouth of hell*, and *theirs not to reason why, theirs but to do and die* . . . The Malta convoys were just like that, she thought, men and ships sailing into a killing field, a shooting gallery all the way from Sardinia and past Sicily to the north, and Algeria and Tunisia to the south, sent to do or die.

This part of the Med was called the Strait of Sicily, but "jaws of death" was more appropriate. She'd have to ask Diggers for the Latin translation.

Some ships would get through, with a combination of guts and luck, but others would not. Some, like the destroyer *Grand* in the harbor, would limp into Malta to die. Malta had enough aviation fuel for another ten days at the present pace and intensity of Axis attacks, she calculated. After that . . .

The fate of Malta hung by a slender thread.

* * *

Miller waited patiently outside Third Officer Dryden's office. She had assigned him to the ack-ack barge, he reasoned, and therefore she could assign him to something more useful. He'd heard there was a Fleet Air Arm airfield somewhere in Malta, which meant aero engines and jobs for mechanics like himself.

He felt completely bloody useless, to tell the truth. Aimless. He had to do something. Maisie would know exactly what to do, but Maisie was half a world away in Manchester, beyond reach.

He had been in the navy since war was declared back in 1939. He was a motor mechanic by trade, a product of the grimy rows of tiny back-to-back terraced houses packed tightly around the factories and mills in the city of Manchester, in the north of England. He'd left school when he was fourteen and had been lucky enough—in the midst of the high unemployment of the Depression—to land an apprenticeship at a small tool and die company. Here he had discovered an affinity for steel: how to shape it, cut it, and bend it to his will, at tolerances of a thousandth of an inch. It was as if he and steel came to an understanding— a partnership—in which he admired its strength and its dull gray sheen and silky texture and its ability to endure extraordinary forces. In return the steel permitted him to turn it to useful purposes and thereby give its existence meaning and value.

When Dalton Engineering succumbed to England's stumbling, moribund economy, he'd found work at a motor repair garage, where he could literally reproduce broken engine parts from scraps of junk. There was nothing more satisfying than transforming an inanimate hunk of metal hauled ignominiously into the garage by a cart horse into a throbbing motorcar by turning the components of a new camshaft on a lathe or crafting a gearwheel with an accuracy within a thou, thereby revitalizing the engine.

His father had died in an industrial accident when Miller was a toddler. His mother worked in a cigarette factory and scrubbed floors in the evenings for extra money. She coughed herself to death in the saloon bar of the Bunch of Grapes when he was fifteen. She left him a tiny savings account, her reserve against a rainy day, and Miller found that he could just about afford to keep renting their tiny home.

Maisie Wilkins was the girl next door, a little older than Miller. She decided that he needed something to cheer him up, to take his mind off his misfortunes, and that something was "a bit of the other." Their first exploratory couplings evolved into a prolonged primeval compulsion that continued unabated until the war broke out in 1939 and Miller volunteered for the Royal Navy, even though he'd never seen the sea. Maisie fancied the navy's uniform more than the drab khaki of the army, and that was that.

The work at the garage had been satisfying, and one day, perhaps, he might be able to open a small repair place of his own—or even a small machine shop. Maisie, who was a bookkeeper in the local Woolworth's and as sharp as a tack, had thought it all out. She'd leave Woolworth's and look after the business side of things. They'd live over the garage; it was taken for granted they'd get married when they'd saved enough. When she got a bun in her oven—it was amazing they'd escaped so far—she could still do the accounts upstairs and answer the telephone, if they could afford one. It was typical of Maisie to state categorically that a modern business needed a telephone.

Maisie suited Miller very well; she was a right little goer, energetic and always ready. He didn't mind her ceaseless chatter, which continued unabated even through their frequent acts of copulation, because he wasn't much of a conversationalist himself, and he'd rather listen to her than to the radio, and he'd rather look at her than go to the pictures.

Maisie liked to take charge, she was ambitious, and she was clever in ways that Miller could not have imagined. She had found a chart in the newspaper that listed all the ranks and trade ratings in the navy, and she was determined that Miller should rise up through them. By the time he'd left England, he was a leading seaman, with a fouled anchor badge on his left sleeve to denote his rank. When the *Tattersall Castle* had sunk with all the MTB flotilla's officers aboard, he'd been bumped up to acting temporary petty officer in charge of the orphaned crews.

Of even more importance, Maisie had pushed him to take trade examinations, one after the other, so she could put a neat checkmark beside the illustration of the appropriate badge in the chart. He was now, therefore, rated as a skilled tradesman—a chief motor mechanic, second class, with a propeller badge with a crown and two stars on his right arm—and a princely pay rate of nine shillings a day in addition to five shillings and sixpence a day as an acting temporary petty officer. That mechanic badge set him apart from most other hostilities-only working-class youths swept off the streets and into the wartime navy; it made him respectable in the eyes of professional sailors and even officers.

But for Maisie he'd have been a mere ordinary seaman earning two shillings a day. He sometimes chuckled to himself that, with Maisie behind him, he might become an admiral before the war was over.

He glanced down at his right sleeve. The chief mechanic badge ensured that Third Officer Dryden would at least listen to him. Besides, there was something about her, something he just sensed, that made him feel she'd pay attention.

* * *

"We can't just sit back in our own half indefinitely," Park said. "Sooner or later we're bound to fumble the ball and they'll score a try, and one try is all they need."

It took Eleanor a second to realize Park was referring to rugby football, New Zealand's national passion. The All Blacks, their national team, were considered the best in the world.

He stood and gazed out the window of his quarters. Once the view must have been magnificent, Eleanor thought, of Valletta and the length of the harbor beyond it, guarded by medieval towers and battlements like a scene from a fairy tale, but now the view was dominated by bomb-shattered buildings and heaps of fallen masonry. The expanse of the harbor was half obscured by oily smoke coiling up from the listing carcass of the *Grand*.

Park had invited her, Johnnie, and Digby to dinner in his quarters, a rare privilege and welcome respite from the grim offerings of the officers' mess. In truth, Park's raw food supply was no better, but he had his own cook who could weave spells with herbs and spices, and he had an impressive supply of whisky.

"Spitfires simply don't have the range to carry the fight to the enemy," Park continued. "Therefore we can't provide our bombers with escorts. Therefore much of Sicily . . . Sardinia . . . Italy itself are all effectively beyond our reach unless we bomb at night, with all the attendant risks and uncertainties. As I said, we simply can't get out of our own half, and we can't win like that."

He grinned at Eleanor. "Nor can we not lose."

"Quite so," she said, grinning back.

"We can try adding larger slipper tanks, sir," Digby offered. "I've seen them up to a hundred gallons."

"No, I don't think so," Park said. "Slippers may be necessary for ferry runs, but there's a limit to how much you can carry and keep enough maneuverability to fight. As you know, slippers create a tremendous amount of drag."

Spitfires had been designed to fight above their own airfields, Eleanor knew, so they didn't need lots of fuel to travel long distances. In addition, the superb aerodynamic design of the aircraft put the weight of the fuel tanks between the engine and the cockpit, above the wing roots, where space was limited.

"Besides," he continued, "I just got a rocket from the Air Ministry about slippers, among other things, complaining we are making unreasonable demands."

"That must have been me, sir," Shaux said, smiling. "Sorry."

"Please be a little more humble in future," Park said, clearly with mock severity. "They did, however, say that they've formed a committee to assess the desirability of larger slipper tanks for Spits, and they'll notify us of their deliberations in a month or two."

"That's really very kind of them, sir," Digby said. "Good to know."

"Indeed it is. I feel much better now," Shaux said. "'With all deliberate speed,' I think the expression is."

"I am reminded of Longfellow's description of the Air Ministry," Digby said. "It is: *Though the mills of God grind slowly, yet they grind exceeding small.* It's amazing how Longfellow was able to anticipate the Air Ministry's mode of operation all the way back in 1846."

"How true," Park laughed.

* * *

"I just want to be useful," Miller said. "I think I can be more use working on engines than carrying ammunition."

"Well, er, Miller, we'll see," Penelope said. "We'll see what we have available, if anything."

He wasn't your average hostilities-only sailor, she thought. His service record was impeccable, and his badges said his abilities were far above average, even though he'd left school at the age of fourteen. There was even a report he'd saved an officer from drowning in the midst of a raid earlier today. She had never met a working-class person from Stretford, which she took to be some sort of industrial part of Manchester, nor did she wish to, but perhaps he was like the skilled senior craftsmen and shipwrights in her father's yard who took pride in their work and their skills but who also knew their place and were careful to keep it. Her father gave a summer garden party and a Christmas party for these workers and their wives, and, although it was a bit of a bore, she found it easy to chat amiably with them for a few minutes.

Miller seemed honest—he was looking her in the eye—and appropriately deferential, but she had the weirdest feeling that she was playing chess with this sailor.

"Not that carrying ammunition isn't important. I'm not saying that, ma'am. No. But not everyone's a mechanic."

"We all have to do whatever we're asked to do, Miller, in the war effort."

She almost said that she should be doing something using her knowledge of marine design—she knew her way around the Admiralty Research Laboratory at Teddington, on the Thames just outside London—instead of dealing with the detritus of the paperwork overflowing from Commander Thompson's chaotic desk, but she caught herself in time.

"I've worked on the Bristol Mercury, ma'am." That wasn't completely true, a bit of a stretch, but he'd pored over one on *Nonsuch* and helped the maintenance crews, so he was confident he could find his way round a Mercury quickly enough, if given the opportunity.

"Oh, sorry, Miller. The Fleet Air Arm doesn't have any Mercuries on Malta," Penelope said. "We only have Gladiators." She felt as if he'd pushed a knight boldly up the board, but she'd promptly taken it.

"'Scuse me, ma'am, but 'Mercury,' the 'Bristol Mercury,' is the name of the engine in the Gladiator."

"Oh." Damn! She'd taken his gambit, and he'd put her in check.

"Or there's the RAF, ma'am. I could transfer there."

It just so happened that the RAF at Luqa were asking the navy for experienced mechanics. She'd seen a signal to that effect just a couple of days ago.

"I'm familiar with the Rolls-Royce Merlin."

"You're an MTB mechanic, Miller. What engines did the MTBs have?"

"Packard M4 2500s, ma'am."

"Really? My father loved—"

She stopped abruptly. Her father's power boat, *Greased Lightning*, had Packard M4 2500s. She'd been about to say so, but she suddenly found she could not remember what Jimmy looked like. Perhaps it would be best—no, it definitely would be best—to dispatch this Miller away immediately.

"That will be all, Miller. I'll notify you in due course."

* * *

"The mills of God are not a laughing matter, Johnnie," Eleanor said later. "If EF-6—Operation Sort, or whatever it's called—doesn't get through, we probably won't be here in a month or two. We'll be in some Italian POW camp."

"'Type,' El. Operation Type," he said, trying to suppress a yawn.

"Then the Eighth Army will wilt before Rommel."

"True."

"It was nice to see Park laughing, though. He has so much on his plate."

"Yes, yes it was." Shaux stood and yawned outright. "I'll just take Charlie out for his nightcap."

Charlie always seemed to be able to get downstairs without his paws actually touching the steps. It would be interesting to film him with one of those high-speed cameras to see how he did it. Shaux could just make him out in the warm darkness, a white-scarved kernel of blackness loping between piles of rubble. The nighttime anti-bombing

blackout, with no lights showing, should have resulted in a sky glori-
ously full of stars, but, alas, a heavy haze hung over Valletta and the
breeze was marred by the sour taste of smoke. Would the Axis ever
stop bombing long enough for the fires to go out? Shaux wondered
what Malta smelled like in peacetime.

"Can you put more fuel inside a Spit?" Eleanor asked as soon as
Shaux and Charlie returned upstairs. "There's nothing in the tail, is
there? What about that?"

Once Eleanor had the bit between her teeth, Shaux thought, nothing could distract her. "You could, but you'd mess up the stability."

"How?"

"You push the COG, the center of gravity, back too far."

"Well . . . in the wings?"

"No, El. The wings are full of guns and ammunition belts."

"No, they're not. You said so yourself. The Mark IX doesn't have
eight machine guns and all the ammunition. It just has a 20-millimeter
cannon and a 50-caliber machine gun in each wing."

"Good lord, you're right! I've never thought of that. They're all
packed together, with drums instead of long belts. The outboard—"

"Would that upset the COG?"

"Shouldn't . . . I'll take a look tomorrow."

"If you'd have asked me, Johnnie, instead of the Air Ministry, you'd
have had extra fuel tanks weeks ago." She struck a pose. "Why is it that
men never ask women to solve their technical problems?"

"Good question."

"Seriously, Johnnie. You think it might work?"

"It's a very good idea, El. Seriously. We'll have to look at the practical details, but it's an excellent suggestion."

"Are you grateful?"

"Very grateful."

"Truly?"

"Truly grateful."

"Exactly how truly grateful are you? Please be specific."

TEN

"Are there records—logs or reports—of all the convoys for the last two years, Commander Thompson?" Eleanor asked.

Thompson's office, commanding a superb view of the harbor—even better than the view from Park's quarters, she thought—was awash in paperwork and extremely hot. At least her own underground office was cool, even though it had no view and no fresh air and she hated it.

"What the devil do you want those for?"

She wondered if belligerence was his normal mode of operation. He had medal ribbons from the last war, and she guessed he'd been brought back from retirement.

"We're reviewing strategies for defending incoming convoys from the air. We want to see what we can do to improve. Looking at what worked and what didn't work will give us some ideas."

"Sounds like a waste of time to me," he grunted. "Pointless," he added, and picked up a piece of paper.

Was he actually in the process of dismissing her?

"I asked the flag officer commanding HMS St. Angelo," she said, wondering if he responded to formality. In the time-honored and mysterious ways of the Royal Navy, their shore headquarters, such as Fort St. Angelo, were given ship's names. Thus "the flag officer commanding HMS St. Angelo" was the admiral who was the boss of Thompson's boss. "He offered the navy's full support and said you would supply any information and staffing support I might require."

He stared at her, evidently absorbing the news that he had been far outranked. She decided to press the point.

"Perhaps you have not yet received your orders."

She wondered if he might leap across his desk to strangle her but lacked the necessary energy and agility. He certainly looked as if he was considering it.

She prepared another barb but did not deliver it. It occurred to her that he was probably more than twice her age, even older than Park, and might be struggling, doing the best he could, in a job beyond his abilities. In another minute I'll be feeling sorry for him, she thought. Poor old thing. He should be home, pruning his roses, or tending to his compost pile, if compost piles, or perhaps heaps, needed tending. Perhaps, thirty years from now, she'd be trying to do a job she couldn't manage in some future war, and some child half her age would be sneering at her, just as she had been tempted to sneer at Thompson.

And so she simply stared and waited.

"Orderly, fetch . . . fetch . . . fetch that girl, that Wren!" he yelled though his door, finally goaded into action.

An awkward two minutes of silence followed while he moved papers on his desk, as if working, and she stared out over the harbor.

A young, blond WRNS third officer appeared in the doorway.

"I'm placing you on temporary duty with the RAF," Thompson said to her without any preamble or explanation. "This . . . this . . . ," he began, clearly undecided on how he should refer to Eleanor.

"She'll explain," he managed. "Carry on." He picked up his piece of paper again, and this time Eleanor welcomed the implied dismissal and took the opportunity to escape.

Penelope Dryden followed the WAAF officer outside.

"My name is Shaux, Eleanor Shaux," the WAAF said. "I work for Keith Park at Luqa."

She had three blue stripes on her shoulder epaulettes, the equivalent of a commander's rank in the navy, and she radiated energy and intelligence. She had a sort of clean-cut, no-nonsense way about her, as if built for speed, almost like a greyhound, it seemed to Penelope. She had short hair with a remarkably nice blue forage cap set upon it and, wonder of wonders, she was wearing trousers.

She shook Penelope's hand—a firm handshake yet not masculine.

"We are going to find out how to improve air support for the convoys. Therefore, we need a record of every convoy for the past two years, what got through, what didn't, and why."

It was like listening to a dynamo, the exact opposite of listening to Thompson.

"What's your name?"

"Penelope Dryden, Commander."

"No, no. I'm a wing officer, but that doesn't matter," the WAAF laughed. "Just call me 'ma'am.'"

She had a wedding band on her finger, Penelope noticed immediately, and she seemed no older than herself.

"Are the files we need in here?"

"The dockyard superintendent's duty office, ma'am," Penelope said. "It's just down the street. The RPO will know exactly what you need."

"RPO?"

"Regulating petty officer."

"What's his name?"

"Edwards, ma'am."

"Good. Lead the way."

Penelope had likened her to a greyhound and that seemed a good analogy, because the WAAF officer was striding along with a long, loping, springy sort of gait, and Penelope had to quicken her pace to keep up.

They met the RPO as he was emerging from the building.

"Good morning, Mr. Edwards. My name is Shaux," the WAAF officer said, extending her hand, and he shook it, clearly surprised. "You know Third Officer Dryden, I'm sure. We need your help, Mr. Edwards."

Now Penelope changed her inner analogy from that of a greyhound to that of an unstoppable steamroller that had just driven over the RPO and flattened him to the extent that she almost felt sorry for him. Within minutes the RPO was barking out orders, and civilian and naval clerks were scurrying. Three cardboard boxes were filled with files, transfer forms were signed with a flourish, and, in a fairly large miracle, an open navy staff car arrived to carry them, and the files, to Luqa.

At the last moment the duty officer with hungry eyes appeared, as if disturbed from slumber by the unaccustomed hubbub.

"Can I help you? I'm the—" he began.

"Thank you, it's really very good of you to offer, but we have all we need," the WAAF officer said, cutting him off. The DO opened his mouth and closed it again, a second steamroller victim.

She turned to the RPO and shook his hand.

"You've been extremely helpful, Mr. Edwards."

"Not at all, ma'am. Just let me know if you need anything else."

Now, a very large miracle occurred: the RPO smiled, perhaps for the first time in several years.

* * *

"It's hard to say from this angle," Jenkins said. The inspection hatches were open on the starboard wing of Shaux's Spitfire, and he was kneeling on it and peering in awkwardly, trying to see beyond the 50-millimeter machine-gun-belt-feed mechanism. Shaux crouched beside him but could see nothing beyond Jenkins's capacious rear quarters.

"We'll have to take the skin off one of the unserviceable aircraft," Jenkins said.

He climbed laboriously into a standing position and stretched his back. He, like many of the ground crew, suffered from chronic back pain caused by hours of reaching above their heads with heavy tools. Bad backs were even more common than twisted ankles from falling off ladders or scaffolding; it was remarkably easy for someone to forget where they were as they worked on an aircraft and take a step backwards or sideways into thin air.

Jenkins led Shaux through the dusty scrub behind the disposal hut towards an outer area where damaged aircraft underwent major repairs or were taken apart for scrap. Charlie trotted ahead on anti-weasel patrol—or, heaven forfend, they might even get attacked by a rogue rabbit. The area looked a bit like an RAF version of a junkyard, Shaux thought, filled with aircraft and their constituent components in varying degrees of damage and disrepair. A short corporal named Dobson crouched beneath one aircraft. He held a hammer and cold chisel in his hands as a cigarette dangled from his lower lip. He struck what looked like an exploratory blow upwards, and grimaced.

"Dr. Dobson, I presume," Jenkins greeted him. "What's up with G for George?"

Dobson extracted himself and stood up, stretching his back.

"Main spar's come a cropper. Done for."

"Done for?"

"Kaput."

Jenkins shrugged. Shaux noted that Jenkins did not question Dobson's judgment; on Dobson's verdict alone, an aircraft costing thirteen thousand pounds would be written off and broken up for scrap and spare parts. Its replacement would have to be brought all the way from England at a hideous cost in men and money. Shaux chuckled to himself: the Air Ministry would have formed a committee.

"Well then, Dobbo, I want the starboard wing open to the ribs, leading edge and all, quick as you like."

"What for?"

"Extra fuel tanks. To see if they'll fit."

"Internal, not droppers?"

"Internal."

Dobson narrowed his eyes in thought. Shaux knew he was an expert rigger, perhaps the best in Malta, and awaited his reaction. He was a corporal, Shaux also knew, instead of a flight sergeant or a warrant officer, because he had a long history of becoming drunk and disorderly and resisting arrest. His professional skills raised him up through the ranks until the next payday, when his encounters with the law laid him low again so that his RAF career resembled the peaks and valleys of an alpine range. Indeed, Shaux had heard it said that payday must be imminent because Dobson was again wearing WO badges on his sleeves.

Dobson lit another cigarette from the dying embers of his last.

"Fair enough," he said finally, and Shaux breathed a sigh of relief. If Dobson thought the idea had merit, it had merit.

* * *

The car carrying Eleanor and Penelope slowed to a crawl behind a horse and cart followed by a long line of women and children. The parade picked its way along rubble-strewn streets. The horse's ribs stuck out from undernourishment, and the cart had a broken spring. This, Eleanor guessed, must be a delivery of food to a Victory Kitchen, as the government food distribution centers were known. These "kitchens" provided measly daily food rations that pretended to be meals—often *minestra* soup consisting of a "marriage" of vegetables and meats.

In besieged, convoy-dependent Malta, the marriage was usually between lettuce or cabbage leaves and chicken stock. Occasionally, depending on the convoys, there might be beans, or tinned fish or meat. Rationing was strictly enforced, with an elaborate system of cards to record each family's allowances and severe penalties for cheating.

The caravan reached its destination, an empty shop. The sign over the shop window announced it was a butchery, recalling the days long ago when meat was available for purchase. The women and children stood waiting in an apathetic line. Eleanor recognized a tall civilian who stood to one side, consulting a clipboard of reports.

"Good morning, Dr. Dryden," she called.

"Why, good morning, Mrs. Shaux," he said, turning to greet her. "How do you do?"

He walked over to the car and saw Penelope.

"Well, good morning to you, too, Penny! What are you doing here?"

"Good morning, Uncle Bert," Penelope said.

Something in her voice made Eleanor guess that Penelope was feeling as if she were eight years old and in the presence of adults.

"Good lord, Dryden and Dryden," Eleanor said, jumping in to provide cover. "I didn't make the connection. How are we doing, Doctor?"

She was not certain whether Dr. Dryden had an official capacity or whether he was one of those natural leaders who just emerge from the crowd in an emergency. She had met him several times in meetings to prioritize what goods should be carried on convoys, an endless balancing act between military and civilian priorities. He was a doctor, he appeared to know everyone, he refused to be browbeaten and had the governor's reluctant respect, and he seemed to have an excellent brain.

"Not well," he said, lowering his voice. "We've just had to cut rations down to fifteen hundred calories a day, when we really need at least twenty-five hundred. That makes everyone weaker and more vulnerable to disease, particularly the youngsters and the elderly. And people are spending hours at a time cooped up in unventilated air raid shelters, where it's easy to spread things like bronchitis. We're seeing more typhoid, more cases of severe vitamin deficiencies . . ." His voice trailed away.

This is our true vulnerability, Eleanor thought. She was usually preoccupied with Spitfires and pilots and all the things they needed to defend the island from the endless bombing. But it didn't matter in the least how many Spitfires they had if the people were starving to death.

She glanced at the bony cart horse. He was living on borrowed time: soon all horses, goats, and any other farm animals still alive would be slaughtered, in part for their meat and in part so that their food could be fed to people instead.

In April the king had awarded the people of Malta the highest decoration for bravery, the George Cross, equal to the military Victoria Cross: *To honor her brave people, I award the George Cross to the Island Fortress of Malta to bear witness to a heroism and devotion that will long be famous in history.* It was a unique, unprecedented honor, she thought, but you couldn't add heroism to *minestra* soup to make it heartier or give devotion to infants to stop them coughing.

A convoy was at sea, another was in preparation, and doubtless another after that. Sailors and merchant seamen were risking their lives at sea; Johnnie and Diggers and the other pilots were risking their lives in the air. Everyone was being stretched to their limits and beyond, including the civilian population.

A woman in the queue tried to comfort an infant wailing in her arms, while another child sat at her feet, comforting her teddy bear. The bear was missing an eye, Eleanor noticed, and the child had a persistent cough. The woman's face seemed drained of expression, as if she were too exhausted to feel anything. She and Eleanor were no more than ten feet apart, but it seemed to be ten thousand miles: the woman in her dusty dress and worn-down shoes, with her children and her empty grocery bag and empty face, waiting for her *minestra*, and Eleanor, in her clean khaki uniform and comfortable car, with breakfast already in her stomach. She was suddenly ashamed of her empty arms.

The little girl was talking softly to her bear in Maltese as she rocked it in her arms.

"What is she saying?" Eleanor asked.

"She's telling her bear she knows it's hungry too," Dr. Dryden said.

The girl coughed and spoke again.

"What is she saying now?"

"'Don't cry, little one. Don't cry.'"

* * *

Eleanor lay in Shaux's arms in the warm darkness, pressed against him and wrapped around him tightly.

"Johnnie, I don't want any children."

"Well, not now, of course, El, in the middle of—"

"Not now, not ever. The world is far, far too cruel for children."

She shuddered, and he felt tears on his shoulder.

"Don't cry, El," he murmured. "Don't cry."

She began to weep in earnest and would not be comforted.

ELEVEN

Eleanor did not feel the least like springing from her bed the following morning—the urge to ignore the alarm clock was almost overpowering—but spring she must. She seemed to remember having nightmares but could not be sure, and there was no time for that sort of nonsense. Harry Hopkins was on his way back from Egypt and had requested a follow-up meeting.

Just as she and Johnnie arrived at Luqa, still bleary-eyed, Hopkins's Dakota growled over their heads and touched down in a miniature dust storm of its own making.

She headed for Park's office while Johnnie took the car in pursuit of the Dakota, obviously hoping to be invited to inspect it. She sometimes had to remind herself, as now, that Johnnie really loved flying and aircraft for their own sakes, while she regarded aircraft as instruments of death—some elegant but deadly, like Spitfires, rapiers in the skies, and some just blunt instruments, flying sledgehammers, like the Sparvieros droning over Malta every day, scattering death and destruction in their wake.

Harry Hopkins looked ill and exhausted and sagged in his chair; he had obviously been unable to sleep during the flight. He winced as he sipped his tea and swallowed three large pills.

"Look, Mr. Hopkins," Park said, clearly concerned. "This is absolutely none of my business, but shouldn't you rest? My private quarters are at your disposal—a bath and a comfortable bed? Perhaps a light meal later? Can't you manage a few hours? Surely you could conduct your business better if you're fresher?"

"Believe me, sir, that sounds absolutely wonderful. But unfortunately I have to get to Gibraltar and on to London as soon as possible."

Hopkins closed his eyes for a moment, as if engaged in an internal struggle to overcome his infirmities. When he opened his eyes, Eleanor saw he had summoned up his steely willpower. He had a lot in common with Johnnie, she thought. They both had the ability to overcome great challenges—in Hopkins's case, his agonizing illness, and in Johnnie's case, the excruciating tensions of combat—and function despite them.

Hopkins straightened himself, glanced at her, and smiled. She knew he knew what she had been thinking, and he was grateful, but business had to come first.

"I'm sure you will recall, Eleanor, the various plans for invading Europe that we started debating last year."

She had attended endless planning conferences—mostly a waste of time—when she was still in Military Intelligence running Red Tape.

"Indeed I do—everywhere from Norway in the north to Morocco in the south."

Images of dreary conference rooms sprang to mind, rooms filled with dreary men arguing—bickering, as often as not—before vast wall maps of Western Europe. Most of these men were in smart uniforms, she always noted, fighting theoretical battles in the safety and comfort of bombproof underground conference rooms, rather than fighting real battles in danger and discomfort in places vulnerable to real bombs.

"Well, the final decision was for three amphibious landings in Morocco and Algeria."

"Oh dear."

"I seem to recall that you were very much opposed, even though it was the plan advocated by Churchill."

"Yes, I thought it was a terrible idea."

Terrible idea or not, it seemed Roosevelt and Churchill had approved it.

"I recall you saying that three bad ideas did not add up to one good one, but they certainly did add up to one really abysmal one." Hopkins smiled.

"Well, I don't recall saying that, but I'm afraid it certainly sounds like me," Eleanor said, smiling back.

Churchill had, at one point, summoned her to No. 10 Downing Street and gazed at her through his customary cloud of cigar smoke.

"I am told, Wing Officer, that you are being difficult," he had rumbled.

"No doubt, sir."

"I am told you oppose amphibious landings upon the northwestern shores of Africa."

"Yes, sir, I do."

"Pray tell me why?"

"Because the shortest way from London to Berlin is eastward, sir, through Antwerp or Rotterdam, for example. Germany is to the east. Instead, we seem to be heading southward, away from Berlin, completely in the wrong direction."

Churchill grunted.

"Any plan based upon deliberately going in completely the wrong direction, away from the target, must be deemed unlikely to be prudent."

Churchill glowered but said nothing. He had a history of unsuccessful campaigns far away from the main arena, she thought—Narvik in Norway just a year or so ago and the tragedy of Gallipoli in World War I.

"In addition, sir, a disinterested observer might point out that we're at war with Germany, not with France. Why, then, are we intending to attack unoccupied French territory instead of German-occupied territory?"

Churchill grunted again.

"Germany is in Europe, not Africa. Could we at least invade the correct continent, sir?"

When did irony turn into sarcasm? She'd better stop.

"Would it change your mind, Wing Officer, to know that this is the plan I favor?"

"It would not, sir."

"Ha!" Churchill beamed. "Now I see it is true: opposing a plan is exercising judgment, an entirely legitimate and often noble activity—indeed, your duty—but opposing me is the very essence, the very soul, of being difficult."

"What do you want me to do, sir?" She was never quite sure what he wanted.

"Continue, Wing Officer. Continue."

Then he had taken up his fountain pen and begun to write. Churchill never dismissed her, she had come to learn; he simply moved on to something he considered to be next, leaving her to depart and, on this occasion, she presumed, to continue being difficult.

"Well, Eleanor, George Marshall agreed with you," Hopkins said, bringing her back to the present. "But Roosevelt overruled Marshall and finally sided with Churchill, and that's the plan."

"Well, sir, it's an argument I thought I would lose." Eleanor shrugged. "So be it. What can we do to help?"

Hopkins became more animated, no longer the husk of a mortally sick man.

"The assault is called Operation Torch, and it will take place in November, three months from now. There are three prongs aimed at Casablanca, Oran, and Algiers. About a hundred thousand troops in all, and eight hundred or so ships. British forces in Malta can play a crucial role by keeping the Eighth Army supplied in Egypt so that it doesn't get overwhelmed by Rommel before the Torch landings take place, and, of course, denying Rommel the supplies he needs to defeat the Eighth Army."

"Three months?" Park asked. "We'll do our best."

"Three months," Hopkins said. "The Eighth Army must stand up to Rommel another three months. If Rommel wins in Egypt, he'll race back across Africa and throw us out of Algeria and Morocco as soon as we land."

"Exactly so," Eleanor said. "If, on the other hand, the Eighth Army can hold Rommel at bay and you get established in Algeria, we'll be able to squeeze Rommel in Libya from both sides and push him out of Africa."

Hopkins nodded in agreement, and Eleanor was almost certain he was wishing she was back in her old job.

"Precisely. That was exactly my message in Cairo, and they said they could hold him if they are kept supplied and if Rommel is starved of supplies."

Well, Eleanor thought, she wasn't sure Auchinleck could hold Rommel even with ample provisions.

Hopkins seemed to read her mind.

"Churchill is about to field a new team, Eleanor," he said. "I mentioned our recent conversation to him, and your opinion of Rommel, and he agreed. He had already reached the same conclusion and taken steps."

Now all the pieces fell into place. Churchill had gone to Egypt—also travelling in great secrecy—to assess the situation in person, and Hopkins had gone to meet him. Evidently Churchill was bringing in new generals to try to stop Rommel. The Eighth Army and the Afrika Korps were both dependent on convoys, and Malta could keep the sea lanes open for Allied shipping and closed for Axis convoys. It all came down to the convoys, and the convoys came down to who held the airfields on Malta.

"The US Congress will not look kindly on a defeat in Africa," Hopkins said, shaking his head. "They'll lose interest in fighting Hitler and put all their resources into the fight against Japan."

"So we must hold Malta for the next three months?" Park asked. "Or we risk losing American support for an invasion of Europe?"

"Yes, exactly," Hopkins said.

"Then we shall," Park said.

Eleanor looked at Park. Not five minutes ago, he'd only said he'd do his best. Park was not a rash man nor prone to histrionics, and it was not clear that he could hold Malta for three weeks, let alone three months, given the shortages. He returned her look, and she knew he knew exactly what she was thinking.

"We have no choice," he said. "We will find a way, Mr. Hopkins."

"Churchill concurred. He said: 'With Keith Park in Malta, I'm confident we'll win.'"

"Well, that's very kind of him," Park murmured, modestly embarrassed by praise, as always.

Hopkins chuckled. "He also said: 'And with Eleanor Shaux in Malta, I'm equally confident we won't lose.'"

* * *

"I like that man, Eleanor," Park said as Hopkins's Dakota roared down the runway and rose smoothly into the air, carrying Hopkins onward to Gibraltar. Eleanor crossed her fingers that he'd be able to get some rest. She wished she had slipped a sleeping pill into his tea.

"Yes," she said. "When Churchill was briefing me before I met him last year, he told me Hopkins has a 'flaming soul.' I think that's very apt."

"Apt, indeed. Well, I have just committed myself to holding Malta for three months. Any ideas, Eleanor?"

"The convoys must get through, sir. That's the only way we'll last. That should be our top priority, even above defending Malta from Axis bombing."

"You know, Eleanor, I sometimes wonder if I'm being greedy keeping you here. Nobody thinks quite as clearly as you. Perhaps it would be better if you were back in your old job, particularly if they're planning a major operation."

"Oh no, please! All the endless meetings, all the petty jealousies, all the preening, all the bureaucratic mumbo jumbo! Oh no!"

"Well—"

She moved on quickly in order to avoid admitting he was right.

"I'm going through the convoy records with the navy, to see if we can learn anything new."

"The Axis powers are hammering the convoys," Park said, shaking his head.

"Well, sir, then we'll simply have to hammer the Axis. We have no choice."

* * *

"I need your opinion on a couple of things," Park greeted Shaux. "I'm going to stroll over and see how they're doing on the wing tank idea. Perhaps we can talk as we go?"

Eleanor emerged from her office as they passed her door.

"I think wing tanks were your idea?" Park asked. "Let's see how they're getting on."

Charlie followed, ready to provide defensive cover as necessary.

"Look, Shaux, I'm going to try putting RP3 rockets on the Mark IXs," Park said as they emerged into the open air. "They've tried them out on Hurricanes in the desert, and I want to do the same with Spits."

Shaux made his automatic search of the sky. "If we manage to put the extra fuel inside the airframe, sir, we'll have room to hang armament under the wings."

"I just don't think we'll ever make a Spit into a fighter bomber. We'll leave that to the Typhoon," Park continued. "Small, two-hundred-and-fifty-pound bombs aren't much use anyway."

Jenkins and Dobson stood on G for George's right wing in deep conversation.

"Good morning, Dobson," Park said. "Any progress on the wing tank idea?"

Dobson climbed down. He seemed unabashed by the gathering. He stubbed out his cigarette, saluted Park, took a stance as if he were a lecturer addressing a class, and pointed to the wing.

"This here's the Mark IX C-Type wing using the Mark V-C Spitfire specs, with the raked undercarriage and the Chatellerault belt drive, right, sir?" he addressed the group at large.

"Er, right," Park responded for the throng.

"Your C-Type's got twenty-one ribs, right?"

"Right."

"Ribs numbers one to five have the radiators under them and the undercarriage struts in them, right?"

"Right."

Dobson began to walk in front of G for George's wing, which had much of its skin removed and its spars and ribs exposed, pointing and speaking rapidly as he went.

"Ribs five to eight have got the wheel well, right?" He tapped the ribs.

"Right."

"The 20-mil cannon is between eight and nine, and the 50-caliber's between nine and ten, right?"

"Right."

"Ribs ten to thirteen have the ammo boxes. The ammo for the 50-caliber is on the leading side, in front, with the feed belt passing under the barrel of the 20-mil to get to the 50-caliber chamber—in other words, a Chatellerault belt drive. The ammo box for the 20-mil is behind the 50-caliber ammo box. Right?"

"Right."

Eleanor listened, fascinated. She was used to seeing the smooth elegance of Spitfires, a magical combination of grace and raw power. Now she could see beneath the surface. The smooth, slender wings were packed tight with a bewildering collection of mechanisms and devices, wires and tubing, all shoehorned in between the bones of the aircraft's skeleton. This was Dobson's worldview, she realized, rather like a surgeon's worldview of the myriad organs and other bits and pieces that made up the human body, all packed together seemingly higgledy-piggledy beneath a person's skin.

A vision of a senior surgeon instructing a group of medical students leapt unbidden into her mind: "Directly behind your left ribs three to six over here, this here's your left lung, what you use for breathing, right?" "Right, Doctor."

She made a note to ask Johnnie why this short rigger was only a corporal; certainly Park was treating him with considerable deference.

"Then, since they took all the 303-caliber Brownings out of the Mark IXs, there's basically nothing all the way to rib number twenty-one," Dobson was saying. "Just some lights. Wide open."

Eleanor could not tell if Dobson approved of removing the machine guns or not; she suspected not. Park offered him a cigarette.

"Thanks, sir, but I'll stick to mine," Dobson said, pulling a hand-rolled cigarette from behind his ear. He tapped the leading edge above the wheel.

"There's an unused eighteen-gallon tank in front of the wheel well between rib numbers five and eight, here, in the leading edge, left over from the Mark V."

He pointed back out towards the wing tip.

"From rib thirteen out, we have room for three more tanks. From rib ten out, if we use the leading edge."

"So we could add at least a hundred gallons, making two hundred in all, or over a thousand miles," Johnnie said. "We could actually reach Gibraltar!"

"Course, it wouldn't be just the tanks," Dobson said, drawing deeply on his cigarette. "A longer flight would need more oil, more fluids, more—well, more of everything, like as not."

"Where are we going to get the tanks?" Park asked. "That could take months."

"Wouldn't need to, sir," Dobson said. "Bladders."

"I beg your pardon?"

"Bladders, sir."

"Ah, of course," Park said. "Mareng bags."

"What are Mareng bags?" Eleanor was compelled to ask.

"Flexible tanks made out of fabric and rubber, ma'am," Dobson said. "We can just sort of squish them in, and they're self-sealing."

"There's bladders in the stores already, old bags for Gladiators that was brought in a couple of years ago and never used," Jenkins said.

"Never used?"

"No."

"Would they fit?"

Dobson paused for reflection before saying, "Like as not."

"Do you think it might work?" Eleanor asked.

"Like as not, ma'am, if the rats ain't got the tanks in the meantime. There's nothing worse than a leaky bladder."

* * *

Penelope sat in a dusty corner of Eleanor's office, compiling a list of every convoy that had sailed since Italy entered the war in 1941. Penelope had been here on Malta that whole time, and in the navy that whole time, but she had never fully appreciated how badly the convoys had been mauled. A catalog of near disasters and complete disasters was emerging from the dockyard superintendent's filing boxes, punctuated only rarely by an undamaged run without losses of lives and ships.

Unlike the dispiriting chaos of Commander Thompson's office, the dusty rabbit warren that made up AHQ Malta was a beehive of purposeful activity filled with very able people.

Wing Officer Shaux, "the greyhound," as Penelope had first thought of her, was unlike any other woman she had met. She was quick at everything, good at everything, and carried herself with complete self-confidence without an ounce of arrogance or hubris. With Wing Officer Shaux—Eleanor—you just knew that every problem had a solution, and every difficulty could be overcome. All you had to do was get on with it. And she was no older than Penelope; Penelope could not decide whether to be in awe of her or jealous of her.

Air-Vice Marshal Park, tall, gaunt, and severe-looking, was a perfect gentleman. He was the first senior officer she had met who treated her as a human being rather than as an underling. They said he had won the Battle of Britain through superb leadership. He never shouted or demanded. He had the trick of suggesting something and everyone jumped to obey, not because they had to but because he was obviously right.

Eleanor's husband was the complete opposite of what she expected. They said he was one of the Few, a hero of the Battle of Britain, one of the ones they wrote about in the newspapers, and she expected he would be a dashing, larger-than-life person in the mold of Errol Flynn. Besides, anyone who could win the hand of the extraordinary Eleanor Shaux would have to be pretty extraordinary himself.

But soon after Penelope arrived, someone in flying gear had appeared in the office doorway and knocked diffidently.

"Excuse me. I'm sorry to bother you, but do you know where she is?" He spoke softly—so softly she could scarcely hear him.

"She's with the AOC, I think. Can I help you?"

"No, no. Thank you," he said. He bobbed his head as she imagined a schoolboy might bob his head in apologetic deference to a librarian he had interrupted. "I'm so sorry to disturb you."

With that, he slipped away. Eleanor returned shortly thereafter.

"Someone was here a minute ago, ma'am, looking for you."

"Oh yes. My husband. He found me."

So the deferential schoolboy was the famous fighter pilot Johnnie Shaux.

TWELVE

Miller checked the settings on his lathe and pressed the Start button. If he had been a more emotional man, he would have whistled or hummed a tune under his breath. Instead, as he often did, he composed a letter to Maisie in his head, describing his miraculous transformation from loading ammunition on a sinking ack-ack barge commanded by a wanker to a mechanist working at a lathe in a machine shop filled with high-precision tools operated by men who understood and respected metal.

His supervisor was a warrant officer named Dobson. Dobson had raised his eyebrows when Miller first appeared in his naval uniform, as if he expected Miller to dance a hornpipe or burst into a sea shanty or ask where the mainsail was, but his attitude changed as soon as he led Miller to a lathe to see if he could work it.

"He's got very good hands," Miller overheard Dobson telling another warrant officer named Jenkins, and Miller felt he had finally found a home.

They were installing additional fuel tanks—collapsible, self-sealing bags—between the ribs of Spitfires. The tanks were connected in series by piping so that the fuel was forced down under pressure from the outermost tank through the inner tanks into a larger tank located beneath the cockpit, and then on into the engine. It wasn't a perfect design, a bit jury-rigged, but considering the supplies and parts available, it was a minor miracle, a testimony to Dobson's ingenuity.

The whole thing depended on carefully crafted fuel lines, and the fuel lines depended on small couplers and leakproof valve fittings that had to be fabricated by hand. That kind of precision work—shaving metal to a thou—was exactly the sort of thing that Miller liked to do and was good at.

Maisie would be pleased. He'd put the "good hands" comment in the letter; Maisie would get a big giggle out of that, understanding a very different meaning.

* * *

"As you know, we're planning on being a little more assertive," Park said. "As we move forward, I want us to carry the fight to the enemy, rather than vice versa, and we're starting with doing a better job of convoy protection."

The Operations Room was filled, and the crowd overflowed into the corridor. The room was hot and sticky at the best of times; this afternoon it was hotter and stickier yet.

"We've been looking at past convoys to see what we could learn," he continued. "Based on that, I've authorized some changes. Wing Officer, the floor is yours."

"Thank you, sir," Eleanor said. "As the AOC said, we've been reviewing the effectiveness of the air defense of past convoys and seeing what lessons we could learn."

Penelope watched in admiration. Eleanor had the entire room instantly at her command. The AOC and even the flag officer, HMS St. Angelo, who had appeared for the briefing, were paying close attention.

"We've gone through the records of past convoys with the assistance of the navy. Third Officer Dryden, here, has been invaluable."

Penelope felt herself blushing, although she almost never blushed, as the entire roomful of men turned their eyes towards her. For once, men were not looking at her speculatively.

"There have been thirty-five significant convoys to date," Eleanor was saying. "I exclude solo dashes, Club Runs delivering aircraft, and our submarines making Magic Carpet runs, although I do not do so to diminish these magnificent efforts. Fourteen merchant shipping convoys sailed in 1940, fifteen last year in 1941, and six have sailed so far this year. Some of these have been complex multipart operations involving several naval task forces, such as the combined Operations Harpoon and Vigorous sailing from Gibraltar and Egypt simultaneously this past June."

She paused, as if considering how to continue.

"Needless to say, these operations have been successful in the sense that we are still here. The purpose of the convoys is to supply us, and we have been supplied. However, these operations must be considered, from a mathematical assessment, to be disasters. The combined Harpoon and Vigorous convoys, for example, consisted of seventy naval vessels, not counting MTBs, submarines, and other auxiliaries. These seventy fighting ships escorted eighteen merchant ships."

She paused again.

"Of the eighteen merchant ships that sailed, only two reached Malta. Sixteen did not. Two out of eighteen is not a winning ratio."

It was as if she had reached out and rapped everyone in the room on the knuckles.

"This in no way, of course, diminishes the efforts and sacrifices of the men involved. It simply points out that those efforts and sacrifices were in vain."

She had a way of saying things, Penelope thought, that made it impossible to disagree.

"The westbound convoy, for example, Operation Vigorous, sailing from Egypt, delivered no merchant ships at all, while losing one cruiser and three destroyers and being forced to turn back due to lack of ammunition. Air defenses were inadequate, and sixteen Spitfire pilots were lost."

No one seemed to be breathing.

"We must reluctantly conclude that any future efforts from that direction, from Alex, will be both costly and futile and therefore should not be attempted."

Penelope stole a glance at the admiral and the AOC, who were sitting together. Both were stone-faced but neither seemed about to reject her statement. Penelope wondered if Eleanor was a schoolteacher in normal life. She had that air of command; the way she said "therefore" allowed no argument. Penelope had spent the last twenty-four hours combing through old reports and logs made by convoy commanders and compiled a messy summary with no real organization or sequence and interlaced with jumbled statistics. She had given it, with some embarrassment, to Eleanor. Now, two hours later, the messy jumble had been turned into an impeccably structured analysis.

"We can therefore address the remaining question, which is how we can provide significantly improved air support for convoys coming from Gibraltar. First let us clarify our objectives and establish benchmarks."

The room held its breath.

"At our current levels of rationing, which are set at approximately fifty percent of a healthy diet, Malta can survive approximately four weeks. Third Officer Dryden's analysis of past convoys suggests that each merchant ship with a mixed cargo gives us, on average, two weeks of life. Therefore we must receive the equivalent of at least two ships' mixed cargoes per month to survive, and more than two if conditions are to improve."

She had made no such analysis, but now, hearing the words, Penelope suddenly realized that yes, hidden in the jumble, there really was such a conclusion.

"That becomes our benchmark, our measuring stick."

There was general nodding of heads around the room.

"As far as air defenses are concerned, the records of the past convoys are very clear."

How could they be clear, Penelope asked herself, when she had seen no pattern?

"It is a truism that an aircraft can only attack a target the pilot can find. There are two places to find targets with a high degree of confidence: on the ground at enemy airfields, and immediately ahead of convoys, where enemy E-boats and U-boats must position themselves in order to attack at close range. Everywhere else we might look, we are dependent on luck to find the enemy; the sea is simply too big, and so is the sky."

There was more nodding.

"Luck is important in warfare, but it is not a viable basis for planning a successful campaign. Therefore, the AOC has approved plans for attacks on enemy airfields and E-boat and U-boat bases and for standing patrols ahead of convoys to find them at sea. Third Officer Dryden's analysis indicates that bombers, E-boats, and U-boats account for the clear majority of merchant marine losses, rather than larger enemy surface ships; hence the need to focus our efforts on those threats."

Yet more nodding, and Penelope had a sense that there was a rising tide of concurrence and enthusiasm in the room.

"These plans are dependent on being able to reach the targets and then hitting them very hard. As you know, we are retrofitting the Mark IXs with tanks for long-range operations and with rockets to increase their firepower."

Now it all made sense, Penelope thought; the whole thing fit together and everyone knew what was going on and why. She found herself contrasting this presentation with Commander Thompson's explanation of the orphaned MTB crews only days ago; nothing could be more different.

"Obviously I'll defer the operational planning to those far better qualified than I."

With that Eleanor sat down, and, for the first time since the war had started, Penelope felt she had found a place where she could be useful. Funny—that was exactly what that sailor, Miller, had asked for.

"That's it," Park said, standing. "We're not just going to wait for them to hit us. I'm calling this new initiative Operation Counterpunch. There's no time to lose; the next convoy is already on its way, so we need to get cracking. Thank you, everyone."

"Good work," Park murmured as he passed Penelope on his way out, while the admiral stared at her in surprise, clearly wondering why he had never heard of her when she was under his command. Yes, she thought, this is where I want to be.

* * *

Digby climbed into the cockpit of his Mark IX and strapped in. His was the first aircraft to be fitted for extra fuel capacity, and it was a big enough change to warrant a full test flight.

"You're carrying the best part of an extra thousand pounds, Diggers," Shaux said. "The extra fuel and the tanks and the plumbing must add up to that. She'll probably be a bit mushy."

"True," Digby said. "She might even roll off the end of the runway before she gets airborne! But, just in case I do manage to make it into the air, I'll fly a hundred miles east and back with my first escort, and then change escorts and repeat. A total of five round trips will give me a thousand miles, using about two hundred gallons of fuel. If I cruise at about 250 miles per hour, it should take me about four hours altogether."

"Did you pee?"

"I did."

"Excellent. If all goes smoothly, we'll know we can reach places like Cagliari in Sardinia without a problem. Good luck, old chap!"

"Piece of cake."

Shaux jumped down from the wing, and Digby began his starting sequence. The Merlin started without hesitation, and Digby raised his arm in salute as he began to taxi, followed by Granger in Yellow Two, Digby's first escort. Shaux wondered if there was any way of telling that Digby's wings were almost a thousand pounds heavier than Granger's, but nothing was obvious to the naked eye. It was yet another reason to admire R. J. Reynolds's superb design. A Spitfire weighed about five thousand pounds empty; Digby's must weigh not far short of seven thousand.

The new tanks would give the Spits a range of a thousand miles, but it would be best to set a maximum operational range of four hundred miles from Malta. That would allow eight hundred miles to and from the target, with enough fuel left to fight an engagement if they encountered enemy aircraft.

He returned Digby's wave and set off for the dispersal workshops. Assuming the extra tanks worked and gave them the range to take the fight to Axis airfields on Sardinia, the next piece of the puzzle was to give the Spitfires a more powerful punch. It was an interesting tradeoff. Putting the fuel inside the aircraft, rather than putting the extra fuel in slippers or drop tanks, made the design much more aerodynamic and therefore more fuel efficient. But then those nice, smooth surfaces under the wings would get covered in drag-inducing weaponry.

Shaux reached the dispersal workshops and stepped into one of the smaller sheds that served as a machine shop—it was shockingly dark inside in contrast to the mid-morning glare—to see what Miller was doing. It had been a pleasure to see him again since they had met on *Nonsuch*. There was no question he was a skilled tradesman—no, Shaux corrected himself as he watched Miller at work at his lathe. He was a craftsman.

It was unbelievable that the navy hadn't recognized his talents and put them to use, but it was the RAF's gain that they hadn't. He'd been shunted off into the Fleet Air Arm base at Hal Far, HMS Falcon as the navy called it, and they'd sent him on here, where the need for skilled ground crews was urgent, on temporary secondment. HMS Falcon had been heavily bombed by the Regia Aeronautica—it was ironic, come to think of it, that HMS Falcon had been attacked by Italian Fiat CR.42 Falchi—Falcons.

Park had had the idea of fitting rockets to the Spitfires. The RAF's RP3 rockets were fearsome-looking weapons. Park had used Hurricanes to launch rockets against the Afrika Korps when he was in Egypt, and they were starting to be mounted on Sea Hurricanes, he'd heard.

That's what Miller was working on. Park had an old snapshot of a Hurricane with rocket racks under its wings—the picture was grainy and slightly out of focus, probably taken with a Brownie box camera—and, based on that alone, Miller had fabricated a prototype rack that Dobson thought might be "fair enough," his highest standard of praise.

Dobson and Miller were in deep conversation, and Shaux did not intrude. Park had jumped Dobson back up to warrant officer, at least until the night after payday, and Miller had found himself oily khaki denims and now looked exactly like all the other fitters.

Using rockets to amplify a Spitfire's punch was all well and good, Shaux thought, but firing a rocket from an aircraft would be like firing an arrow: the aim had to be exact, adjusted for the speed and movement of the aircraft and also for whatever the target might be doing. It would be like a hunter standing on top of a moving car and firing a bow and arrow at a racing rabbit.

* * *

"So, the most likely time that the Regia Aeronautica will strike at EF-7 will be on Saturday morning, Eleanor?" Park asked.

"That's correct, sir. EF-7 will come into range of attacks from Cagliari on Friday night, so they'll probably take off at dawn on Saturday. The convoy has been shadowed by a Focke-Wulf Condor, so the enemy knows exactly where they are."

"That's less than two days from now. Will we be ready?"

It was typical of Park's hands-on, no-nonsense style, Penelope thought, that this meeting was taking place in a ramshackle area off to one side of the airfield, with half-demolished buildings and wrecked aircraft all around but yet with a sense of purpose and industry, with officers and other ranks mixed together as a team. Eleanor had invited her to attend, and Penelope felt proud of herself for the first time since . . . well, probably since she'd won her degree at Imperial College.

"We'll have the new tanks fitted on the remaining aircraft by mid-day tomorrow, sir," a short warrant officer named Dobson said. He must be the man in charge of the tanks. "They'll need short test flights, of course, but not full flights like what Squadron Leader Digby did, sir."

"I agree," Digby said. He was another famous pilot, Penelope knew, like Eleanor's husband. She had passed him in the hallways a couple of times, and he also carried himself without any airs and graces.

"What about the rockets?" Park asked.

"We're going to test-fire one first thing tomorrow morning, sir," Shaux said. "If that works, we'll give everyone a couple of practice shots from the air tomorrow afternoon. It's not much, but that's all we'll have time for."

"We can fit the rails so quickly?" Park asked.

"It's a very simple design, sir, very nicely thought out," Shaux said. "I don't think you've had a chance to meet the chap that did it, Petty Officer Miller, on loan from the navy?"

Miller—good lord, *that* Miller, Penelope thought—emerged from the group, obviously surprised to be summoned into the spotlight.

"How are you, Miller?" Park said, holding out his hand. "Welcome on board."

Miller wiped his hands with an oily rag before taking Park's hand. Penelope couldn't help noticing Miller's bare arms looked very strong, and he was nicely tanned.

THIRTEEN

The target was a derelict Morris "Quad" lorry used for pulling field guns, a squat-looking truck with four big wheels, somewhat resembling a constipated turtle. It stood two hundred yards in front of Shaux's Spitfire on the outskirts of the airfield.

Miller watched as the ground crews maneuvered the Spitfire until it was pointing straight at the Quad. Dobson had jury-rigged a scaffolding device to hold the tail in position so that the rocket could be fired horizontally. The rails Miller had designed and fabricated were attached below each wing. They looked a bit flimsy, but he was very confident they'd hold; it was interesting what you could do with aluminum if you had the right tools. It wasn't his favorite metal, but it was widely used in aircraft, and he looked forward to exploring it further.

One rail had a rocket hanging below it, held by clamps. The rocket was just a tube about four feet long and was filled with cordite. An electrical fuse would ignite the cordite at the exhaust end of the rocket. The cordite would generate a huge volume of hot gases—flames a hundred feet long—which would escape through the exhaust end of the tube, forcing the rocket along the rail and forward through the air at a very high speed. The front of the rocket had a bulbous shell, a so-called SAP, semi-armor piercing, about a foot long and wider than the rocket tube. At the back, the exhaust end of the rocket, were four fins slightly angled to spin the rocket to give it stability in flight, just as a rifle spins a bullet.

Fireworks rockets on Guy Fawkes Night used black powder inside a cardboard tube to propel them; these rockets used cordite within a steel tube, but the principle was the same. As the cordite burned its way along inside the tube, the rocket would be propelled faster and faster—faster than a bullet fired out of a rifle.

Shaux was in the cockpit. Miller admitted to himself that he was a bit nervous in case the rails didn't work correctly, because he wanted Shaux to be pleased, but, on the other hand, Miller had no doubt the rails would work as he had planned. Shaux and Digby had wondered if gravity would bend the rocket down towards the ground, just as gravity pulls a bullet down, but Shaux had done some sort of calculation in his head—God alone knew how—and concluded that it wouldn't, at least at these distances. They'd called it "ballistic droop." Miller was more concerned about the rocket exhaust burning the underside of the wings and melting his rails but, again, Shaux was unconcerned.

It took a little while to get the Spitfire aimed exactly where Shaux wanted. Miller waited calmly and confidently and was surprised when he discovered he had crossed his fingers.

"Tallyho, chaps," Shaux said at last, and pressed the button that fired the electrical fuse in the rocket's tail. A long streak of yellow-white flame propelled the rocket forward. The sound was somewhere between a very loud sizzling noise and an explosion, like the sizzle/crack of lightning when it strikes a tree, except the sizzle/crack continued as the sound seemed to chase the rocket, just as the streak of fire also seemed to chase the rocket. The Quad lorry disintegrated into its constituent parts as the rocket flashed straight through the lorry as if it wasn't there. The rocket finally exploded with a mighty thud in a grove of olive trees three hundred yards beyond.

The silence that followed was as shocking as the sound.

"Jesus *wept*," Dobson offered finally.

"Exactly so, Dobson," Shaux said. "Ouch!"

"Indeed; probably stings a bit," Digby murmured.

The air above the olive grove was shimmering with heat as flames danced among the trees. A wheel from the Quad was still rolling along one of the runways in the direction of Hal Far. Miller allowed himself a grunt of satisfaction; the rail had worked, just as he had known it would.

* * *

"So, you will take off at 0400 hours and fly northwestward on a compass heading of two-niner-zero degrees for exactly forty-five minutes," Freddie, the controller, said.

A small group was gathered in the Operations Room for this final briefing.

"At a cruising speed of 250 miles per hour, that will put you just north of the Gulf of Tunis. You will then turn farther northward to a bearing of three-four-zero degrees and fly for another forty-five minutes. This route should bring you to the coast of Sardinia at the first peep of dawn."

Freddie had strung ribbons on the big wall map to indicate the route. Shaux, Digby, and several others were taking notes.

"We'll fly at an indicated height of five hundred feet," Shaux said. "Hopefully radar will miss us. I'd like to be lower, but I don't want to risk flying into the drink in the dark."

"I suggest three flights in finger-fours," Digby said. "Each aircraft in the flight should be able to see each other's exhaust manifolds."

Eleanor knew the exhaust gases from the Spitfire's Merlin engines burned at eighteen hundred degrees, turning the exhaust manifolds white-hot.

"Good point, Diggers," Shaux said.

"The moon is waxing crescent," Freddie said. "There won't be much moonlight, so the flights may get separated."

"We'll rendezvous over Cape Carbonara, which should be a very easy landmark to find from the air," Digby said. "It is, after all, the very bottom right-hand corner of Sardinia; hard to miss."

"Then we'll drop down to a hundred feet and fly westwards along the coast to Cagliari," Shaux said. "The airfield at Elmas is just beyond it. As we pass over Cagliari, we may spot some Regia Marina MAS boats in the harbor, but the airfield has the priority. If we have any ammunition left after we rhubarb[3] the airfield, we can take a shot at anything else that looks interesting. We're all carrying eight rockets.

---

3. RAF slang for an air-to-ground attack.

They've been wired to fire in fours, so we each have two shots, as it were."

"The return flight will be in daylight," Freddie said. "A course of one-three-five degrees should bring you north of Pantelleria after an hour. Lower this time. I suggest a hundred feet, no more. We'll have some chaps waiting to escort you the rest of the way in case the Regia Aeronautica spots you."

"What do you think?" Park asked. "Is it doable?"

"It's very doable, sir," Digby said, nodding. "We'll be overhead Elmas just when the Regia Aeronautica is finishing its morning *caffe* and getting ready to take off for a crack at EF-7. We could find twenty or thirty Sparvieros on the ground."

"Do you think so?" Eleanor asked.

"We'll catch 'em with their pants down," Digby said. *"Fragmen massae."*

"Fragmen massae?" Shaux asked.

"Piece of cake."

* * *

Penelope stepped outside the HQ building bunkers and lit a cigarette. The evening was growing darker, but it was still very warm, much warmer than the catacombs below. The breeze should have been delightful after the dank air below, but it carried the taint of smoke from the day's cumulative raids. Several people who had attended the briefing stood in a group discussing the finer details of the operation, and she was grateful to be included. The pilots had gone off to bed; she had seen Eleanor and her husband, Johnnie, climb into their little car with their big black dog and drive away.

They hadn't seemed the least bit nervous that he was going into battle the next day; perhaps they were used to it, but how did you get used to a thing like that? She wondered if they would make love, in case he didn't come back. She remembered, very clearly, the last time she and Jimmy had made love. Neither of them had thought he was going into danger; just that he'd be at sea for three or four days. Would it have been different if they'd known it was the last time forever?

A group of the ground crew stood to one side. They'd be working most of the night, she realized, preparing the aircraft, arming them, fueling them, and fussing over them. One of the crew came towards her in the gloom, and she saw it was Miller.

"I just want to thank you for getting me transferred, ma'am," he said.

"Oh, it's you, Miller," she said. "I didn't know you were here."

She had seen him yesterday. Why was she lying?

"I like it here."

"So do I," she replied before she could stop herself. Why was she starting a conversation?

"Are you here permanently, ma'am?"

"I don't know." She was planning to ask Eleanor if she could stay, but she had been unable to think of a good reason.

She wasn't certain what to say next, and he seemed to understand.

"Anyway, thanks again, ma'am."

He backed away into the gloom, and she discovered, to her astonishment, that she wished he had lingered.

* * *

Eleanor shook her head to wake herself up. They'd returned to Luqa at 0200 hours this morning. Now it was 0700 hours, and she could scarcely keep awake. Johnnie should be back by 0900 hours at the latest. If Park had nothing urgent, perhaps she'd slip off home with Johnnie and catch up on her missing sleep.

The dawn raid on Elmas had been very successful; 505 had arrived over Elmas at sunrise, just as they had planned, having made their way to Sardinia guided only by their compasses. The three flights had found each other and regrouped over Cape Carbonara at the southeastern tip of Sardinia before flying along the coast to reach Elmas—approaching from due east just as the sun rose above the ground horizon, making 505 invisible from the ground—where they had caught a complete Italian *Squadriglia Bombardamento* on the ground and damaged as many as twenty Sparvieros.

Better yet, they had also found a squadron of Macchi C.202 Folgores on the ground and set a hangar building on fire, hopefully with several more aircraft inside it.

And, to cap it off, they'd caught two Italian *motoscafo armato silurantes*, Italian MTBs, in the harbor at Cagliari. One had exploded when a salvo of rockets had hit it like four massive hammer blows, and the second had capsized and sank when a rocket exploded like a torpedo against its side just below the waterline.

Freddie was really a remarkable man, Eleanor thought, glancing over at him as he sat with his headset on and his line of telephones in front of him. He'd devised a set of code words and phrases that allowed 505 to give detailed reports in just a word or two. He was a good controller, she thought, not just because he was always calm and unruffled but also because he devoted a great deal of effort and imagination into planning for every possible contingency.

This was an excellent start for Counterpunch, a new way of preventing the enemy from launching raids on the convoys as well as against Malta. It would also have a powerful psychological effect. Instead of the bomber crews being able to take off at their leisure—after sipping their morning *caffes*, as Diggers had said—in future they'd be rushed and fearful and more vulnerable to the accidents and errors that befall rushed and fearful men.

There could also be a broader psychological impact on the civilian population: 505 had overflown the town of Cagliari on their way to Elmas. Thus, its citizens had been rudely awakened by the sound of roaring Merlins and the spectacle of unopposed Spitfires in perfect formation, flying overhead at a low level and with complete impunity, armed with fearsome rockets. They would have heard the sounds of gunfire and explosions from the airfield, and seen the oily black smoke rising above it, and wondered if *Il Duce*'s new Roman Empire was about to go the way of the old one.

Eleanor half-listened to reports of 505's flight home. Not only had they prevented the Sparviero attack on EF-7 from even taking off, 505 had sustained no losses of its own—in fact, they had not had a single shot fired at them. We should do this as often as we can, she thought, before the Regia Aeronautica and the Luftwaffe can come up with a counterstrategy.

A WAAF brought more tea, and she nodded thanks. While she was waiting, she reluctantly reread the letter from her mother. It was postmarked a month ago and had arrived with yesterday's mail, which was flown in by a Beaufort every few days, weather permitting. Her father had been wounded in the Mesopotamian campaign in the last war and had never quite recovered. Her mother wrote to inform her, almost gleefully, that he was not long for this world. She had offered no details of his condition but had stressed her own frustration that the family lawyers would not give her full and immediate control over his investments. Poor old Dad; all he wanted was a quiet life and an English country garden. Instead he—

"Message understood," Freddie's voice intruded. "Turn to bearing one-one-zero."

She shoved the letter back in her jacket pocket. There was absolutely nothing she could do to help her father, so she might as well try to stop worrying about him. She was here on Malta, and he was in England, almost two thousand miles away.

Her eyes went to the big new maps on the wall. This new raid changed a lot of things. The whole of Sicily and the toe of Italy, as far perhaps as Taranto, would be now be in Spitfire range and vulnerable. Taranto had been the site of the Fleet Air Arm's most brilliant success, the sinking of the battleships at anchor in the harbor last year; could something similar be tried, perhaps with Blenheims escorted by long-range Mark IXs? If—

"Message understood," the controller said, interrupting her thoughts. "Yorker Leader is down. Yorker Leader is down."

"*What?* What do you mean, Freddie, 'Yorker Leader is down'?" Eleanor demanded, breaking every Operations Room protocol in one sentence. "*What?*" How could Johnnie be down?

"Message understood, Blue Leader," Freddie said, speaking into his telephone, holding up his hand to silence Eleanor as if he were a policeman directing traffic. "Continue on bearing one-one-zero."

If Freddie was giving navigational instructions to Diggers instead of Johnnie, then that meant—

Freddie carefully turned his receive/transmit switch back to the Receive position and looked across the map table to Eleanor. He had a strained grimace on his face, and Eleanor felt a chill of dread run down her spine.

"It appears that—" Freddie began and stopped to listen to his telephone.

He switched to Transmit. "Message understood, Blue Leader. Estimated time of arrival three-zero minutes."

Again the ever exact and punctilious Freddie moved the switch.

"Approximately twenty miles east of Pantelleria—"

Again Freddie broke off. Eleanor had never screamed in her life, but now she thought she was going to.

"Message understood, Blue Leader."

Now, abruptly and completely, she didn't want Freddie to be able to finish his sentence. As long as Freddie couldn't finish his sentence, Johnnie was still alive. Everyone seemed to be holding their breath and staring at her—Park, Freddie, Penelope, the WAAFs, the liaison people, the girl who was just about to hand her a fresh cup of tea.

Freddie began to speak, but it was her turn to silence him.

"Sorry for the interruption, Freddie."

She had to get away immediately before she made a spectacle of herself—immediately!

"Excuse me, sir," she said to Park.

The door was perhaps twelve steps away. It seemed a very, very long way, almost halfway across the room, but she had been walking since she was a year old and was confident she could make it—"piece of cake," as the pilots said.

FOURTEEN

The sea was very wet, very cold, and very salty. Rich people spent a fortune to holiday in the Mediterranean; well, in Shaux's opinion, they were wasting their money. The most important thing was to keep his mouth shut, because swallowing seawater dehydrates the human body. He wasn't sure if it was a good idea to pee, or not—although he had very little choice in the matter. Try as he might, he could not keep the water entirely out of his mouth or prevent it from splashing up his nose. His throat was burning, but he had to resist the urge to open his mouth to cough or gag.

It was probably important to stay as motionless as possible in order to conserve energy, but, on the other hand, that could make him colder, therefore using up more energy to maintain his internal temperature. This was the Mediterranean in the middle of summer, so that shouldn't be an issue. At what temperature did hypothermia set in?

Although he was floating on the water, it seemed it was always higher than his head, washing over him. He could see nothing but wave tops, even though he knew that the sea was unusually calm. Was saltwater bad for the eyes? Should he keep them closed?

It was about four in the afternoon. It would get dark—and colder—in about five hours. Then he would have to wait eight hours for dawn. His watch was missing; it must have been knocked off when he hit his arm.

The slight breeze would push him southeast towards Malta but probably past it. In that case, he wouldn't make landfall until he reached the coastline of Tunisia, weeks from now. That is, whatever was left of his corpse wouldn't reach the coastline of Tunisia until weeks from now. There were sharks in the Mediterranean, and probably other carnivorous fish as well, so whatever reached Tunisia would probably just be his skeleton. That assumed that his skeleton would stay intact and various bones wouldn't get bitten off, or just break off, every now and again.

That raised another issue: his left forearm was clearly fractured, either the radius or . . . the other one. He'd hit the gunsight pretty hard when his Spit hit the sea, and his arm had refused to work correctly when he tried to swim up to the surface. Try as he might, he could not ignore the steady pulses of pain coming from his forearm. Perhaps the pulses of pain were in synchronization with the beating of his heart, although he didn't know why. Ulna—that was the other one. It was not good for his arm to be floating around loosely, buffeted by the waves; he'd need to fit it into his life vest, using it as a sort of sling, to keep it immobile until . . . until whatever happened.

* * *

"But what happened, Diggers?" Eleanor asked. "What happened? I still don't understand."

"Well . . ."

"Tell me."

"Well, I don't know what happened, Eleanor," he replied. "We were cruising along in splendid shape at about a hundred feet, at 275 miles per hour or so, in three nice finger-four flights, when, completely without warning, Johnnie flipped over, right wing down, left wing up, and cartwheeled into the sea."

He lit a cigarette with shaking hands as the room waited in silence.

"Just like that. There were no enemy aircraft, of that I'm certain. There was no enemy shipping, I'm equally certain. We were not attacked, and the conditions were calm."

Eleanor was like a statue carved in marble, Penelope thought, or in ice, completely under control. Anyone would think she didn't really care what had happened to him. She had calmly—apparently calmly—left the room when the message first came through.

"He didn't say a word on the radio," Digby said. "The whole thing, from flying straight and level to hitting the sea, was no more than ten seconds.

"We turned back immediately, of course." He drew deeply on his cigarette. "We were back over the spot in a minute or less, but there was no trace."

"Mechanical problem, do you think?" Park asked into the silence.

"I just don't know, sir; some kind of catastrophic structural failure of his right wing, perhaps."

Eleanor stared at him without expression, as if she didn't care.

But Eleanor did care, Penelope thought. She was certain of it. When they'd been getting into their car last night, and he was leaning over to crank the starter handle, she'd seen her give him a tiny, secret smack on his bottom and a tiny, secret smile, and she'd thought with a pang of jealousy: "Oh-ho, we all know what's going to happen the moment they get home."

* * *

It was almost two years since he'd been dumped into the English Channel. A Stuka had dive-bombed the schooner that was bringing him home from Dunkirk. The schooner was part of the miraculous volunteer rescue mission to evacuate the defeated British army; it had been called Operation Dynamo. He'd been in the water for a day and a night. He remembered watching other ships passing without seeing him, some close by.

Finally, sometime after he had decided he would die and wondered if he'd know he was dead, in which case it would matter but otherwise not, a two-masted Thames sailing barge had rescued him. He hadn't seen it or even heard it as it approached him behind his back. The first he knew of it was a violent jerk as a grappling hook snagged his life jacket.

"Don't bother, Nobby; 'e's a dead'un," said a loud voice in a cockney accent.

"No 'e ain't. I saw 'im move," said another voice, presumably Nobby's.

"I am alive," Shaux had attempted to tell them, but his own voice had stopped working.

The grappling hook jerked him around, and he saw the barge with two sailors leaning over the side above him.

"See? I told yer 'e weren't brown bread," said Nobby, a wizened man with a gap-toothed grin and a bushy beard. "Welcome aboard, mate. How about a nice cuppa tea?"

Now he was in the Mediterranean, somewhere between Sicily and Malta, and the probability of a Thames barge rescuing him, with hot tea, approximated zero. There was an RAF Air-Sea Rescue launch based in St. Paul's Bay, and another at Kalafrana, and the navy had a couple of Vosper MTBs that might join the search if they were available, but there wasn't enough daylight left to mount a search today.

Even if they'd seen exactly where he went down, if he was drifting at three knots, for the sake of argument, basic geometry said he'd be could be anywhere in a search area of over a hundred square miles by morning. Every hour reduced his chance of being rescued by a factor of . . . well, it didn't really matter.

If, by a miracle, he was rescued, it could be by an enemy ship—he was drifting into their convoy routes. In that case he'd be back into a POW camp, where he'd languish until the war was over, years from now. He'd escaped after he'd been forced down last year, but that was in France, not in the middle of the Sahara Desert.

There was an old sailor's prayer he remembered hearing that began: *O God, thy sea is so great, and my boat is so small.* Well, the sea was indeed very great, and he didn't even have a boat.

* * *

"They'll go at first light," Park said, putting down the phone. "The search launch chaps say there aren't enough hours of daylight left this evening."

"There's no point in me going to look," Digby said. "I'll never spot him from a Spit—much too fast."

"What about a Catalina?" Eleanor asked.

"By Jove, you're right," Park said. "A Cat cruises at not much more than a hundred. Unfortunately, a Catalina wandering about south of Sicily wouldn't stand a chance. It would be a sitting target."

"We'll cover it," Digby said.

"A Swordfish is even slower," Eleanor said.

"Right again, Eleanor," Park said.

"Or a Gladiator, sir," Jenkins said.

"Let me make some telephone calls," Park said and picked up the nearest. "Operator? It's the AOC. I need to speak immediately with the following three people . . ."

Eleanor couldn't decide whether to scream or just give way to the sobs building inexorably inside her. She could feel waves of empathy from the men around her as they tried to glance away to give her as much privacy as possible. Penelope was looking at her, radiating sympathy, but sympathy was the last thing she wanted. She wanted Johnnie.

The odds against finding Johnnie were less than one in ten, and, even if they found him, he might have been injured when he went down or died from exposure. She was, statistically, ninety percent likely to be a widow. Every time she got Johnnie, it seemed, fate grabbed him away from her. She tried to imagine life without him but couldn't. In fact, she tried to imagine any life but the one she lived every day and couldn't. It was hard to remember there had once been a time before the war when people could just be people and not helpless cogs in the inexorable gears of war. Nothing escaped the war. An air raid siren began to whine, as if to illustrate her thought.

* * *

Shaux guessed it was probably midnight, give or take an hour. The sea was very cold, but it would get colder still, until dawn. Eleanor would be pacing their tiny married quarters with Charlie for company. Charlie would be upset, wondering why Shaux had not returned, and would sense Eleanor's alarm, and she would probably have forgotten that she'd stopped smoking.

It was very comforting to know that they were concerned about him. He had been alone all his life, solitary and unloved, until that day almost two years ago when he and Eleanor had flown in a Defiant and everything had changed. Three Messerschmitt 110s had attacked the airfield at Oldchurch. Shaux had run to the only operational aircraft on the airfield, an obsolescent Boulton Paul Defiant. But a Defiant's guns are in a separate turret and cannot be operated by the pilot. In an act of extraordinary courage, Eleanor had climbed into the turret, insisting that he take off, and had helped him drive the 110s away. That night she had summoned him to her bed, perhaps as an act of catharsis. They had been together ever since.

Charlie had become his dog a few days later, when Charlie's master, Froggie Potter, had been killed when his Spitfire exploded. Froggie was the second pilot Charlie had lost. The first was a Belgian air force officer who had escaped from the German invasion in a small training aircraft with Charlie—all eighty pounds of him—sitting on his lap. The Belgian had been killed a few days later, and Froggie had adopted him. When Froggie was killed, Shaux had adopted Charlie in his turn, determined that Charlie should not feel abandoned or unloved.

Charlie's white silk scarf had once belonged to Froggie; they'd had a tug-of-war and it had torn in two. Froggie's half had gone up in smoke when Froggie burned to death in his Spitfire. Charlie still wore the other half.

Shaux had been orphaned as a baby and brought up in a children's home in south London. He often took long, solitary walks across Blackheath. Sometimes he would find tears on his cheeks for reasons he did not understand, because—as he realized years later—he did not understand that he was all alone and unloved. Shaux was determined Charlie would not have to feel the same, even though dogs don't cry. At least Charlie would not keep being handed from one pilot to the next as each pilot was killed—Shaux was already his third—because Eleanor would keep him.

* * *

If anyone could survive a night in the sea, it was Johnnie, Eleanor thought. He had a unique capacity to absorb hardship and simply shut down his emotions. He wasn't a masochist. He was like one of those ancient saints who could live on top of a pole for years on end or in a cave halfway up a cliff; he simply set aside his difficulties and ignored them. He wouldn't be panicking. If he was injured, he would somehow disregard it. He would wait patiently for dawn, and then patiently for the rescue launch, and then for the next dawn, and so on. He would enter a state of suspended animation, like a hibernating bear. He wouldn't be thinking about the sea and the chances of survival, or any such things; he was probably comfortably adrift in erotic daydreams of her.

* * *

Shaux considered trying to solve the mathematical constant pi in his head by dividing twenty-two by seven. Pi had the advantage of being an irrational number, so there was no actual solution. He could spend the rest of the night, and all of tomorrow, keeping his mind occupied, all the way to Africa. So, twenty-two divided by seven is three, remainder one; add a zero for the next decimal place. Ten divided by seven is one, making 3.1, remainder three; add a zero for the next decimal place. Thirty divided by seven is four, making 3.14, remainder two . . . Alternatively, he can recall, in as much exact detail as possible, on a minute-by-minute basis, a night with Eleanor . . . That seemed far more practical . . .

* * *

Eleanor recalled that Erwin Schrödinger, one of the fathers of quantum mechanics, had designed a thought experiment that involved a cat trapped in a box. The cat could be alive or dead. You couldn't know that cat's state until you opened the box and looked inside. Schrödinger had postulated that the cat was in a state of "quantum superposition," both alive *and* dead, until you opened the box. It was the act of opening the box that either saved or killed the cat. Johnnie was similarly both alive and dead. He'd remain so until they found him, when he would be forced out of superposition into everyday reality and be one or the other.

It might be best if they never found him, because he couldn't be dead until they did. There was therefore a fifty percent chance, on a scientific basis, that the search parties were setting out not to rescue him but to kill him.

* * *

Shaux, adrift in the sea and a sea of memories, both real, was catapulted back into the present by the loudest sound he had ever heard. The aircraft passed him so swiftly he didn't see it, but the sound, the roar, of a Merlin 61 twenty feet above his head was unmistakable. The stillness that followed was almost as shattering. The sea was silent.

Now, for the first time since he had crashed, Shaux felt fear, not of pain or death but fear that the pilot had not seen him. There was no need for fear, because he was certain that the pilot was Diggers, and Diggers always saw everything. But nothing else happened, and perhaps he'd been mistaken.

Then, after a very long time, or so it seemed, a yellow rubber lifeboat intruded into his field of vision, and above the lifeboat faces peered down at him. He wondered what Nobby was doing in the Mediterranean, so far from home, but it was really very good of him to come all this way. Nobby, or one of the others, grabbed his arms and started pulling him up out of the water. Nobby didn't realize that his arm was broken, and Shaux couldn't speak.

Why not? Well, perhaps this was a dream, or a hallucination, and in his dream he couldn't speak. In real life, he'd be screaming in pain. Silent pain, he decided, as they hauled him onto the raft, was more painful than screaming pain—somehow the ability to yell had an analgesic effect.

Now they were bobbing about on the surface, and the warm breeze was not warm at all. It was freezing. Abruptly the hull of a Catalina appeared beside and above them, rocking in the swell, its engines idling. One of the blister turrets was open, and someone was pulling the dinghy in on a long rope. The sound of a Merlin engine roared overhead, and Shaux was more certain than ever it was Diggers.

Now the dream shifted again and a dog was barking. Charlie's big black head appeared in the blister. Charlie was gathering himself to leap down, but someone with a voice just like Eleanor's told Charlie to stay. Now the Catalina was high over them, and Nobby and his mate were lifting him up. Shaux wished, he really, really wished, that they'd realize his arm was broken. He wished he could yell, but he couldn't. This was more like a nightmare than a dream. Funny thing—Nobby was much younger than Shaux remembered, and he had all his teeth.

Now he was lying on the floor of the Cat, and its mighty Twin Wasp engines were getting louder as the pilot turned into the wind and prepared to take off. Perhaps all American aircraft were powered by Wasps. He'd sometimes toyed with the idea of joining Rolls-Royce after the war to work on aero engines, but perhaps he should consider Pratt and Whitney also, and move to America. The sun always shone in America, and they probably had coconut trees.

The Mediterranean seemed much calmer now he was in the Cat, less bouncy, and they'd be able to take off without any difficulty. Charlie was licking his face, staring into his eyes, and Shaux knew that Charlie knew he was in pain—Charlie could smell pain. Charlie was licking his left hand—he'd already found the problem. Somehow he would communicate that to Eleanor. She was leaning over him. Why was she crying? Why was this dream so complicated?

PART TWO

Podium

FIFTEEN

"Well, I think that's about it," the doctor said. "I'll see you in, let me see, in eight weeks."

"Eight weeks, Doctor?" Shaux asked. "I thought you said it was a clean break that would heal quickly."

"I did, it is, and it will." The doctor scribbled a note in his file and closed it with finality. "You'll just have to be patient and let nature take its course, Wing Commander, a *patient* patient, if I may say so. Good day to you."

He was extremely young to be a doctor, Shaux thought, guessing he'd only just arrived in Malta. He was wearing an immaculate blue RAF uniform with a pristine white coat on top of it. He seemed to carry his stethoscope as if it were a badge of office rather than a clinical device, and his pockets were bulging with an array of pens and medical instruments. Shaux noticed he did not use his glasses when he wrote his notes and guessed they were a theatrical prop to add to his gravitas.

He looked no older than Shaux—just twenty-three or twenty-four. Everything was rushed in wartime. Pilots were being pushed through training and posted out to operational units whether they were ready or not, do or die—too often, die—and Shaux supposed it might be the same for doctors, who were probably hurried through medical school and sent off to practice in the hope they wouldn't kill too many patients before they learned their trade.

The doctor's desk was piled with medical books stuffed with book-marks. One thick volume lay open; Shaux wondered if it was turned to a page headed "Arms, Broken, Treatment Thereof."

"Look, Doctor. It doesn't take much strength to fly a Spit. I think if I rest it for a couple of weeks, I'll be—"

"Out of the question."

"But—"

"Your physical injury is not the only condition requiring treat-ment, Wing Commander; perhaps it is the lesser. We also have to treat your psychological injury."

"What psychological injury?"

"You crashed into the sea because of some unknown failure in your aircraft, I understand, and spent twenty-four hours in the water before being rescued."

"Oh, that. It wasn't so bad, Doctor. It—"

"These events were traumatizing by definition, and you need time to let your psychological wounds heal."

"Oh, I don't think—"

"And, judging by your service record, this is just the latest acutely stressful episode in a long line of such episodes, stretching back over two years to the Battle of Britain or even before. Prolonged stress is extremely harmful. I am, frankly, amazed that you are still—"

"Doctor, some people can deal with stress better than—"

"Rubbish! I know it's not considered manly to show fear, Wing Commander, particularly in wartime, but suppressed fear can and will cause emotional damage. Prolonged fear can cause psychosis. When you come back in eight weeks, I'll make an assessment of how much emotional damage has been done. Hopefully not too much, but it may be time to end your flying career before the damage becomes permanent."

"End my—?"

"That is my opinion, Wing Commander, and with due respect, my opinion is the only one that counts. Good day to you."

Shaux bit his tongue. He had seen this kind of thing in inexperi-enced officers before, this kind of dogmatic certainty on the outside disguising complete uncertainty on the inside. There was no point in arguing. He'd wait a week or two until his arm stopped aching, and then quietly take a practice flight. The doctor wouldn't be able to say he couldn't fly if he already had. Besides, Park wouldn't let this raw novice end his career, Shaux was certain—well, almost certain.

He thanked the doctor as politely as he could and stepped outside into the heat of the day, automatically checking the skies for 109s. There were none. He lit a cigarette. "Psychological wounds? Emotional damage?" What rubbish! His left arm ached; that was it.

He was completely normal, untouched by two years of battle, sustained by Yeats's poem and Eleanor's love. After all, everyone has the occasional nightmare, even though he'd thought it best not to bother Eleanor by mentioning his own.

In the meantime, what was he going to do for eight weeks?

* * *

"It had to be some sort of structural failure," Digby said.

"He flipped over, just like that, for no reason?" Jenkins asked, scratching his head.

"Flipped over and went straight in, like an uncontrolled roll," Digby nodded. "He said he tried to catch it but couldn't."

"You know, Dobbo, we gave those wings a right old bollocking," Jenkins said. "I mean, when you think about it, we took the skin off, put the tanks in, and put the skin back on."

"It could've been an error, I suppose, in the rush," Dobson said. "One of the lads didn't secure the skin proper. The leading edge, like as not."

"If I checked those wings once, I checked them a thousand times," Jenkins said.

"We all did," Digby said. "It may not have been an error; it may have been something else."

"Such as what?"

"Well, we put four hundred pounds of extra weight in each wing, and we hung rocket rails under them, and then rockets under the rails. That's a lot of weight, even though they seemed to fly normally."

"You think it was my rails, sir?" Miller asked. "I'll swear to God—"

"No, no, t'wasn't your rails. Don't you fret, lad," Dobson said. "You mean we overstrained it, sir?"

"It's possible," Digby said. "We must have changed the geometry, surely? Perhaps we warped the profile or the dynamics of the way the wing flexes?"

"If he started to roll, he'd have applied his ailerons, without thinking, to correct it, but he rolled all the way, you said, sir?" Dobson asked.

"Yes. I read something about that once," Digby said. "Something about ailerons; let me see if I can find it."

"In the meantime, every single Spitfire gets checked and checked again," Jenkins said.

"Should we take everything off again, sir, just to be on the safe side?" Miller asked.

"Oh no." Digby smiled. "Those rockets are far too much fun; nothing quite like sticking a firecracker up the enemy's fundamental orifice."

* * *

Eleanor had never snapped or snarled or even humphed at Shaux, but she felt she was moving rapidly in that direction. Park had said he would not overrule the doctor, at least for a while, unless there was a dire emergency in which Shaux must fly. Shaux had therefore taken to moping around their quarters, making deep sighing noises and driving her to distraction. If the telephone rang, he would snatch at it in the hope that Park was overruling the doctor and recalling him to flying duties.

He had begun construction of a model Spitfire made of wooden matchsticks and glue but lacked the necessary dexterity and patience, or, she thought, it was very possible that he had mistakenly purchased the kind of glue that sticks wood to fingers rather than wood to wood.

He had borrowed a scorched volume of Shakespeare's plays from the bombed public library and started diligently working his way through it. Unfortunately the book was more damaged than he had thought, and he had tossed it aside when Brutus's stabbing of Julius Caesar was followed immediately by Hamlet's contemplation of Yorick's skull.

"'Et tu, poor Yorick'? Bit of a non sequitur, one would have thought," Digby had murmured when Shaux mentioned it.

At her suggestion, he began spending his days with the ground crews, and his attitude brightened immediately. He had been a fitter when he first joined the RAF, and working as Dobson's assistant made him feel useful, he told her, although he still felt he should be in the air. And that sailor, Miller, was evidently another mechanical soul mate; Shaux had begun to speak of steel as if were alive.

He did not seem to be in any significant pain. His lower arm was in a heavy plaster cast, but he could move his arm quite freely.

"I know I can fly, El. I know it, doctor's orders or not."

"Well, look, there's an operational Swordfish at Hal Far," she said. "You could take it up with Diggers and see if you can manage it."

He rewarded her with a bear hug, despite his injured arm, and set off to find Digby.

* * *

The doctor seemed even worse than Johnnie had described, both combative and dogmatic. He had ginger hair and a bad case of sunburn—a particularly unattractive combination.

"Why do you think my husband is suffering psychological damage, Doctor?" Eleanor asked.

"I don't usually discuss patients' conditions with third parties. It's unethical, Mrs., er, Mrs. Shaux, but in this case I'll make an exception."

She added the word *irritating* to her growing list of unfavorable adjectives.

He positioned himself on a corner of his desk, perhaps to disguise the fact that he was shorter than she was, and adopted an instructional tone, pursing his lips as if marshalling his thoughts.

"He is suffering—how can one put it in lay terms you can understand—from cumulative stress. He has been exposed to danger on an almost daily basis, and emotional trauma can have physical as well and psychological effects. He may delude himself into thinking he is invulnerable, but—"

"Delude? Emotional trauma? How—"

"'Trauma' is a medical term meaning—"

"I am well aware of what 'trauma'—"

"Obviously, Mrs. Shaux, wartime amplifies these dangers."

He seemed uncertain as to whether wearing his glasses gave him more or less authority.

"You may have heard of your husband's condition in layman's terms such as *shell shock* or *battle fatigue*." Glasses off. "Unfortunately men are told that such things are signs of weakness, just as boys are taught that it is unmanly to cry." Glasses on. "In your husband's case—"

"My husband is a case, Doctor?"

"I haven't made a final decision yet. Emotional trauma is a fascinating and growing field, in which I intend to specialize."

So that was it. This ginger-haired, red-faced runt fidgeting with his glasses was going to make a study of Johnnie in order to advance his own career.

"Before you make that decision, Doctor, I suggest you seek competent medical advice on your burned face. You seem to be unaware that a Mediterranean summer is very different from an English summer. Such foolish overexposure to solar rays often leads to permanent damage."

It wasn't much of a shot, but it was the best she could come up with on the spur of the moment.

"That's none of your—"

"One tends to lose confidence in doctors who make such obvious and elementary medical mistakes, particularly with their own health. Good day to you."

* * *

Park put down the telephone and grimaced.

"Bad news, Eleanor, I'm afraid. They've put Podium on hold—again."

"Why, sir? What is it this time?"

Following the failure of EF-7—only two ships had reached Malta, and one of them had been so badly damaged it sunk at its moorings before it could be unloaded—another convoy had been planned and named Operation Podium.

"There's been an outbreak of some sort of food poisoning in Gib," Park said. "A lot of the crews are laid up. There's some speculation that it was sabotage, but more likely some tinned food got spoiled. Tins sit in hot warehouses or the holds of ships in bilge water for weeks on end. Who knows? It really doesn't matter. All that matters is that Podium lacks adequate air cover. The Fleet Air Arm doesn't have enough pilots. In fact, they've even asked for help."

"How long is the delay?"

"I don't know, nor, apparently, do they," Park said. "It's all a bit of a mess. They've replaced their Gladiators and Fulmars with Martlets, which is a good thing, but they haven't had time to train the pilots fully, and they can't complete their training if they're ill."

He gestured in frustration. "How long have we got? What's the governor's latest estimate?"

"Less than a month, according to Dr. Dryden. I think he's a better judge than Lord Gort. In four weeks, we won't be able to feed ourselves or defend ourselves. The civilian population is on half rations and cases of dangerous illnesses are shooting up."

Park shook his head.

"Well, Podium cannot defend itself either—there simply isn't enough time for adequate carrier training, and half the chaps have no operational experience. In any case, as you know, Podium has been thrown together at the last minute with all sorts of loose ends. And now, the coup de grace, half their chaps are in the hospital."

She had seen him facing long odds. She had seen him facing agonizingly difficult decisions. She had seen him within hours of defeat. Never had she seen him so pessimistic.

"And the other half is on the toilet, sir," she said. It was the first thing that popped into her mind.

"True!"

Thank God he chuckled, Eleanor thought.

* * *

"They've been re-equipped with Martlets?" Shaux asked. "I flew one when I was at the A&AEE last year. Not a bad aircraft."

"You flew a Martlet?" Park asked.

Park had invited them and Digby for dinner. Such invitations were becoming more frequent, Eleanor realized. Perhaps Park grew lonely in the long, splendid summer evenings, half a world away from his wife. Perhaps he grew depressed as his marvelous view of the harbor became ruined by half-sunken wrecks and a perpetual haze of smoke from smoldering dockyards. The civilian wartime radio service offered little but scratched recordings of classical music interspersed with bleak news broadcasts and announcements about yet more rationing—nothing to let Park escape from the weight of his responsibilities.

"Well, a Grumman F4F to be exact, sir. But yes, it was being considered as a possible replacement for the Hurricane. We thought it very airworthy, good and solid, but it simply wasn't big enough, unfortunately."

Park rose as if restless, stared out the window for a moment, and began to pace back and forth.

"Incidentally, I've had a complaint from the FAA," Park said. "They're complaining about our chaps wasting their fuel joyriding Swordfishes. I'm not going to take any action, but I expect this practice to cease immediately."

"Sorry, sir," Shaux and Digby murmured in unison, with identical sheepish grins.

"How's the arm, Shaux?" Park asked.

"Absolutely fine, sir. Not a problem at all."

It was most unlike Park to engage in idle chatter or to keep changing the subject like this, Eleanor thought. It was as if his mask of disciplined control was slipping a little and opening a spyhole into his inner turmoil.

"Well, in the meantime, we're getting to the crisis point," Park said. "The governor's going to pick a date to surrender before supplies run out completely."

So that was it, Eleanor thought. Park was staring into an abyss, facing the possibility of surrender. The island would run out of food, and Park would run out of fuel for his aircraft. Lord Gort, the governor, did not approve of Park's offensive fighter strategies and would doubtless blame Park for failing to defend the island. Gort had presided over the collapse of the British army in France in 1940, and had indirectly blamed Park on that occasion also.

"Podium may have to sail without adequate air cover," Park said. "They simply don't have enough fit pilots. If they sail, they'll be risking a slaughter."

He looked at Eleanor. "Kesselring must be gloating."

She looked back. There were no words to comfort him, for it was true.

"I promised Harry Hopkins we'd hold," Park added, staring out over the harbor. "So much for my promises."

* * *

"Perhaps you should go to Gib, Johnnie."

She lay curled beside him, her head on his shoulder.

"What?"

"Well, Gib is presumably out of the doctor's jurisdiction, and it saves me from hearing you sighing all the time. Dr. Sunburn wouldn't know you've gone."

"Do you think so, El? Are you trying to get rid of me? Do you suddenly find me inadequate?"

"Of course not," she giggled. "Although I admit I'm tired of finding sticky matchsticks in the bedclothes."

It was obvious that a crisis point was coming, he thought. Park was clearly unusually worried. Podium was vital to Malta's survival, which was in turn vital to the Eighth Army's survival, which was in turn vital to the success of the plans for Torch . . . If Podium had no air cover, it would get blown to pieces . . .

He was fit to fly. He'd managed the two-seater Swordfish without difficulty, although he was secretly surprised how much his arm ached afterwards. He was confident he could handle a Martlet. He'd done a carrier takeoff, although not the much more difficult landing. The Fleet Air Arm was fiercely independent ever since they'd been transferred back from RAF to Royal Navy control at the beginning of the war. They might not welcome his presence, but silly interservice rivalries were irrelevant. Besides, the FAA's *Faith, Hope,* and *Charity* had saved Malta in 1940 when the RAF couldn't, so it was probably time to repay the debt as best he could.

"I don't know what the FAA would say," Shaux said. "We could speak to Park, I suppose."

* * *

"*Nonsuch* has fifteen Martlets on board," Park said. "Twelve of them are serviceable. They have seven fit pilots and one chap who might recover well enough to sail. They're even considering taking the ill pilots out of the hospital and putting them on *Nonsuch* in the hope they'll recover on the way here. They're going to sail in two days, come what may."

The navy must be desperate, Eleanor thought.

"What did they say about Johnnie, sir?"

"In a word, they said come immediately."

This was her idea, she thought. It was her idea to send him away to fight. Not only would he have to face all the dangers of aerial battle, he would have to endure the dangers of sailing in a convoy under attack, potentially—God forbid—finishing up in the Med again. What kind of a wife volunteers her husband for such hazardous duty? A wife who secretly wants to be a widow? How would she feel if he didn't return? Perhaps she should ask Park to overrule—

"There's a Blenheim leaving for Gib this evening, as soon as it gets dark," Park said. "I'll tell them to squeeze him in."

Too late, she thought. Before going into war, the ancient tribes had sacrificed their dearest possessions to the gods—their fattened calves, for example, or a virgin or two—seeking divine favor in the coming battle. She wondered if she had just sacrificed her husband to the gods of war.

SIXTEEN

Shaux came aboard *Nonsuch* feeling almost as if he was coming home—it was only a couple of months since *Nonsuch* had carried him out to Malta. Some small part of his brain had questioned if, after spending a day and a night floating in the Med, he would be frightened of going to sea, but the mighty carrier felt reassuringly solid beneath his feet. That particular small part of his brain had probably been in secret communication with the RAF doctor about "cumulative stress" or "delayed shock" or some such baloney. He stamped on the armor plating on the flight deck. A hole did not appear and seawater did not gurgle up through it. Enough of this nonsense!

The Gibraltar naval dockyard was busy with warships and merchantmen, and there were more ships anchored beyond the mole. Unlike Malta, the Axis powers had conducted only sporadic operations against the Rock, as Gibraltar was known. A tangle of warehouses and barracks and repair docks lined the waterfront, with shops and houses and offices crammed in behind them until the hillside grew too steep. The airstrip where he had landed stuck out improbably into the sea. He had grown used to Malta, a small island, but Gibraltar was tiny in comparison.

The naval vessels were dazzle-painted[4] in shades of dull gray, and the civilian merchantmen were shades of grimy black. All were streaked

---

4. A form of naval camouflage making range-finding inaccurate.

with rust and looking worn and weary, hunkered down at their moorings as if they didn't want to put to sea again. In vivid contrast, the sky was a brilliant blue, and white gulls cried harshly as they flashed and wheeled, indifferent to peace or war.

The Rock loomed above it all. This was one of the great nerve centers of the world, the frontier post between Europe to the north and Africa to the south, the northern Pillar of Hercules. To the east lay the Mediterranean, the center of the ancient European world; to the west lay the vast and trackless Atlantic, the end of that world. It was said that the Rock once had a warning sign carved upon it: *Non plus ultra*—there is nothing beyond.

For this convoy, there were no Spitfires IXs lashed down on *Nonsuch*'s flight deck, waiting to be carried out to Malta. On this trip *Nonsuch* would be a fighting ship, not a ferry. There were three or four Martlets clustered together at the aft end of the flying deck with their wings folded up, as if the planes were origami paper birds. It seemed extraordinary to Shaux that you could build a wing that could be folded up and yet still be robust enough to bear the weight of a fully loaded aircraft. The joints must be incredibly strong. And wings were not solid, rigid lumps of metal, of course, his thoughts ran on. They are constructed of thin metal sheets stretched over ribs and spars, constantly flexing in response to the complex stresses of flight, which meant that the folding joints must not only be very strong but also be capable of similar flexibility. He walked over to examine them in detail.

A couple of fitters, stripped to the waist and bronzed by the sun and the salty breezes, were working on them.

"Can I help you?" one of them asked.

"I've come to learn how to fly these things," Shaux said. "I've been transferred. I'm amazed at how much stress these joints can take."

Within a minute the fitters were explaining the exact workings of the hinging and locking mechanisms, while Shaux admired their elegantly and deceptively simple design. Some expert draftsman in America must have conceived them and drawn them at his drafting table, skilled metal workers had fabricated prototypes, and doubtless they had been tested and redesigned and refabricated many times until a final version, the progenitor of this one, was exactly right. Then, just to complete the process, some advertising chap in a smart suit in the front office had dreamed up the name Sto-Wing.

"Wing Commander Shaux?" a voice asked behind him. "I'm Cameron."

Shaux squirmed out from under the Martlet's wing. A Fleet Air Arm lieutenant in a tropical white uniform stood before him.

"Ah, good morning, Lieutenant. I'm just trying to understand the Martlet's wings."

Cameron had a certain Viking look about him, a hard look, or so Shaux imagined, as if his face had been constructed using an impermeable material. He led Shaux a little way from the Martlets and came straight to his point.

"Look, Wing Commander, I don't want to be offensive, and I know you've volunteered, and I appreciate that, but, well, 839 is my squadron."

Shaux should have felt sorry for the man. As the commander of an FAA squadron, he had an immensely difficult job to do at the best of times, not to mention an incredibly dangerous job. The stakes were even higher because the convoy was vital to Malta's survival, and Cameron's task was to provide the backbone of its aerial defenses, flying in the teeth of the Regia Aeronautica and the Luftwaffe. The eyes of the Admiralty would be on *Nonsuch* and on his squadron. Therefore, the idea of some senior ex-Battle-of-Britain tallyho Spitfire chap second-guessing him at every turn must be icing on the cake. Shaux would normally have sympathized, but it worried him a little. If ranks and pecking orders were at the top of Cameron's list of worries, rather than the fitness of his squadron for the task at hand, then . . .

"Look, Cameron, I completely understand. I'm under your orders. That's it."

Cameron's face did not reveal whether he believed Shaux or not.

"That's all," Shaux said. "Now, I've never landed on a carrier, and I need to practice."

"Oh," Cameron said, as if he had expected the question of rank to be more contentious. "Well, we have a set of arrester wires at the end of the airstrip for simulating landings. You can practice on those. We have one Martlet over there for training purposes. You'll have to learn to fly it, somehow, although there's no time, God knows. I'm not sure if attempting to fly an unfamiliar—"

"I evaluated the F4F Wildcat for the Air Ministry last year. I think it's essentially the same aircraft? I'd appreciate a few circuits and bumps to get used to it again, if I may?"

"Oh," Cameron said, as if trying to find a problem but failing to do so. "You did? Oh, well, I'll call the tower and tell them you have permission to fly. Ask for Sublieutenant Lingard. He's our deck landing officer. He can take you over and show you the ropes."

"Thank you," Shaux said, not knowing if this was meant to be a pun. Judging from Cameron's general demeanor, he assumed it was not.

* * *

"And, finally, this is the 'cut' signal." Lingard held his left paddle down beside his leg and brought his right paddle in front of his face. The paddles were the size of tennis racquets and painted a dazzling white. "You cut the throttle and pull up the nose to make a three-point landing. I give this signal when you're in the slot just off the stern, so you can drop your tail hook down on to the wires."

"The slot?"

"The correct glide path and attitude. It's like a gramophone needle being in the right groove."

"I understand, but what if I miss the wires?"

"Throttle wide open and take off again, just like a circuit and bump, sir."

"How do I know exactly where the wires are?"

"I'll be standing next to them. As your starboard wing goes past me, you should feel the hook catch."

"How close are you?"

"Well, ten feet from your wing tip, more or less."

"All right, Lingard; now give me some signals. Let's see if I've got them."

He stood twenty feet in front of Lingard, who raised the paddles above his head.

"Too high, reduce altitude."

Lingard brought the paddles up and down to shoulder level in a waving motion.

"A little high."

The paddles stopped at shoulder height.

"In the slot."

Lingard began to resemble a semaphore signal.

"I forgot to put my flaps down . . . I'm not banking fast enough . . . Complete balls-up. Go round again."

At last Shaux was satisfied, and they paused for a cigarette.

"I was on *Nonsuch* before, on a Club Run, a few weeks ago," Shaux said.

"We go back and forth once or twice a month," Lingard said. "I must have been to Malta six times this year without setting foot and actually coming home."

"You're from Malta?"

"My father was commodore back in the twenties."

"Oh, so your family's still there. Lingard . . . Don't think I've met anyone with that name."

"No, my parents are back in England, and my brother was killed last year when his destroyer went down."

"Oh, I'm sorry to hear that," Shaux said. These kinds of tragedies were so common these days there was nothing else to say. "Shall we give it a try for real, Lingard?"

"Whenever you're ready."

* * *

The Martlet was not an elegant aircraft, Shaux thought. It had a big, bulbous nose encasing its Twin Wasp engine and a short, stumpy tail, with none of the smooth lines and graceful curves of a Spitfire—a bulldog rather than a greyhound. No, Shaux thought, not a bulldog but a Bouvier: Charlie has a big nose and a stumpy tail, and he looks just fine. He decided, quite irrationally, that he would like the Martlet and think of it as a Bouvier like Charlie.

He waited while three ponderous Halifax bombers thundered along the airstrip and took off towards the west and then eased his Martlet into position at the end of the runway, where painted lines indicated the length of a carrier's flight deck. A Very flare rose above the control tower to give him permission to take off. He opened the throttle to let the revs spin up before releasing the brakes, and the

Martlet jumped forward. It was ready to fly in a remarkably short distance. He could see Lingard standing by one of the white lines to see exactly where he became airborne.

He climbed to ten thousand feet and tried some maneuvers, remembering in the nick of time not to fly into Spanish airspace—that would create an embarrassing international complaint at least and possibly a burst of ack-ack fire at worst.

It was important to have a sense of how tightly he could turn the Martlet before spinning, how steeply he could climb before stalling, and how the aircraft responded to problems like putting the undercarriage down in the middle of a simulated dogfight.

Aerial combat was not just pilot against pilot but aircraft against aircraft. He would have to be able to outmaneuver Fiat Falchi and Macchi Folgores, and perhaps he'd run into 109s. The purpose of aerial combat was to get one's guns to bear on the enemy and to avoid him doing that to you. The enemy seldom flew in a nicely predictable straight and level line, waiting patiently for one to aim and fire. To the contrary, the enemy threw his aircraft wildly right and left, up and down, to escape the deadly lines of tracer, just as a hooked fish thrashes and leaps and throws itself against the pull of the line. Dogfights were fought at the limits of the aircrafts' structural capabilities, on the knife edge of the possible.

He closed his eyes and operated the controls by feel, rolled over and maneuvered while inverted, stalled out in several attitudes to understand how the aircraft dropped and how to catch it. An inverted power-off stall was one of his least favorite things to do, particularly with a full stomach, but he'd used it in battle to good effect on more than one occasion. Fighter pilots survive not by shooting down the enemy but by avoiding being shot down themselves—it was an aerial application of Eleanor's zero-sum principle of not losing. Any idiot can fly in easy conditions, but survivors can fly successfully when conditions become adverse.

The Martlet felt robust and steady and responsive without being twitchy; the Twin Wasp pulled nicely without a hint of fuss. The Martlet was slower and less sharp than his Spitfire—but the Martlet could land on a carrier and his Spitfire could not. That led to the remaining question, Shaux thought, whether he could pilot the Martlet to land on a carrier, and he returned to circle the airstrip. The tower gave him approval for an arrested landing. He flew a final circuit, brought his height down to two hundred feet, put his wheels and flaps down, and extended the hook beneath the tail—that last part felt a little odd.

He made a banking turn towards the end of the runway where Lingard stood, his white paddles clearly visible. Surely he was too low? Lingard's paddles were raised above his head—Shaux was too high! Damn! Cut the revs, raise the nose. Paddles down—too low, damn it! Just a few revs more.

The trick, Shaux suddenly realized, was not to simply respond to Lingard, which would always make him too jerky, reacting and correcting the last mistake, but to look at the runway and come down the glide path—the slot—as he normally would, using Lingard for confirmation, not instruction. Raise the nose. Lingard's paddles rose to the slot position. Good. Ease her down . . . lift the nose a trifle but not too much . . . almost down . . . paddles still outstretched . . . almost down . . . almost down . . . it looked as if he was almost going to cut Lingard in two with his right wing . . .

Paddles in "cut" position. Throttle to idle. Nose up to let the hook drag down. Right wing flashes past Lingard—damn, that's close!

BANG!

The hook snagged one of the arresting wires, and the Martlet was caught just as a fisherman catches a fish. The wires screamed to their limits and stopped the Martlet in its tracks. Shaux was flung forward violently in his straps, with his nose stopping just short of the gunsight, as the Martlet decelerated from 60 miles per hour to zero in twenty feet.

Wow! Shaux felt as if he had just driven his aircraft into a brick wall. He pushed the canopy open, catching his breath. Wow! Lingard appeared on the wing beside him.

"How did I do, Lingard?" There was no point pretending to be calm and casual.

"Not bad, sir."

"I thought I was going to hit you."

"Missed me by a mile."

"Let's do it again."

* * *

"Very well, gentlemen," the rear admiral said. "The essence of this convoy will be speed. Any vessel not capable of maintaining fifteen knots will be left behind. No stragglers; no exceptions. At fifteen knots it should take us a little less than three days to reach Malta, if we can hold our course."

Shaux was seated in the officers' mess aboard the escort carrier HMS *Woodstock*. There must have been close to a hundred men jammed in for this briefing, the captains and first lieutenants of all the escort ships and the senior civilian officers from the merchantmen they would be escorting. The room was hot and sweaty, and the ceiling fans achieved little more than blowing the tobacco smoke back and forth. He noticed that the navy's dress code was not as casual as the RAF's; the officers were in white shirts with sparkling gold braid badges and shorts. A couple of them glanced curiously at Shaux's crumpled RAF khaki as if he were a member of a different species.

"We have ten merchantmen in the convoy; they will form as two parallel lines of five. There will be a quarter-mile gap between each ship in the line, and the two lines will be a quarter mile apart. The portside line will be code named Drake, and the starboard line will be Jellico. This formation is designed to minimize the target profile the merchantmen will present to any U-boats we encounter. Is that clear?"

There was a murmur of affirmation.

"Midway between the two lines, we will position the ack-ack cruisers *Gosport* and *Savannah* to provide covering fire. Drake and Jellico and the two cruisers will form the core of our operation and, to the extent possible, will remain in their positions, while all other naval forces will deploy around them as the tactical situation dictates."

That meant, Shaux thought, that the Martlets and all the other carrier aircraft would have to operate well outside the two lines of merchantmen to avoid friendly ack-ack fire from the cruisers.

"Now, in addition to *Gosport* and *Savannah*, we have ten destroyers, mostly Havant and Tribal classes. We have four minesweepers, two oilers, and six corvettes we can also use as tugs if necessary. If anyone falls behind the convoy, one of the corvettes will provide an escort and, if necessary, a tow.

"In general, the destroyers will deploy on each flank as two independent flotillas, code named Yoke and Zebra, and will be, with the corvettes, our main defense against U-boats. The minesweepers will lead the convoy, of course, and the oilers will follow, with the remaining corvettes as a reserve."

Shaux imagined how it would look from the air: the two columns of fat merchantmen with the sleek shapes of the cruisers between them, bristling with ack-ack guns like floating porcupines; the smaller shapes of the destroyers and corvettes on the flanks; and the minesweepers out ahead like scouts and the oilers and corvettes bringing up the rear. All would be sailing as fast as possible, the whole procession marked by an accumulation of wakes stretching back miles, a long white streak cut at an angle through the endless lines of blue-black waves.

"Last, but by no means least, we have two carriers, *Nonsuch* and *Woodstock. Nonsuch* will provide our main fighter escort, with potentially fifteen Martlets. Weather conditions permitting, she will fly standing patrols. I say 'potentially,' gentlemen, because several of the pilots are unwell, and we will be relying, in part, on untrained volunteers."

Well, Shaux thought, it was a very long time since he'd been described as an "untrained volunteer," but he supposed from the navy's point of view that's exactly what he was.

Be that as it may, the admiral was expecting a dozen or so Martlets—more like eight or ten in practice—to be able to defend over thirty ships. The entire convoy would stretch for two and a half miles, perhaps three; it would take the Martlets less than a minute to fly its length. The admiral had designed his formation with the ack-ack cruisers in the center so that they could fire at attacking bombers above the columns of merchantmen. A pom-pom had an effective range of about two miles, Shaux thought, in which case the defending fighters would have to stay outside the perimeter of the convoy.

"You will have noted, gentlemen, we have no battleships or cruisers. *Woodstock*'s role is to defend us from heavy enemy forces. She has Swordfish torpedo bombers to attack the enemy, Sea Hurricanes to defend the Swordfish, and Fulmars to act as reconnaissance scouts."

The admiral paused to mop his brow.

"We must expect to be attacked heavily from the air, once the enemy has found us. We can also expect E-boats and MAS boats and U-boats, and mines once we're south of Sardinia. We really don't know if the Italians will bring their heavy stuff out, or not. If they do, we have *Woodstock*."

The admiral paused and looked around the room, and Shaux wondered if he was calculating the odds on how many of these officers would survive the journey.

"Now, let me finish by wishing us a safe and uneventful voyage. Good luck to us all."

SEVENTEEN

Shaux had imagined that their departure would be ceremonious in some way, perhaps with the shrilling of the bosuns' whistles, flags flying from the mastheads, and sailors at attention on the flight deck. But there was none of that; one moment *Nonsuch* lay against the wharf and the next there was a widening gap of oily water with bits of rubbish floating in it. The few sailors in sight were manhandling massive mooring cables and looking as if they wished they hadn't drunk quite so much last night.

Nonsuch's initial movements surprised Shaux. It was almost as if the captain wasn't sure what he was doing or that he couldn't find the rest of the convoy—"Do I want the Med or the Atlantic?"—until Shaux realized that this was a deliberate strategy to confuse watchers from Morocco and Spain.

It took several hours for the convoy to organize itself into the formation the admiral had ordered, and when it was done at last, and *Nonsuch's* engines assumed a more deliberate beat, Shaux could see only the sterns of the last merchantmen in each line. *Nonsuch* was the very last ship in the convoy, behind even the oilers, probably a couple of miles behind *Woodstock* in the van. If he fell overboard, he thought, there would be no one following to rescue him; best not to fall.

* * *

"Podium has sailed," Park said, replacing his telephone. "Let us pray for a swift and safe passage."

"Amen," Eleanor murmured. She still couldn't quite believe she had sent Johnnie away and forced him to endure a long sea journey through waters in whose silent depths U-boats lurked and glided and upon which battleships armed with 15-inch guns stalked their prey. She was used to Johnnie being in danger when he flew, but on this convoy, he would be in danger all the time.

She feared he might be staring at the wall of his cabin or cubicle or wherever he was, wondering if a torpedo would burst through it. She had always admired his ability to sleep peacefully, apparently without dreaming, as if his mind and conscience were clear, while she, on the other hand, tossed and turned as her mind raced unstoppably. But recently, ever since he had been forced down into the Med, he had emanated a certain tension as he slept, with his hands clenched into fists, as if he were defending himself against his dreams.

That doctor had implied Johnnie had deluded himself into thinking he was invulnerable, like a daredevil or a man who walked on high wires in circuses. Perhaps the doctor was right. But when Johnnie flew, he assumed his cloak of impenetrable fatalism—that was a sign of indifference, surely, not of delusion.

He had seized upon William Butler Yeats's poem about an Irish airman to convince himself his life had no value. But how could his life be valueless if she was in it? She slept naked in his arms every night, and yet it seemed she didn't know him at all. She knew his smell but not his soul.

If you unwrapped Johnnie like an onion, layer after layer, until the real, essential Johnnie stood revealed, he would be an orphan boy, alone and unloved, perhaps sensing he was missing something vital but not knowing what it was. His caretakers did not love him; nor did they ask for his love in return. Love was therefore new and extraordinary for him, for he had not felt it as a child nor had he been taught it.

Perhaps he didn't love her at all, because he didn't know how to; perhaps he only felt carnal desire, which needs no instruction. He had always hungered for her as if he were a poor urchin boy staring into the window of a cake shop, but now his hunger was somehow tinged with melancholy, as if savoring the moment for fear it might be the last.

That odious little prick of a doctor—there was simply no better way to describe him, ignorant and arrogant and sunburned—had, she feared, poked a hole in their most fundamental tenet of belief, that Johnnie was invulnerable. She did not know if either of them could handle vulnerability well.

"Amen," she said again—louder this time, to make sure God could hear her.

* * *

Johnnie shook his head to clear away the cobwebs—he'd found it difficult to fall asleep with *Nonsuch's* motion—and flew a wide circuit around the convoy. He wanted a sense of it. If Stukas attacked this ship or that, what were his best tactical options for driving them off? Stukas, he knew from long ago in the Battle of France, are most vulnerable to attack as they pull out of their dives, whereas Sparvieros and Junkers Ju 88s are most vulnerable immediately before they bomb.

The convoy was an impressive sight, driving purposefully eastward in the formation the admiral had ordered. The minesweepers were well ahead, beyond the range of the convoy's main ack-ack firepower. He led his flight past them, in part to reassure their crews that he would come to their defense if necessary and in part to make sure their gunners could recognize a Martlet, as opposed to a Falco or a Folgore, and would at least hesitate before firing at him. He had been unable to convince the navy to install R/T equipment so that the fighters could talk to the ships below them. He was limited to talking to *Nonsuch*, with the hope that they might communicate with the rest of the convoy. He acknowledged the navy's legitimate aversion to radio signaling, particularly in a situation like this where there were enemy listening stations all along the hostile shores that surrounded them, but it meant he couldn't offer any close support.

Cameron had dismissed the idea out of hand, not so much wrong as alien—"This is the navy, not the RAF"—while Captain Lancaster, *Nonsuch's* commanding officer, had simply shrugged and said the admiral would never approve it.

"Every mile we can go without the enemy detecting us is a mile the enemy can't attack us," he had said.

Shaux considered countering that it was likely that the enemy knew where they were if the enemy was in the process of bombing them but kept his mouth shut.

The carrier *Woodstock*, the admiral's flagship, led the main convoy. It struck Shaux that the aircraft were an odd lot, as if made up of whatever odds and ends were available: obsolescent Swordfish torpedo bombers and Fulmar fighters, with a squadron of modern Sea Hurricanes to protect the Swordfish. The Swordfish on her deck, like Gladiators, were the last of the long line of biplanes stretching back to the dawn of flight, produced just in time to be made obsolete by monoplane designs. But, obsolete or not, Gladiators had fought like hell to defend Malta in 1940, when there were no other aircraft available— the famous *Faith*, *Hope*, and *Charity*. Gladiators and Swordfish had achieved amazing successes, severely damaging three Italian battleships at Taranto and last year fatally crippling the battleship *Bismarck*, the pride of the Nazi Kriegsmarine.

Shaux led his flight farther north. Cameron had appointed him as one of his flight commanders with obvious reluctance, but Shaux was vastly more experienced than the other pilots and the only one apart from Cameron who had actually engaged the enemy.

Shaux wanted Red Flight to get as much flying time as possible and as much practice as possible in flying as a unit so that, when the time came, they would be able to fight as a unit. Cameron was unimpressed. After Shaux had led Red Flight past *Nonsuch* in a tight formation, Cameron had snorted: "This is not a bloody airshow."

* * *

"Podium is about twenty miles north of Algiers, sailing eastward at 15 knots," Park said. "They're midway between Majorca and Algiers, about a day away from Tunis and Sardinia."

Eleanor had asked the mapmakers to jury-rig a large-scale map of the convoy route, and it now hung on the Operations Room wall. She wrote an *X* on the map and added the time.

"They're well within range of bombers based at Elmas airfield in Cagliari," she said. "In fact, they're sailing directly towards it."

The mapmakers had added circles to the map indicating distances from major enemy airfields and naval harbors. The farther east Podium sailed, the more choices the enemy had for striking at it.

"Indeed, and they won't pass Cagliari until dawn tomorrow," Park said. "I'm afraid they're sailing into the chokepoint, the narrows between Sardinia and Tunisia."

"Sailing into the chokepoint," Eleanor repeated to herself, with a secret shudder. "Into the jaws of death."

* * *

The sun was definitely lower, Shaux noted. It was important to keep Red Flight between the sun, as it sank west towards Gibraltar, and any Axis aircraft searching for the convoy. If he happened across a Condor or a Ju 88, he wanted to be sure he could see them before they could see him. They were about 150 miles from Sardinia, less than an hour's flying time, and the experienced officers on *Nonsuch* were surprised the convoy hadn't already been attacked.

The convoy was just visible to the southeast, off his right wing, still in the formation the admiral had ordained, steadily plowing a long furrow across the Mediterranean. It all looked so calm and peaceful, but down there the winds were picking up and the waves growing steeper. The small clouds at angels one-zero looked stationary from up here, but they would be scudding across the convoy.

Bravery is a remarkable thing, he thought. All the men in all the ships down there knew that they would be attacked, sooner or later, and some of them would die, but they plowed on as if serenely unconcerned.

The two ack-ack cruisers lay in the center, bristling with weapons. Their aft 6-inch gun turrets had been removed and replaced by no less than sixteen pom-poms mounted on four platforms so that an attacking aircraft would be flying into a hail of shells. On each side of the cruisers came the long columns of merchantmen. Each of them carried enough to keep Malta alive for a fortnight. If half got through, Malta could live three months, and if, miraculously, all got through, Malta could survive until next year. Park had promised Harry Hopkins that Malta would hold, Eleanor had told him; if those ships arrived, the promise would be kept.

Beyond each column was a shepherding line of destroyers and corvettes, the convoy's principal defense against U-boats. Shaux hadn't been seasick, but his stomach was not fond of *Nonsuch*'s motion; he dreaded to think what it would be like to be on one of those destroyers or corvettes down there, swooping and plunging and rolling to the rhythm of the waves as the wind hurled salt spray at you.

The leading merchantman in the port column disappeared beneath a cloud—no, that wasn't a cloud, it was smoke. Surely it wasn't smoke—the convoy had done a wonderful job in making sure their furnaces burned cleanly so that the smoke from their funnels wouldn't betray their presence.

But it was undeniably smoke, a thick, black, oily, trail of smoke, and now the destroyer next to the merchantman turned sharply to the left, away from the line of convoy, heading north.

"Red Flight, eyes in the skies," Shaux said. Some unknown enemy was attacking the convoy. Shaux didn't see how it could possibly be an attack by enemy aircraft, but he didn't want Red Flight to be distracted. He had assigned a quarter of the sky to each Red pilot to maximize their chances of spotting another aircraft. It was a bit like Vulture, except that he didn't have the benefit of Diggers's eyesight. His own segment was from twelve o'clock to three o'clock, but there was nothing to see.

He spared a single glance downwards. The merchantman was belching smoke and seemed to be moving in a crablike manner, sliding towards *Gosport*, the leading ack-ack cruiser. Its wake was shortening—presumably it was losing speed. Now the destroyer was also belching smoke and heading northwest and seemed, from its wake, to be turning a complete circle.

The admiral's perfect formation had been rudely interrupted.

* * *

"Podium is under attack," Park said, replacing the telephone handset. "Evidently a U-boat managed to fire a salvo that hit a merchantman and a destroyer. Both are on fire. The rest of the convoy is continuing as planned."

Those poor men, Eleanor thought, trapped on burning ships many miles from the nearest shore. If they had to abandon ship, they'd be floating on little life rafts or in the water hanging from lifejackets, and night was falling. She remembered the agony of searching for Johnnie just a few weeks ago; the miracle of Diggers finding him; the way Johnnie looked, all but drowned; the way Charlie barked in an inexplicable frenzy until she realized Charlie was telling them that Johnnie was hurt . . . Those poor men, she thought, and they wouldn't have Diggers's eyes to find them or Charlie to sense their pain . . .

"Eleanor, did you hear me?" Park's voice intruded.

"What? Sorry, sir?"

"I said I want you to give me our best options for supporting the convoy. The enemy will surely follow the U-boats with a bombing run from Elmas or Borizzo—or both. They've still got enough light to attack this afternoon and doubtless tomorrow morning as well."

"Then I think we should launch a dawn attack on Borizzo, in Sicily," Eleanor said.

"Go on?" Park asked.

"If we send 505 off at, say, 0430 hours tomorrow morning, and they follow the southern coast of Sicily, they'll reach the town of Trapani, just east of Borizzo, just as the sun is coming up."

"Indeed so," Digby said, nodding. "We should be able to catch them on the ground again, just as we did at Elmas, just when they're finishing their morning *caffe*."

"Very well," Park said. "We'll do it. In which case—"

He was interrupted by the telephone. She could tell from his expression that the news was not good. He replaced the telephone carefully, as if it was a hand grenade without a pin.

"Another merchantman," he said. "They think there are probably several U-boats in a pack."

Podium had started with ten merchantmen, each carrying vital supplies, each representing two weeks of life for Malta: food for children's hungry bellies, medicines for the wounded lying in hospitals, 2-pounder pom-pom shells to protect the hungry children and the suffering wounded, and a thousand other necessities for an island that had been besieged and pounded for two years. Above all else, two of the merchantmen were tankers bringing high-octane aircraft fuel. If even one tanker arrived, Park would be able to fight for months; if neither arrived, Park would not be able to defend Malta for more than two or three weeks.

Ten merchantmen had started out, sailing into the jaws of death; now there were eight, and Malta had lost a month. Park had promised Harry Hopkins that Malta would hold. The odds had suddenly become less favorable.

* * *

"I've been looking through some physics books at the library," Digby said. "The place has been badly damaged, but quite a few books have survived. I think there may be an explanation for Johnnie Shaux's crash."

"What did you find, sir?" Dobson asked.

"There's a thing called *aeroelasticity* and—"

"'Aero' what, sir?"

"Elasticity. The ability to bend. Wings are flexible structures capable of withstanding enormous pressures. I think we may have changed the geometry of the wings sufficiently to make them distort abnormally under some high air-pressure conditions."

"You mean like this?"

Dobson held out his hands and twisted them to mimic a Spitfire's wings warping.

"Exactly so. It was one of the problems the Wright brothers had to solve before they could get their original aircraft to fly."

"That's what happened to Wing Commander Shaux?"

"It could be. There's a condition called control reversal under which the ailerons will cause the wing to go down instead of up. Spitfires are designed not to do that below about 600 miles per hour, but we may have changed that."

"So, if I understand you, he thought he was correcting a roll but in fact was reinforcing it?"

"That's my theory."

"Well, then, we'd better take off the tanks and rockets immediately," Jenkins said.

"No. I think we should keep the outer tanks empty. That should reduce the distortion in the wings and correct the problem, at least in part."

"I'll get the lads started on it, sir."

"No, not yet. We have another rhubarb at first light," Digby said. "We'll do some experiments when I get back."

EIGHTEEN

Shaux rearranged his limbs in search of comfort, yet again in vain. His bunk was too narrow. There was something about *Nonsuch's* ponderous motion that prevented him from slipping away into sleep. Shaux was in the upper bunk and could not entirely escape the idea that *Nonsuch* might suddenly heave to some unusually steep wave and dump him down onto the deck several feet below. His tiny cabin was dank and airless, and his cabinmate, Sublieutenant Lingard, was an aggressive snorer. The cabin was no more than a small metal box below the waterline into which the Mediterranean might pour at any moment.

Lingard's snoring, emanating from the bunk below him, interrupted itself, paused, and then restarted at a deeper, more resonant pitch.

Shaux was used to the comforts of his double bed with Eleanor's naked body sprawled beside him. There had been a time when he could sleep anywhere under any conditions, he thought, but apparently no more; perhaps he was growing older. He was already twenty-four. Soon, perhaps, his waistline would expand, and his temples would turn gray. He'd become crotchety and spend his postwar days teaching algebra to dull boys who would be counting the minutes until the bell rang, releasing them from class. Eleanor would grow impatient with his declining vigor and cast about for a younger, more energetic companion. None of those things would really happen, of course, because they all assumed he'd survive the war—the "cumulative stress" of war, as that doctor had put it—which he was certain he would not.

Just when he finally managed to disregard Lingard's snoring, it interrupted itself again and, after a pause, commenced a different rhythm.

Shaux resettled himself and stared into the darkness. Was there some way he could quiet Lingard without actually suffocating him? This was getting ridiculous. Shaux would be flying at dawn and needed to sleep . . .

But, as he reluctantly admitted to himself, he didn't really want to sleep because he had begun to have dreams, for the first time in his life, and he didn't like his dreams one little bit.

* * *

Shaux opened the throttle wide. As the revs spun up and the engine rose to a roar, his Martlet began to quiver. The Twin Wasp's exhaust ports spat out acrid smoke and angry flame. The propeller was a pale gray transparent circle. Now the quiver accelerated to a faster, more urgent, thrumming vibration. Something loose in the instrument panel rattled insistently. The roar of the engine sharpened to a snarl. Torque pushed the nose down and to the right. Surely the brakes would yield? If the Martlet were a beast of prey, it would be gathering its muscles, coiling itself to spring.

The trembling rev counter shook up to 2,500, and Shaux released the brakes.

The Martlet bounded forward. Torque tried to yaw it wildly to the right so that, if Shaux hadn't been waiting to catch it, he was certain the aircraft would have careened off the deck and crashed into the sea below. As it was, with the merest correcting tweak on the controls, the Martlet straightened and bolted forward down the flight deck. Three hundred feet of deck left, tail up, halfway to flying speed . . . two hundred feet left, wheels thumping harshly over the seams of the flight deck plates . . . the controls feeling lighter but not light enough to fly . . . one hundred feet . . .

Straight ahead the sea awaited him. Perhaps the Martlet would fail to reach flying speed and crash over the bow, hit the sea, and perhaps flip over onto its back as the prop drove madly into the waves. Then, even as he was underwater struggling to disentangle himself from his straps and get out of the cockpit, he would be crushed beneath the bow of the onrushing mass of *Nonsuch*, dragged beneath her full length as the Martlet was torn apart around him. As his throat and lungs burned with saltwater, he would finally reach the stern, where her huge racing propellers would be waiting to shred him into shark bait. Perhaps, or perhaps not.

The wind was blowing at fully twenty knots, and the carrier was doing almost thirty—fifty knots of wind flowing over and under his wings as if he were in an experimental wind tunnel—and that was before the snarling Twin Wasp's fourteen cylinders applied 1,200 horsepower to the propeller blades, dragging the Martlet forward at 40 revs per second. The wheels were barely on the flight deck—indeed, he was holding the Martlet down.

Shaux forgot about everything—the war, the enemy, Park, even Eleanor—in this moment of primal delight, this split second of supreme anticipation, this instant when gravity was at his mercy and all the laws of physics were bending to his will. This was as close to ecstasy as he had ever come, even in Eleanor's arms. If there was a heaven, it would feel like this. He flew off the bow, and the transition from the flight deck to the air was so smooth he could scarcely detect it, except that it was much quieter and steadier in the air. If there was ever—

Something—ingrained self-discipline or the habit of experience or something like that—snapped him back to reality. He had learned long ago in the Battle of Britain—no, even before that, in the Battle of France—that pilots are at their most vulnerable when taking off or landing, when their movements are predictable and the pilot's attention is focused on the job at hand. He had stooged around Luftwaffe airfields in his old, banged-up Defiant in the hope of catching an enemy aircraft off guard and unwary, and he had been jumped more than once himself. He tucked the moment of takeoff away in his memory for when he could relive it at his leisure.

Here and now, there were Macchi C.202 Folgore fighters to chase away and Stukas or Sparviero bombers to hunt, chase, and kill. He flew a circuit around *Nonsuch* and then two more. It took about a minute for a Martlet to be manhandled into position on the flight deck and take off, and Shaux timed his circuits so that another Martlet could slot in behind him, and two more behind that, each time he flew by. Four aircraft were as many as could take off one after the other, because of the extremely cramped conditions on the flight deck and the limited capacity and speed of the lifts. Now there would be a fifteen-minute delay before they could do it again.

But a flight of four Martlets, maneuvering and fighting as a cohesive group, was still a powerful weapon. Shaux wished the navy hadn't changed the aircraft's name to Martlet, a small imaginary bird with no feet that Diggers, the ultimate avian authority, dismissed as "a myth of no consequence or virtue." Grumman had originally named the aircraft the Wildcat—that was much better: a small scrappy predator, unafraid, on the prowl, bred to fight, with sharp claws and sharper teeth.

It occurred to Shaux that Wildcat would make a perfect radio identifier. Shaux wondered why he was getting so sensitive to names—he hadn't liked Vulture and now he wanted Wildcat. Perhaps he was turning into a prima donna . . . Douglas Bader's radio call sign had been Dogsbody, using his initials, and the Tangmere wing had been known as "Bader's bus company" . . . Shaux's Wildcats . . . No. Bader, now sadly a prisoner of war, was a legend, whereas he, Shaux, was merely lucky, no more.

Shaux led them up through the clear Mediterranean sky until they were positioned between the convoy and Sardinia, open for trade and looking for prey. Almost immediately *Nonsuch* vectored them north to a point that Shaux estimated lay halfway between the Regia Aeronautica airfield at Cagliari and the convoy. Shaux guessed that Hat-Rack, a lone Bristol Blenheim night fighter flying high above the coast of Sardinia, had reported sighting enemy aircraft or seeing radar images on its AI screens. Height was safety for the Blenheim, all alone and essentially undefended and helpless. It would be way up there above twenty-five thousand feet, where few aircraft could reach him, but they said the new version of the 109, 109 G Gustav, could reach up to thirty thousand feet. Bert Rogers, the Blenheim pilot, was a very brave man.

Ah, here they came: a formation of ten or a dozen Sparviero bombers with a cluster of Folgore fighters behind them, perhaps twenty aircraft in all, appearing to the northwest at angels one-zero. Shaux was higher, and there was a reasonable chance they couldn't see him in the glare of the sun. The Italians had the advantage of numbers, but their radio equipment was poor at best, and Shaux was banking on their inability to communicate among themselves.

As Shaux rounded their flank, easing round to the left as they passed him a couple of miles away to the east and perhaps three thousand feet below, the Folgore fighters showed no sign of having seen him. They were flying in what seemed an almost random pattern behind the Sparvieros. Their position was worse than useless, far too close to the Sparviero bombers to defend them. They should have been a couple of thousand feet above and a couple of thousand yards behind, waiting for Shaux to close in on the bombers so that they could jump him from behind. As it was, they had simply made themselves into an even bigger target.

The Folgore fighters should have had a significant speed advantage over Shaux's Martlets—they had the same engine as Messerschmitt 109s, built under license by the racing car chaps at Alfa Romeo—but the Folgores had stuck themselves behind the Sparvieros and were dragging along at least 100 miles per hour below their maximum speed. Shaux's plan was simple: jump the Folgores, hoping that the shock would scatter them and that their poor communications would prevent them from regrouping, and, by punching through the middle of the escort, be lined up on the Sparviero bombers just ahead of them. Simple plans were always best, particularly in formation flying and particularly when Red Flight's pilots had not had time to get to know each other's idiosyncrasies.

"OK, chaps. Just go straight through the middle," Shaux said, as they completed their turn behind the Folgores. "All tucked in and cozy." The Martlets were wingtip to wingtip, no more than twenty feet apart. The FAA was not known for formation flying, but he had to admit these chaps were doing really well. Besides, if they were concentrating on keeping formation, they'd have no extra thoughts left over to be scared.

They swept down on the bandits while the Italians seemed unaware of their presence, doubtless looking forward and down in search of the convoy.

"Follow me, chaps. Tallyho."

Shaux opened fire when he was only one hundred yards behind his target Folgore, the leading fighter, and continuing to close. Instant lines of light, cut through the sky by tracer fire, connected Shaux's Martlet with the Folgore. At fifty yards, bits and pieces started breaking off the Folgore, and it began to hemorrhage a trail of white liquid. Shaux was aware, in his peripheral vision, that the Folgore next to his was also under fire.

Four Browning 50-caliber guns firing ten rounds per second delivered forty rounds per second. The destructive power of a 50-caliber was not really in the weight of its rounds—an API armor-piercing incendiary 50-caliber round weighed only four ounces—but in the fact that four ounces was delivered with the kinetic energy of four ounces travelling at half a mile a second, and energy, as Newton had shown, was mass multiplied by speed. Shaux was firing from only three hundred feet behind so that each round struck the Folgore only one tenth of a second after it left the muzzle.

The effect could be likened to a pneumatic jackhammer smashing concrete or a chainsaw cutting wood.

The rear fuselage and tail of Folgores were unarmored. The API rounds ripped through his target's canvas skin, snapping the spars and ribs beneath like matchsticks. The elevator and rudder control rods, the oxygen supply, the radio, the supercharger coolant reservoir, and the rear fuel tank were all vulnerable.

The armor plating behind the pilot's seat was almost half an inch thick, but 50-caliber API rounds can penetrate armor thicker than that. After passing through the armor plate, they still had more than enough kinetic energy to pass through the pilot, the control panel in front of him, and the fuel tank beyond that before being finally being stopped by the steel casing of the supercharger. One round of the 120 Shaux fired snapped the elevator control rod in two and jerked the Folgore into a catastrophic vertical dive at full power.

Half a second later, the Folgore immediately to the right of Shaux's target exploded. Shaux flew into a ball of fire filled with jagged shards of metal that tore and slashed at his Martlet. A massive object—it must have been the second Folgore's engine block—flashed past Shaux, barely missing him. It struck Red Four's left side and sliced off the left wing, just as a mediaeval axman might amputate a limb. Red Four, spinning like a top, followed the Folgore down.

Now the Sparviero bombers were ahead and a little below. Their rear gunners would have seen their defensive escort blown apart and the Martlets closing fast. But perhaps they were confused, for the head-on profiles of Martlets and Folgores were quite similar—indeed, Shaux knew it was very hard to tell most fighters from each other if you couldn't see their wings and fuselages, particularly in the stress of battle. He had been fired on more than once by an RAF bomber rear gunner who thought he was a 109 or 190.

There were still far more Regia Aeronautica aircraft in the sky, and Red Flight was down to only three aircraft, but the odds had shifted decisively in Red Flight's favor. The Folgore fighters had scattered—indeed, Shaux couldn't see any—and each Sparviero would have just one Breda-SAFAT machine gun to defend itself against each Martlet's four Brownings.

The Sparviero pilots would not be sure exactly what had happened. Doubtless their eyes had been fixed on the sea below, searching for the convoy, assuming that the Folgores would keep them safe from attack. Now their rear gunners would be sounding the alarm, but they might not be reporting accurately or coherently. From their perspective, at one moment the Folgores had been following them and the next a Folgore had exploded, another had nose-dived, another had lost a wing, and the rest had scattered into the glare. It could have been a catastrophic but innocent midair collision. Radio communications between the Folgores and the Sparvieros were probably nonexistent.

In any event, the Sparvieros flew on, perhaps out of discipline and determination and perhaps because they failed to grasp what had happened.

Shaux led Red Flight a little below the Sparvieros as the range closed so they would be hidden—or at least difficult to see—beneath the Sparvieros' rear fuselages and tails. Then, at two hundred yards, he drifted upward and opened fire.

A fighter is a small target to hit, particularly if it is approaching head-on and particularly if it is spitting forty rounds of 50-caliber ammo at you every second. A Sparviero, on the other hand, is a big target.

Shaux focused his tracer on the nearest Sparviero's dorsal gunner's position. The dorsal gunner immediately stopped returning fire—he'd scarcely fired a shot—and Shaux transferred his attention to the port engine and wing. Thick smoke started pouring from the engine, and the wing began to sag. If the Sparviero continued to press its attack on the convoy—assuming it could still fly—it would be an easy target for the navy pom-pom gunners to spot.

The remaining Sparvieros began to break left, right, up, and down at random as they sought escape from this totally unforewarned attack.

"Red Flight, follow me," Shaux said, turning away as the Sparviero formation descended into chaos. Breaking it up was as good as shooting it down, Shaux thought, because they'd never get reorganized and they'd arrive over the convoy—if they arrived at all—in vulnerable ones and twos.

Shaux searched carefully through all four quadrants of the sky, above and below. The convoy's leading minesweeper screen was just coming into sight to the south. If Shaux continued to engage the Sparvieros, he'd interfere with the convoy's antiaircraft defenses and risk being hit by friendly fire. It looked as if at least two Sparvieros were on their way down, and the Folgores had disappeared completely.

"Red Flight, follow me," he said again.

He led them in a wheeling turn to the west so that they could circle round the convoy at a safe distance. *Nonsuch* was stationed in the rear, and, with luck, Red Flight wouldn't be taken for bandits.

Red Flight had done well, he thought. The chaps had stayed in formation and in control—Shaux knew how incredibly easy it was for inexperienced pilots to forget all their training and instructions when they first came into contact with the enemy and into the shock of live machine-gun fire. The Martlets had also performed well, he thought. They were not super-fast silky-smooth Spitfires, but they were steady gun platforms and had a good, solid, trustworthy feel about them—Bouviers of the skies.

As for the enemy, it was absolutely outrageous that brave young men should be sent into danger so poorly organized and so relatively defenseless. Shaux guessed he had killed one Folgore pilot outright as soon as he attacked, although the crew of the Sparviero might make it down alive and ditch in the sea. If they did, they would endure, by his hand, what he had endured in the Med just a few weeks ago, and they wouldn't have Diggers's eyes to find them and a Catalina to bring them home.

Victory, as always, had a bitter taste.

NINETEEN

The dawn raid on Borizzo, the airfield at the southwestern corner of Sicily, just east of Trapani, had been another success, with 505 surprising a *Squadriglia Bombardamento* on the ground just as it was preparing to take off, presumably to attack Podium. On the way back, flying at very low levels along the coast, they had also caught an MAS boat in the harbor at Marsala and another at Mazara.

This corner of Sicily—the bottom left-hand corner on the map—formed the upper jaw of what Eleanor had imagined to be the jaws of death through which the convoys must pass.

"Good name," Diggers had said, when she mentioned it to him. Being Diggers, of course, he had immediately translated it into Latin and inscribed it on the map in his beautiful handwriting.

"Ora Mortis," he'd said. "Very apropos."

Perhaps the Regia Aeronautica and the Regia Marina had become complacent, too used to dishing out destruction on the convoys and on Malta and not expecting to be on the receiving end. These raids might well force them to retreat northward beyond the range of the rocket-armed Spitfires. This was the second time in a few days that Spits had rudely interrupted their morning *caffe*.

"Message understood, Yorker Leader," Freddie said, speaking into his telephone. Eleanor idly wondered how many times a day Freddie said, "message understood." It must be hundreds.

Johnnie and Diggers thought that the rockets were probably a bit more dramatic than effective—they were remarkably difficult to aim— but Eleanor thought that this didn't matter. Just as the Luftwaffe fitted their wailing *Jericho-Trompete* sirens to their Stuka dive-bombers to terrify people on the ground, the sight of rockets propelled by long jets of flame being fired from the unmistakable and unmatchable Spitfires must have a similar effect.

If the Counterpunch strategy was successful in pushing the Axis forces back north, away from Malta and the convoy routes, it would make an important contribution to Harry Hopkins's plans by making it a little more likely that Malta would hold. The balance of naval power in the eastern Mediterranean was probably tilting in Italy's favor, as the failure of Operation Vigorous indicated. All the more vital, there-fore, that western convoys like Podium should be successful.

"Message understood, Yorker Leader," Freddie said. "Position beta."

"Podium reports All Clear," Penelope said, holding her own phone. Eleanor had brought her into the Ops Room team on a full-time basis as the naval liaison controller, replacing the naval petty officer who had been recalled for duties aboard the submarine tender *Silkworm*. In his absence, everyone had been grabbing that phone whenever it rang—even Park. Eleanor had guessed Penelope was dreading returning to Commander Thompson's tender mercies and had taken pity on her.

Diggers's success at Trapani meant one less attack on Podium for Johnnie and the Fleet Air Arm to fight off. Penelope's All Clear was probably the resulting benefit of Diggers's attack. Let's see, Diggers and 505 should be safely home in another thirty minutes, give or take. It would be interesting to know if—

"Message understood," Freddie said, breaking into her thoughts yet again. "Yorker Leader is down."

Eleanor froze. How could Diggers be down? This was like some hideous case of déjà vu, some monstrous repetition of a nightmare: first Johnnie, now Diggers.

She couldn't speak. Freddie simply looked at her as he spoke into his telephone. He did not need to respond because his face said it all. Diggers was down. Penelope was staring at her. The second hand on the wall clock was moving.

She didn't know the Latin word for "down," but she knew the word for "death," because Diggers had written it less than twenty-four hours ago. Her eyes were drawn to the map on the wall, and then, against her will, to the place where Diggers had elegantly inscribed *Ora Mortis*.

How would she ever be able to tell Johnnie?

* * *

"Cameron didn't return," Captain Lancaster told Shaux. His manner suggested that he was reporting a fact rather than the loss of a human life; there is no room for sentimentality in battle. "Lieutenant Smith will take his place, but I will welcome your advice. You are, after all, the more experienced man."

"I'll do whatever I can, sir," Shaux said.

Lancaster nodded, turned back to the sea, and raised his binoculars.

Cameron's flight, Green Flight, had taken off with five aircraft and returned with three. Cameron had attacked what he had thought was an unescorted formation of Sparvieros and been jumped by Folgore fighters he had not seen. Shaux wondered how many times he had tried to teach inexperienced pilots that it wasn't the enemy you could see that you should worry about but the enemy you *couldn't* see. Thousands of lives had been lost on both sides for failure to learn this simple rule.

Nonsuch now had, Shaux estimated, eight operational aircraft at most, commanded by a pilot, Harry Smith, who had flown his first operational sortie yesterday. How were they going to defend the convoy like that?

It occurred to Shaux that, from Lancaster's perspective, his ship might be what mattered and the aircraft and their aerial operations were secondary. It might seem to Lancaster to be an unsatisfactory and indirect way of fighting; aircraft departed and perhaps returned, having fought or not fought, successfully or not, far beyond the horizon. Lancaster's medal ribbons suggested he had been in the navy for at least twenty-five years, coming up through the ranks when battleships and heavy cruisers were the unquestioned lords of the sea. *Nonsuch* had no big guns and could not, in that sense, engage the enemy. She had started life as a cruiser, a formidable fighting ship armed with 8-inch guns, but now *Nonsuch* was, in essence, a floating garage with a flat roof, with its bridge and upperworks all jammed over on the starboard side in a most inelegant, asymmetric manner.

Perhaps Lancaster secretly wished that the guns could be restored and the flimsy aircraft sent away so that *Nonsuch* could regain her dignity. If Lancaster really did wish that, Shaux thought, then he was probably mistaken; the Battle of Midway had been fought in June entirely between American and Japanese aircraft carriers.

Shaux saluted Lancaster's back—it seemed the right thing to do— left the bridge, and returned to flight deck. The crews had completed refueling and rearming the Martlets. Smith, Cameron's replacement as squadron commander, was reorganizing his diminished forces into two depleted flights.

"I'll take one flight and you take the other, Wing Commander," he said. "You know what you're doing, frankly, and we'll seldom be together as a single squadron."

"If there's anything I can—" Shaux began, but a seaman interrupted him.

"Captain to speak to you, sir," he said, and led Shaux to a voice pipe—one of several—projecting from the side of the bridge. "Listen an' speak 'ere, sir," the seaman said as Shaux hesitated.

"Shaux here?" he said into the bell-shaped tube end.

Lancaster's voice sounded hollow, and it seemed bizarre to be speaking to someone through a metal tube.

"Malta has signaled that there are Junkers 87 Stukas and Macchi C.202s or Messerschmitt 109s taking off from Triscina."

"Then we must get as many aircraft in the air as soon as possible, sir," Shaux said.

"Triscina is at least a hundred miles away," Lancaster said. "Isn't that premature?"

"Triscina is thirty minutes away, sir." Shaux wondered how loudly he should speak into the tube. "It will take us fifteen minutes to climb to their altitude, by which time they'll be halfway here. We need to get at least two flights in the air as fast as possible."

"Why two flights?"

"We need one to attack the Stukas, sir, and one to try to keep the Folgores away from the Stukas."

"Oh, very well. Carry on."

This is ridiculous, Shaux thought. The Stukas and 109s had probably been spotted by Wardrobe, another of the high-flying recce Blenheims like Hat-Rack. Wardrobe had told Malta, Malta had told the senior air officer aboard *Woodstock*, who had told Lancaster, who had asked Shaux's advice before taking action. A Stuka could climb two thousand feet in a minute, he thought, so we've probably given away ten thousand feet and we're not even airborne.

He stared at the voice pipe. It seemed bizarrely old-fashioned with its big brass mouthpiece, a hangover from a mechanical age before the invention of electricity. Nelson had used a voice pipe at Trafalgar, for God's sake! Minutes had been lost while he was chatting through a tube. How can we hope to fight a modern war like that? And how are Martlets supposed to fight 109s?

Then he stopped. These men, with their obsolete voice pipes, were risking their lives to bring fuel to Malta for his Spitfire, and ammunition for its guns, and food and water to keep him alive. Six hundred men in *Nonsuch* were risking their lives to supply him. Perhaps the captain didn't understand the basics of aerial defense, but he did understand the limits of his knowledge and had therefore asked for advice. So, Shaux told himself very firmly, if the navy wanted to communicate through a hollow tube, that was fine with him.

* * *

Eleanor walked blindly along the taxi path at Luqa, wracked by guilt. She had killed Diggers. She wanted to cry, but her guilt wouldn't let her.

She often thought that if you dug into someone deep enough, you'd find their bad side. But Diggers didn't have a bad side. He was the same all the way through, a gentleman on the surface and a gentleman at his core.

He was the big brother she'd never had. He had a sharp wit and a soft heart and a mind like a sponge, absorbing everything. He had the bluest eyes in the world. He could do delicate watercolors and the *Times* crossword. He was the only person she had ever known, or even heard of, even at Oxford, who could carry on a casual conversation in Latin. He was happiest when he was sitting in some damp bog or in a thicket of thornbushes or stinging nettles or somewhere like that, for hours on end, waiting to catch a glimpse of a rare bird. He could have been anything, but he wouldn't be, he'd be nothing—he was already nothing—because she had killed him stone cold dead, just as certainly as if she had shot him between the eyes, by coming up with the idea for the raid on Trapani and sending him off.

She remembered his favorite joke: "If I have to translate 'ad nauseam' one more time, I'm going to be sick."

He was one of the two men she knew Johnnie had loved. The first had been Froggie Potter, a superb, natural fighter pilot, a boy for whom life was an incredible madcap adventure. Johnnie, she was certain, had secretly longed to be Froggie, to throw caution to the winds and savor each moment, every breath, to its limit. But he couldn't be, because Froggie lived freely in his own skin while Johnnie, like a turtle, needed protective armor plating. Diggers was the other man she was certain Johnnie loved, because Diggers was the complete man that Johnnie, believing himself incomplete, wished he could be.

Froggie had been killed in the Battle of Britain, cut into pieces by a propeller and then burned alive. Diggers had now been shot down, or gone down—she still didn't know; he had been spared the agonies of burning because he had experienced the agony and despair of drowning instead.

Now she would have to tell Johnnie that Diggers was dead too. Johnnie would never again have the benefit of Diggers's eyesight on Vulture patrols, be told the exact differences between a Fulmar and an ern; be told to "stop carping and seize the day," and receive a signed copy of Diggers' *A Short Introduction to Scottish Birds of Prey*, the draft of which would lie unfinished in curling, yellowing pages on Diggers's desk, written in Diggers's elegant copperplate script and embroidered with Diggers's delicate illustrations, until someone bundled it up with his other effects and sent it off to his mother.

The newspapers would note that Acting Squadron Leader Alistair Quinton Digby, DFC and two bars, was missing, presumed dead, lost on patrol over the Mediterranean. The legend of the pilot who could see everything would one day make its way into Fighter Command mythology, if Fighter Command survived the war.

Meanwhile Johnnie, born friendless, would be friendless once more.

She closed her eyes and prayed as fiercely as she could that Diggers's death had been painless, an instant transfer from one set of wings to another.

"*Fragmen massae,*" she thought she heard his voice reply, in his customary murmur, or perhaps it was just the breeze whispering in the olive trees: "Piece of cake."

Now, at long last, Eleanor began to weep.

* * *

Shaux had first encountered Stuka dive-bombers just over two years ago, when the Germans had launched their invasion of Holland, Belgium, and France. They were, he thought, brilliantly designed killing machines, with their gull wings, diving brakes, and automatic pullout system permitting near vertical dive bombing. Their wailing *Jericho-Trompete* sirens were inspired propaganda devices, designed to terrorize civilian populations.

They might be brilliant, Shaux thought, but they were also very vulnerable, because they had been built to do only one thing, and they were slow and cumbersome and predictable in most other things. Spitfires and Hurricanes and even Defiants had chewed them up in the early days of the war, and they had been withdrawn from the Battle of Britain.

They were, unfortunately, very effective against unarmored shipping; even a small bomb delivered from a dive-bomber could smash through two or three decks and explode deep within a ship's hull. Of all of Podium's ships, only the two cruisers, *Gosport* and *Savannah*, had enough ack-ack firepower to be reasonably safe. *Nonsuch's* flight deck had only two inches of armor plating—enough to keep the rain out, as they said, but not much more.

"Eyes wide open," he said to Red Flight. "Keep searching the skies."

The key, as always, was to find them before they could find you. Shaux led Red Flight along a straight line drawn on an easterly bearing between the convoy's position and the airfield at Triscina in Sicily. When Shaux left Malta, Park and Eleanor had been considering a Counterpunch raid against Borizzo; it would be interesting to find out if Diggers had done so.

The enemy had the benefit of approaching reciprocally from the east, with the sun to hide them, but Martlets had high service ceilings, and with a bit of luck, he could get Red Flight high enough to look down on the enemy rather than trying to see them in the glare of the sun. Every minute gave him another two thousand feet. The more he flew the Martlet, the more he liked it. The aircraft was very solid, and the muscular Twin Wasp was pulling like a train.

He had told Lancaster he needed one flight for the Folgores and one for the Stukas, but the truth was that they needed at least two full squadrons to have a good chance of breaking up the Folgores and preventing the Stukas from getting through.

"Eyes wide open," he repeated to Red Flight. "Keep searching the skies."

"There!" Red Two yelled, less than a minute later. "Er, I mean, er, three o'clock low."

"Bandits thirty miles," Shaux said, to make sure *Nonsuch* and the convoy knew they were about to be attacked. He looked out a little below his right wing and saw a small dark smudge moving above the sea.

"Red Flight, follow me."

He began a moderate right turn that would bring them round to the enemy's beam. Without Diggers's eyes, he wasn't certain that the bandits were Stukas or how many there were.

"Eyes wide open. Keep searching the skies," he said again. There was no need to look at the enemy, but there was every need to see if there were more enemy aircraft above the smudge. He hoped his chaps would have the self-discipline to keep looking for new bandits and that the Italians, to the contrary, would focus their attention downwards as they searched for the convoy.

TWENTY

A Stuka had a very distinct profile, Shaux thought. To the untrained eye, a Martlet and a Folgore looked quite similar, but there was no other aircraft quite like a Stuka. It had big wheel spats and a long, droopy nose, as if the engine was too heavy for its mountings, an impression exaggerated by a big radiator cowling sagging beneath it. The canopy was long and narrow, like one of those little cloches that gardeners used to protect baby vegetables from frost. The radio mast was stuck improbably on top of the canopy like a flagpole, and a peashooter dorsal gun stuck out the back. A chubby bomb was slung below the fuselage.

This particular Stuka leader had foolishly painted a shark's face on the engine cowling, complete with a red mouth and white teeth and angry eyes. Such designs might impress newspaper photographers and lure the pilots' girlfriends into bed, Shaux thought, but up here they simply made their aircraft easier to spot. "Look at me. I have a very high opinion of myself," these paint schemes seem to say. Shaux always regretted the need to shoot down his fellow pilots, but he felt a little less sympathy for this chap.

The Stukas were flying in closely bunched formations. The Folgores were tucked in right behind them, too close and too low to be an effective escort. It would be impossible for the Folgores to cut Red Flight off or to follow it after the attack. Whoever was in charge of the Folgore escort had no idea of fighter tactics, Shaux thought, but at least he hadn't painted teeth on his aircraft.

He was closing rapidly on the shark-nosed Stuka, approaching from behind the pilot's right shoulder. A two-second burst would put a hundred or so rounds straight through the cockpit. If he missed the crew—anything could happen in the chaos of battle—he might still cripple the Stuka by damaging the controls; aircraft have many vulnerabilities.

He could see the white face of the rear gunner. The man could not train his machine-gun round far enough to aim at Red Flight, and his pilot could not turn to enable him to do so because the Stuka formation was jammed too close together. Shaux had, on more occasions than he cared to remember, been in a similar situation—watching an approaching enemy without the ability to retaliate.

Shaux did not know how many times he had opened fire on the enemy in the last two years—at least a hundred times, he was sure—and each time he saw not the fuselage of the aircraft, or the wings or tailplane or engines, but the aircrew inside, as if their aircraft was made of glass.

He fired a short ranging burst and saw tracer above the canopy. Martlets tended to fire a little higher than Spitfires from the pilot's perspective, Shaux was beginning to recognize—he'd remember next time. The Stuka countered immediately, plunging into a sudden dive so abruptly that Shaux was surprised the pilot was able to induce his inherently clumsy aircraft to react so quickly. The shark, *il pesce-cane*, might be arrogant, Shaux conceded, but he had lightning-fast reflexes—he should have been flying a fighter instead of a dive-bomber. Nevertheless, Shaux had the advantages of speed, height, and position. He nudged down, just a hairsbreadth, and opened fire into the side of the fuselage.

The Stuka flipped over and fell into an inverted dive. *Il pescecane* was returning to its natural habitat. It had been ill-considered, Shaux thought, to paint one's aircraft to resemble a fish and then fly over open water.

"Red Flight, follow me."

He led Red Flight round in as tight a turn as possible. The Folgores turned to follow, but that simply put them out of the fight—they were unprepared, too tightly packed together, and too slow. They were only halfway through their turn, flying away from the Stukas they were supposed to be supporting, as Shaux completed his turn. The Stuka formation was still together, still in level flight, as if uncertain what to do. Shaux had long observed that bomber squadrons stayed in formation when under attack far longer than fighters. Perhaps it was discipline, perhaps it was reduced maneuverability, or perhaps it was a sense of safety in numbers. Whatever it was, the Stukas stayed together while Red Flight circled back to their flank for a second attack. Perhaps the Stukas were counting on the Folgores to protect them, but the Folgores were far too far behind.

It occurred to Shaux that because the leader of the Stuka formation—the self-aggrandizing *il pescecane*—had been knocked out, and because Italian radios were notoriously bad, perhaps no one was making a decision or communicating it. Shaux had been convinced since the Battle of Britain that clear decisions, clearly communicated, were vital to survival in aerial combat. Pilots—particularly new pilots—were highly stressed, fearful, and indecisive, flinching at shadows while failing to see real dangers. The Stuka crews would be looking at each other, looking over their shoulders wondering where their protecting Folgores had disappeared to, and then over their other shoulders, with sudden horror, at the tight formation of Martlets already lining up for another attack.

Finally, to Shaux's relief, the formation broke up as one Stuka after another turned for home. This was prudence, not cowardice, in Shaux's view. The Stukas would live to fight another day, and he could see no honor in dying in a futile gesture.

"Let them go," Shaux said. The objective was to stop them from bombing Podium: objective obtained. Better to let them go home with their tails between their legs, wounded and discouraged, than risk Red Flight's inexperienced pilots in a second encounter. It was best to get back to the convoy in case there were other threats. The next time the Stukas flew, they would be less confident, less trustful of their escorts, and therefore a little more willing to abandon their mission when danger struck.

Shaux led Red Flight back to the convoy. Smoke billowed from the leading merchantman in the Jellico line. A second *Squadriglia Bombardamento* must have managed to reach the convoy, or perhaps they'd been found by more U-boats. The merchantman was still underway and holding her position, so perhaps the damage was not too severe.

Woodstock, however, had stopped in the water, and she had fallen back as far as the ack-ack cruiser *Savannah* as the rest of the convoy pressed on around her. Shaux remembered the admiral saying: "The essence of this convoy will be speed. Any vessel not capable of maintaining fifteen knots will be left behind. No stragglers; no exceptions." Now the admiral was watching the convoy leaving him behind.

Woodstock's flight deck seemed to be canting at a strange angle, and he saw she was listing badly, with much of her port side exposed above the water. There were several aircraft on the flight deck; Shaux wondered whether they would slide off into the Mediterranean. A corvette was pulling alongside *Woodstock*, looking diminutive in comparison. Shaux did not know if *Woodstock*'s captain had given the order to abandon ship, but if he did, it seemed unlikely that the corvette could accommodate all *Woodstock*'s crew. The flight deck seemed to shimmer, and Shaux guessed there must be a fierce fire raging below it. Perhaps a bomb had ignited the aviation fuel supply. God alone knew what it must be like down there. If anyone had been trapped, he hoped they had died quickly.

Shaux led Red Flight once around the entire convoy to make certain there were no enemies in the immediate vicinity. It struck him again how vast the sea was. How could they hope to spot a small MAS boat or an E-boat, let alone a U-boat periscope, amid the endless waves? No wonder the damage to the convoys was so great. More than twenty naval ships, including two aircraft carriers and two cruisers, sounded in theory as if a whole fleet had been assigned to protect the convoy, but looking down from angels one-five, it seemed pathetically inadequate in practice.

* * *

Penelope's telephone buzzed. She both loved and hated her new job as the liaison officer between the Luqa Operations Room and HMS St. Angelo. The job put Penelope in the thick of things in the Operations Room, a part of the team, but it also cast her as the bearer of bad tidings, because the telephone connected her to the Signals Center in

HMS St. Angelo, which relayed reports from Podium. When the phone buzzed, as it was buzzing now, it probably meant more news, and the news was almost always bad, to the extent that she had begun to cringe whenever the phone buzzed, and people would turn their eyes on her to find out what had gone wrong now. There was the principle of not shooting the messenger, but she wished that occasionally she had positive news to report.

At Eleanor's suggestion, she'd constructed a chart of all the ships in Podium and then updated it as reports flowed in. She had two carriers, two cruisers, ten destroyers, four minesweepers, two oilers, and six corvettes on her chart, for a total of twenty-six naval ships. She also had ten merchantmen. Against two of the merchantmen and one of the destroyers she had been forced to write "sunk."

She answered the phone and listened, acknowledged the information, and replaced the phone in its cradle.

"Podium reports another attack," she said into the expectant silence. "HMS *Woodstock* has sustained torpedo damage and has stopped, with a corvette standing by. Another merchantman has been hit but is continuing without loss of speed."

Woodstock was the flagship, she thought. If they lost *Woodstock*, what were the chances of the rest of the convoy getting through? At least Peter Lingard wasn't in *Woodstock*; he was in the other carrier, *Nonsuch.*

* * *

Shaux counted to himself using the fingers of his left hand as a guide. He had boiled the extra things he needed to remember for carrier landings down to five essentials. He'd realized that it was a bad idea to give himself a list of negatives to think about: "Don't undershoot or you'll fly slap into the stern," "Don't come in too flat or you'll miss the wires," and so on. Instead he had a list of positives, like "Put the hook down," to remember and then, once that was done, he could just let his Martlet slide down the slot.

There was Lingard, with his white paddles at the ready. Paddles aslant: Lingard wanted a tiny bit more bank. Paddles level: Lingard was happy. *Nonsuch* growing rapidly as the distance closes. Lingard still happy. Now the flight deck seemed large enough to land on, with the afterdeck black with the cumulative rubber skid marks from hundreds of previous landings. Lingard still happy. Almost there. Now *Nonsuch* is no longer an exquisitely detailed model of itself, it is a full-size twenty-five-thousand-ton ship filling his forward vision. "Cut!" said the paddles. Throttle down. A little right rudder. Let the nose begin to drop and now pull back. Drop down—a controlled fall, not a stall; tail down; nose up; still flying under control; hook dangling. *Bang.*

The Martlet stopped as the arrester wires grabbed the hook, but Shaux continued forward until his straps grabbed him with his nose an inch from the gunsight. The abrupt stillness was shocking. The deck crews swarmed towards him. He opened the canopy and took a deep breath. Piece of cake!

Carrier operations were only possible because of the skilled teamwork of the deck crews, Shaux thought as they folded his wings and manhandled his Martlet to its designated parking area so that the rest of Red Flight could land. He climbed out of the cockpit and lit a cigarette. Red Three was banking in. Red Three had done a decent job up there, Shaux thought. He'd have to compliment him. Lingard's paddles were moving rapidly. Shaux thought Lingard might have to wave him off—he looked a bit steep to Shaux—until Lingard gave the cut sign, and Red Three settled neatly on the deck.

Lingard was really very good at his job, Shaux thought; it would be very easy to confuse the pilot rather than correct him. If he didn't snore so much, he'd be a very decent chap. He kept a bible by his bunk, Shaux had noticed. What was it the bible said? "Snore ye not, lest it shalt be snored unto thee," or something like that?

Red Two came in next. Lingard's paddles were telling him he was too low, too low, still too low. Now Lingard waved him off urgently, telling him to apply full throttle and climb and go round for another try, but Red Two must have thought he could make it, or perhaps he simply reacted too slowly. The Martlet caught its wheels in the arrester cables rather than its hook and tipped forward on its nose with its tail in the air.

The prop met the deck and disintegrated, the blades flying off like scythes. Two blades flew into the air just past the funnel while the third decapitated Lingard before burying itself in the side of the bridge like a giant dart. Lingard's head arced high over the stern before plunging into the wake; his body, with his paddles still raised in warning, stood for a moment before collapsing. Red Two skidded along in an impossible vertical position before flipping forward over the side, as if it were an Olympic diver executing a skillful summersault into the sea below.

* * *

Every blow against Podium was a blow against Malta, Penelope thought, a blow against her past and her future.

And she had become used to it, when almost every day the Regia Aeronautica blew away another piece of her life or another person she knew. It was just a question of which building would be turned into rubble or which person would be the next to die—a friend, a neighbor, perhaps a relative. Nobody went to funerals anymore. There weren't enough hours in the day, and the priests raced through the services, one after the other. In any case, all this was probably just a dress rehearsal and things would get worse: if the convoys couldn't get through, there'd be starvation and then invasion.

Her uncle Bert thought that starvation—actual starvation and not just hunger—was an increasing possibility. Malta's farm production was limited in the best of times. If they couldn't feed the animals, the goats in particular, they'd have to kill them, and the children would have no milk. If they had to kill the horses, there'd be no more farming and no more civilian transportation. Maltese women relied on kerosene for cooking, but kerosene had all but disappeared, and consequently hot meals and even tea were becoming rarities.

Uncle Bert had always been a thin man, but now he was looking skeletal. His housekeeper had told Penelope, in the strictest confidence, that he was eating one poor meal a day and giving the rest of his rations to his neediest patients.

Penelope updated her chart, writing "remaining with *Woodstock*" next to one of the corvettes and "damaged" next to one of the merchantmen. That particular ship was a tanker, she noted, one of two in the convoy. Half of the fuel necessary to keep Malta fighting was now at risk. Each merchantman, Eleanor had calculated, represented two weeks of life for Malta. Penelope counted the remaining merchant-men; Malta would die before the end of September.

* * *

Shaux watched the flight deck crews turning the Martlets around. Just like the ground crews at an RAF station, these men were the unsung heroes of the battles in the sky, which were not only duels between pilots but duels between aircraft. The best-maintained aircraft—with guns that didn't jam, an engine that didn't overheat or misfire, smooth, clean surfaces over which the air could flow without turbulence, and a thousand other details—had a distinct advantage.

That Stuka pilot, *il pescecane*, had moved like lightning. If he hadn't been hemmed in by that tight, boxy formation, he'd have evaded Shaux. Every once in a while, you encountered a truly superior opponent, someone who was simply better than yourself. Shaux was certain that he'd encountered Adolf Galland in the Battle of Britain and survived only because Galland had chosen another target. *Il pescecane* was that kind of pilot, Shaux thought, but unlike Galland, he was flawed. Why had his ego compelled him to paint his aircraft in such a childish, garish manner?

Shaux strolled on until he reached the stern and lit a cigarette. The long white wake stretched back forever, and the sun was pleasantly warm. He was becoming a sailor, he chuckled to himself. He could light a cigarette in spite of the stiff breeze, and he was confident that the ship would not sink in the next ten minutes—well, fairly confident.

Red Three—Shaux thought his name was Walsh—approached him. Walsh had fluffy blond hair, pimples, and an air of innocence that suggested he was far too young to be engaged in warfare; he should be in some boring sixth-form class listening to a droning schoolmaster or playing cricket on the school fields.

"I was going to ask you, sir, about the way we attacked the Stukas, coming in from the side and hitting them like that. What do you call that plan of attack, sir?"

It was a good question, Shaux thought, and it deserved an honest answer.

"I call it butchery."

"What, sir?" Walsh asked, his eyes opening in disbelief. "What did you say?"

"A beam attack. It's referred to as a beam attack."

"Oh, I see, sir," Walsh said, his face clearing. "Beam attack—of course. Thank you."

He watched Walsh turn away, evidently satisfied, but "butchery" was a far more honest answer.

Shaux shook his head. Perhaps he should consider getting a job in a butcher's shop after the war, or, better, in a slaughterhouse. He seemed to have a natural talent for it.

TWENTY-ONE

Dear Eleanor,

 I have wavered back and forth on how to write to you, but we have always agreed that honesty is the best policy in the long run. Therefore, I am sorry to tell you that your father's condition is not improving. It is so sad that this wretched war keeps you from him. He asks for you every day . . .

A large tear fell with a splat on the word *sad*, and Eleanor could not see clearly enough to continue.

This is August, she thought. Operation Torch would not take place until November. Even if, against the odds, the Eighth Army defeated the Afrika Korps, it would take months to bring all of Libya, Tunisia, and Algeria under Allied control, months during which Malta would continue to be the most important theater of air operations in the whole Mediterranean. It would be the middle of 1943, almost a year from now, before there would be any chance Park might be assigned elsewhere and that she might request a posting back home.

Aunt Charlotte's letter made it sound as if her father would not last that long. Eleanor would therefore fail him as a daughter, just as she sometimes thought she was failing Johnnie as a wife. But how could she be a good wife if the war was consuming both of them? How could she comfort her father if she was stuck here, in an underground bunker in Malta, day in, day out?

She pretended to yawn lest anyone see that she had tears in her eyes.

* * *

The thing about Eleanor, Penelope thought, was that she had this restless energy—not in a fidgety way but in a way that all problems and challenges in life were solvable, easily solvable, and would indeed get solved in the next ten minutes. In fact, whatever it was would not so much get solved as get overpowered. She was like a dynamo. She was a wing officer, the same rank as a naval commander like Thompson, and she was no older than Penelope. She wore a ribbon on her jacket, indicating she had won the Military Medal.

Penelope, stringing together a half-dozen rumors and secondhand anecdotes, had formed the impression that Eleanor was a brilliant mathematician who had studied at Oxford. She'd worked for the AOC during the Battle of Britain and even for Mr. Churchill in some secret role. She had been wounded somehow and sent here to recuperate. It was even suggested that she had been involved in shooting down an enemy aircraft. Half the world seemed to think that was ridiculous, but the RAF did not give out medals for being good at arithmetic.

Penelope stole a glance at Eleanor, who was sitting on the other side of the table. Her husband was flying in the teeth of danger, and their best friend had just been killed, but you would never know it from looking at Eleanor; indeed, in the midst of all the tension and danger, she was actually suppressing a yawn!

Well, perhaps Eleanor was not really so calm beneath the surface. How could anyone be? She had started smoking more heavily, and you could sometimes see her clenching her jaw. It had begun when her husband had crashed into the sea and worsened since the fighter pilot with the amazing blue eyes had been killed. The three of them had been very close friends, ever since the Battle of Britain, Penelope had been told.

Everyone had a limit beyond which they could not go. She must have known literally dozens of pilots who flew off and did not return or who did return but were mangled by hideous injuries. Perhaps their friend Digby's—"Diggers," they'd called him—death was a death beyond her limit. Perhaps she was beginning to crack; after all, even a dynamo can't overcome death.

Penelope had accidentally overheard a snatch of conversation between Eleanor and the AOC, evidently debating whether to send a message to her husband about Digby's death; for once, neither of them seemed to know what to do.

"I'll have to send a signal," Park had said. "I simply have to."

"But what will you say?"

"I don't know."

* * *

"We've lost *Woodstock* and another merchantman," Captain Lancaster said. "Without *Woodstock*, we cannot defend ourselves against their fleet, if they come out. We have whatever aircraft we have on *Nonsuch*. That's all."

"We found a formation of approximately twenty Stukas and Folgores and broke it up, sir," Shaux said. "Some of the Stukas might have pressed on, but those I saw were ditching their bombs and turning for home."

"The attack on *Woodstock* was another U-boat attack. We haven't seen any bombers this morning."

Again Shaux had the impression that the aerial battle was a side-show in Lancaster's mind. The fact that Shaux and Red Flight had prevented a Stuka attack did not seem relevant in comparison to U-boats and the possible intervention of the Italian fleet.

"How long before we reach Malta, sir?"

"We've been at sea two days, forty-eight hours," Lancaster said. "We have another thirty hours to go."

"There's seven or eight hours of daylight left today, sir; I strongly suggest we need to send up standing patrols."

"Very well. As you wish." Lancaster did not shrug, but again he conveyed the impression that aerial tactics were a minor concern.

"We just have to get through the rest of today, sir," Shaux said. "We'll be much safer tomorrow morning as we approach Malta; we'll be within our chaps' range, and we'll get good fighter protection. I suggest—"

A dull boom interrupted him, sounding across the water from somewhere ahead.

"*Aretha* signaling, sir," the officer of the watch reported to Lancaster. "Merchant ship *Benedict* has been struck by torpedoes."

Aretha was the last destroyer in the Zebra column, Shaux remembered. Lancaster turned away to deal with this new development, and Shaux ran down the flights of steep ladders as fast as he could until he reached the hatch leading to the flight deck. Next to the hatch was a line of telephones and voice pipes he didn't understand. Fortunately, Bentley, the deck chief petty officer, was speaking into one of them.

"Tell the first lieutenant that we will take off immediately, with two aircraft," he said to Bentley and ran to the Martlets parked on the afterdeck. Etiquette and his own indeterminate status did not give him the authority to make such a decision, but it was essential to get at least a couple of Martlets in the air as soon as possible, just in case the attacker could be found. U-boats fired their torpedoes from periscope depth or even from the surface and could be seen under the water if they were not too deep.

He found Walsh, Red Three, by his aircraft, gazing in the direction of the stricken merchantman.

"We're taking off immediately," Shaux said. "A low search pattern for U-boats."

"Forebridge says you are clear for takeoff," the deck CPO gasped, trotting up. He was a stout man—to be polite—and clearly not designed for speedy physical maneuvers. But he knew his business, and the deck crews had Shaux's Martlet started and ready within two minutes. A green flare erupted from the bridge high above their heads to give him permission to take off, and Shaux opened the throttle wide. He was surprised to realize, as he cleared the bow already at fifty feet, that he had just made a carrier deck takeoff without giving it a second thought.

* * *

Eleanor watched Penelope as she received updates from Podium. At first she'd wondered if Penelope was a bit lightweight, a bit flighty, but

Penelope was still very young and seemed to be trying hard. Perhaps she just needed a chance to grow up.

Eleanor stopped herself. Penelope was exactly the same age as she was. Perhaps Penelope was fine, but she, Eleanor, was the one out of kilter, old beyond her years, eroded prematurely by the war.

"Podium reports another merchantman has been struck by torpedoes," Penelope said, steadily and clearly, and Eleanor guessed Penelope had been studying Freddie's calm demeanor under pressure. Perhaps by next week she'd be saying "mer-chant-man-na."

"How many is that?" Park asked.

"Podium has now lost four merchantmen and one damaged, sir," Penelope said, looking down at her chart. "In addition, they have lost *Woodstock*, the destroyers *Bromley* and *Avery*, and one corvette, sir."

Penelope nodded in secret approval. Yesterday, when Park had asked a similar question, Penelope had begun to answer him by saying: "Well, let me think, sir. If I recall correctly . . ." Penelope wasn't flighty after all.

A WAAF updated Podium's position, sticking the marker into the *O* of *Ora Mortis*. Johnnie, in *Nonsuch*, would soon be sailing over Diggers's watery grave, and he still didn't know.

* * *

There was time for one more circuit, Shaux decided. He was reluctant to give up, even though the chances of finding a U-boat were close to zero. He wished he knew more about U-boat tactics. Most of their attacks had come from the flanks ahead of Podium, he had seen. The U-boat captains seemed to be trying to align themselves so that there were two or more ships in their sights. If their torpedoes missed one ship, they might run on and hit another.

If I were a fighter pilot attacking the convoy, he thought, I'd attack from due west, from behind the convoy, with the setting sun behind me, blinding anyone in the convoy looking back towards me. I'd simply fly out of the sun to within a few hundred yards and then let my rockets go. Perhaps a U-boat captain might do the same, sneaking up behind the convoy and firing torpedoes into the serried ranks of ships ahead of him.

Shaux decided to take a lazy, low-level circuit behind the convoy, just in case. He dropped the revs down until he was flying at no more than 90 miles per hour, not much above stalling speed in level flight. Glancing back, he saw Red Three flying erratically as he tried to follow. The slower the speed, the more an aircraft was affected by shifts in winds and changes in pressure and therefore the more jittery it became. Red Three must be wrestling with his controls.

"Red Three, return to *Nonsuch*," he said.

"Herky-jerky will no workie!" Shaux's old flying instructor had said. There was no point in needlessly putting Red Three at risk, and he'd be too preoccupied with flying to be able to assist in the search.

Shaux saw Red Three climbing away and resumed his search, crisscrossing behind the convoy, but could see nothing. Either his theory about U-boat tactics was wrong, or he simply could not see a U-boat that was really down there. Even if, by some miracle, he spotted a U-boat, he thought, his 50-millimeter guns could do it only very superficial damage. At least he'd be able to tell the destroyers and corvettes, and they could hunt anything he found.

The western sky was turning the heavens into a sublime spectacle of vivid orange and luminescent eggshell blue, God's twice-daily effort to win Shaux's soul. It was tempting to abandon the search and just spend ten minutes tooling around enjoying the sunset. Why look down at the darkling sea when there was such a spectacular—

There! There it was, whatever it was, a tiny anomaly amid the endless rollers playing hide-and-seek with the wave tops. It had a long, high prow butting through the wave tops followed by a fat, black body with a deck gun on a bandstand in front of a conning tower. He'd have missed it completely, the gray-black U-boat set deep in the green-black sea, if it had not been for its wake, a green-white phosphorescent line stretching out behind it, cutting across the natural angles of the waves.

Shaux flashed over it and saw two figures on the conning tower staring up in shock. He'd heard that U-boats were extremely noisy when their diesels were running, so noisy that the crew could not hear aircraft approaching them. He began a sharp turn. Even though he couldn't hurt the U-boat, at least he could scare the crew.

The U-boat was a couple of miles behind *Nonsuch*, the last ship in Podium. Now, that was strange. It had a wake running ahead of it as well as behind. How could it have a wake—no, two wakes—pointing forward as well as backwards, long white lines in the water stretching out rapidly ahead of it?

"Attention, *Nonsuch*," he snapped into his headset. "U-boat astern. Torpedoes running."

A torpedo ran at 40 miles per hour or so. It would take about a minute and a half for the torpedoes to reach *Nonsuch*.

"Attention, *Nonsuch*," he repeated. "U-boat astern. Torpedoes running."

The U-boat crew had disappeared inside the conning tower by the time he'd turned, and the prow was already lower in the water as the U-boat dived to safety. If he had his rocket-armed Spitfire, he could do it serious damage, but a short burst of fire from his Martlet's machine guns was at least a gesture. He didn't know if he could even puncture the skin, but at least there'd be a loud rat-a-tat-tat hammering sound inside the hull.

On board *Nonsuch*, the R/T signals rating would have had to hear him, understood the message, and relayed it accurately to the bridge. The officer of the watch would have to understand the message and react. He'd have to decide if the threat was credible. Flight ops R/T messages were a very unlikely source of tactical navigational information requiring an immediate change of course. Would the officer of the watch understand? They'd be able to see him circling behind them, making tight spirals, and perhaps they—

"Repeat signal," said his earphones.

Nonsuch had failed to understand, or somewhere in the communications chain the message had broken down, perhaps lost in the labyrinthine coils of endless voice tubes.

"Red Leader to Forebridge," he tried. There was an R/T repeater loudspeaker on the bridge. Perhaps they'd turned it on, and the officer of the watch could hear him directly. "U-boat astern. Torpedoes running."

He opened the throttle and turned towards *Nonsuch* as the revs spun up, following and then overtaking the torpedo wakes. They were, he judged, directly aligned with *Nonsuch*'s stern: long, white, malevolent streaks in the water. He reached *Nonsuch* in just a few seconds, flying the length of its deck at twenty feet at perhaps 250 miles per hour, level with the bridge and his wingtip no more than ten feet from it; at least he would have their attention!

"U-boat astern, *Nonsuch*. Torpedoes running. U-boat astern, *Nonsuch*. Torpedoes running."

He had probably broken every single rule it was possible for an FAA pilot to break. But, as he turned yet again, he could see, at long last, *Nonsuch* turning ponderously to starboard. The torpedoes would reach her any second; either they'd strike her or pass by harmlessly.

He waited. *Nonsuch* continued to turn. Still nothing. If they were going to hit her, it would have to be now, on her port quarter.

Two white streaks appeared in the water beside her port side, running parallel to her and overreaching her rapidly, heading for Tunisia.

* * *

"That was a little too close for comfort," Captain Lancaster said.

"Indeed it was, sir," said the first lieutenant. "Those torpedoes went past us no more than twenty feet off the port quarter. Thank God for—"

"I was referring to your fly-by, Wing Commander, if I am using the correct terminology," Lancaster said. "Please do not do that again during your remaining time on board."

"Very well, sir," Shaux said. He had absolutely no idea whether Lancaster was joking or not but guessed he was not. The first lieutenant instantly drew his features into a study in indifference and gazed into the middle distance as if in contemplation of eternity, and Shaux did not blame him; the first lieutenant had to live in close proximity with Lancaster on a permanent basis.

Shaux saluted. As he turned away, one of the signals ratings approached him—Shaux congratulated himself on beginning to recognize at least some of the hundreds of seamen who transformed *Nonsuch* from twenty-five thousand tons of metal into an efficient fighting machine.

"Excuse me, sir, but there's a signal for you from RAF Headquarters in Malta."

"Yes?"

The telegraphist looked down at his signals pad.

"It says 'From AOC AHQ Malta. Regret to inform you Digby MPD, signed Park.'"

Shaux noted that the white ensign still fluttered from the mast-head. The Mediterranean rollers still advanced in their endless serried ranks, and *Nonsuch* still heeled before them with solemn gravity. The maintenance crew working on the Martlet with the faulty engine still couldn't get it to stop missing and coughing—could it be the magneto?—and a work crew still had several deck inspection plates up around the arrester wire mechanisms in case Red Two had broken something when he crashed. The world appeared to be exactly the same without Digby in it as it had been with him: *plus ça change, plus c'est la même chose*—the more things change, the more they stay the same, Digby would have said.

"Thank you," Shaux said.

"Aye-aye, sir." The telegraphist saluted and turned away.

Well, Shaux thought, it's actually something of a relief. It was inevitable to wonder if a fighter pilot would survive his next flight. It was hard to resist glancing around the mess bar in the evening, with the air filled with tobacco smoke and raucous conversation and laughter, and guess who wouldn't be there tomorrow night. Diggers had flown against the enemy hundreds of times. The ending—KIA, killed in action, or MPD, missing presumed dead—was all but unavoidable. He had joined Froggie Potter and dozens and dozens of others. In fact, it would be interesting to calculate whether, after almost three years of war, there were now more dead Spitfire pilots than live ones.

The message didn't say how Diggers had been lost, but it didn't matter, Shaux thought. MPD was just as final a death sentence as any other. Yes, it was definitely a relief. Diggers had been his only friend, and he had worried about him. Now Diggers was dead, there was one less thing to worry about. Life was therefore a little simpler.

He found himself on the flight deck and looked up automatically, searching for enemy fighters, but there were none in sight. He wondered if, when the time came, he'd see the enemy who killed him or whether he'd just be blown out of the sky without warning. It didn't really matter—he'd be dead in either case. When you came right down to it, nothing really mattered.

Pity about Diggers, though; he'd have to make sure to write to Diggers's parents when he got back to Malta.

TWENTY-TWO

Now that he had the cabin to himself, Shaux couldn't sleep a wink, listening in vain for Lingard's snoring. He'd been an extremely competent deck landing officer, Shaux thought, but he'd also been a morose sort of chap, with a large bible he consulted frequently, with numerous bookmarks among the gilt-edged pages and a photograph of a pretty blonde girl stuck on the bulkhead by his pillow. The girl seemed strangely familiar to Shaux, although he couldn't put a name to her face—but he'd never been able to tell one film star from another.

Shaux turned over and rearranged his pillow. Perhaps the bookmarks detailed Lingard's favored sins, although there were far more than seven bookmarks . . . Shaux had no photograph of Eleanor to stick on the bulkhead beside his head; should he have one? Let's see; there was envy, gluttony, sloth, lust . . . Lingard had never struck him as suffering noticeably from any of those, and gloominess was not a sin . . . He hoped he had a decent snapshot of Diggers . . . He needed sleep; he'd be in the air at first light . . .

The truth was that he didn't want to sleep, because he didn't want to have that dream again, the dream in which he arrived at a river—the Styx, he assumed—and saw a group of people waiting for him on the other side. It was a shallow river, narrower than he had first thought and easy to wade across and pleasantly warm: the transition from life to death was surprisingly easy. Perhaps this wasn't the Styx or the caverns of the underworld; in fact, the sky was deep blue and the sun was shining brightly.

Some young men in the group—well, it was more than a group; it was a crowd, a totally silent crowd—were in flying gear, and Shaux knew that these were airmen he had shot down and killed. With each young man stood his mother and father, and his wife or girlfriend, and most of the groups had little children, except the little children were strangely ethereal. Shaux knew that these were the children the airmen would have had if Shaux had not killed them. No one said anything. They just looked at Shaux, and he understood they just wanted him to see the lives he had ended, damaged, and denied.

Shaux passed slowly through the crowd, looking wordlessly into every face, and came to a stage set on a grassy knoll above the river bank. An elderly man sat at a desk on the stage and beckoned Shaux to approach. The crowd pressed forward and watched in silent witness.

"Ah, here you are at last," the old man said, picking up an old-fashioned quill pen and preparing to take notes. "Now, please evaluate your life."

The old man—he had bushy eyebrows raised in query—and the crowd waited for his answer.

At that point Shaux always awoke, grappling with the old man's question.

* * *

Podium was now six hours from Malta. The convoy looked very different, Shaux thought, looking down from angels zero-five, compared to when they sailed from Gibraltar just three days ago. Instead of two lines of merchantmen with the ack-ack cruisers between them, there was now only one column with a cruiser on each side. There were now just four merchantmen instead of ten. The two columns of destroyers and corvettes, Yoke and Zebra, now each had four ships instead of eight. All the minesweepers had survived and still led the convoy; *Nonsuch* still brought up the rear.

A fifth merchantman, MV *Avery*, was still heading for Malta fifty miles behind Podium, being towed by a destroyer with a corvette as an escort. Thirty-six ships had left Gibraltar three days ago; now there were twenty-one left in the convoy with three following. From the first attacks on the convoy until now a ship had died, on average, every four hours.

Stretching out behind *Avery* were no more surviving ships. Doubtless there were life rafts bobbing about here and there, all the way back to the narrows between Sardinia and Tunisia, and doubtless at least some of their crews would still be alive. Far beneath the life rafts lay the wrecks of *Woodstock* and the others, forming a trail of sunken aircraft, drowned ships, and drowned crews resting together, British and Axis, to mark and memorialize the route that Podium had followed.

They were the just latest additions to the detritus of war scattered across the floor of the Mediterranean, Shaux thought. Half-buried in the sediments around them would be ships dating back to the dawn of written history—Assyrian biremes powered by rows of slaves and Egyptian square riggers carrying the pharaohs' grain, Roman and Carthaginian galleys, fat Venetian frigates *da mercato*, Viking long-ships like killer sharks, and mighty ships of the line from the days of Napoleon and Nelson. Men had fought on these waters and died beneath them for eight thousand years.

The air above and around Podium was positively thick with Spitfires and Hurricanes from Malta. Park was clearly pulling out all the stops. It would take a suicidal bomber or surface vessel to attempt an attack now; the remaining danger, if any, still lay beneath the waves. U-boats had claimed two more victims overnight; perhaps one of them was the U-boat that had fired at *Nonsuch* yesterday evening. If he was going to fight U-boats, Shaux thought, he should know a lot more about them. When he got back to Malta, he'd make a point of talking to the anti-submarine chaps in Force K, if there were any there, or, better yet, the navy's own submarine chaps at HMS Talbot.

Shaux led Red Flight—well, it was a flight made up of all the remaining serviceable aircraft aboard *Nonsuch* and they had to call it something—back westward to check on the struggling *Avery* and her escorts. At a speed of only four or five knots, the ships would be sitting ducks if the enemy found them. Unfortunately the merchantman was belching oily smoke; any enemies in the vicinity would find them immediately.

They were just north of Pantelleria, taking yet another slow lap around *Avery*, perhaps eighty miles from Malta, when Shaux thought he glimpsed, or felt, or sensed, something was down there, although he looked again and there was nothing to see. He blinked his eyes rapidly and led Red Flight lower; still nothing. He shook his head to clear it, but he could not shake off this strange feeling, this whatever it was. They went round again.

Whatever it was had to be very small, if it was there at all. Perhaps it was a life raft or the conning tower of a semi-submerged U-boat. There was no wake, so it wasn't a marauding Italian MAS boat. No, there was nothing, at least—

Then, in an instant and very much against his will, he knew exactly what it was.

He didn't believe in ghosts or life after death or any of that sort of nonsense, and he had no idea how or when Diggers had died—that was the whole point of MPD. You just vanished without explanation, in a sort of existential magic trick; first you see it, then you don't—but he had a sudden intuition, a sort of silent buzz, that made him stare down at the waves, as if Diggers were somehow sending him a message, that this was where Diggers lay, far below the surface.

He flew on and the feeling faded; on the next circuit, the feeling strengthened again. Yes, this was where Diggers had died. There could be no question. And it had to be Diggers and not some other lost soul, for the message he was sensing was in Latin: *fragmen massae*. It was Diggers beyond a doubt; no one else communicated in Latin, at least not for the last thousand years, and no one else, in the entire history of the human race, had ever said *"fragmen massae"* instead of "piece of cake."

Shaux pulled off his flying helmet. The practical side of his brain was still functioning reliably and independently, like an accurate mechanical autopilot, and it told him it would be really, really messy to weep into an oxygen mask.

* * *

Eleanor stood and stretched. She was due for the regular weekly staff meeting between Park and Lord Gort, the governor. Podium was almost here—that is to say, she corrected herself, what was left of Podium was almost here. *Nonsuch* and all the other escorts would be turning around in the next hour and heading straight back to Gibraltar. Podium's four remaining merchantmen would be escorted into Valletta by a motley assortment of naval ships—whatever St. Angelo could scrape together—and unloaded as soon as possible by men working through the night until the job was done; the Regia Aeronautica was bound to attempt to bomb them as soon as they arrived and again tomorrow morning.

There had been several disastrous occasions when vital supplies had finally reached Malta only to be destroyed the moment they arrived. In March, for example, the last two surviving merchantmen from convoy MW10 arrived safely in the Grand Harbour but were bombed and sunk before they could be unloaded. In April forty-seven Spitfires had been flown off the carrier USS *Wasp* during Operation Calendar, only to be destroyed on the ground as soon as they landed at Ta Kali.

Dozens of ships and thousands of men were involved in each operation, and many had been sacrificed. It was a particularly bitter loss when all those ships and all those men were sacrificed in vain, with the enemy snatching victory from the jaws of defeat.

Park had standing patrols up and waiting to spot the incoming bombers, and three more squadrons of Spitfires and Hurricanes standing by for takeoff as soon as the bombers were detected. It would not be impossible for the Sparvieros to get through, but it would be very difficult and very expensive.

Johnnie was supposed to be transferred from *Nonsuch* to an RAF search-and-rescue HSL—high-speed launch—to bring him back to Malta. If they didn't make the transfer, he'd have to go all the way back to Gib. It would be a sad homecoming; they would mourn Diggers together. Well, perhaps they'd mourn together, or perhaps Johnnie had shut himself down and retreated inside his impenetrable armor plating.

In the meantime she began to assemble the papers Park needed for the meeting. Lord Gort had a mixed reputation. In the First World War, he had won the Victoria Cross for great personal heroism and was considered one of Britain's finest soldiers, rising quickly through the ranks. He had, however, been in command of the British Expeditionary

Force in France and Belgium in 1940 when it collapsed in the face of the German blitzkrieg and had to be rescued from Dunkirk. Gort had not been reprimanded but had been shuffled off into administrative duties rather than battlefield commands—like being governor of Malta.

The leader of the German spearhead in that battle had been Erwin Rommel, who was now torturing the Eighth Army in Egypt. Perhaps Gort feared he would lose to Rommel twice.

Gort, she had come to realize, had an exceedingly dim view of the RAF, believing he had been let down in France. Since Park had been AOC 11 Group during the Germany's attacks on France, Belgium, and Holland, that meant Gort thought Park had let him down. Now he was objecting to Park's Counterpunch tactics. He wanted Park to stay close to home, to conserve fuel for defensive patrols against bombers, whereas Park was taking the fight to the enemy, arguing that offensive operations consumed less fuel than endless defensive patrols.

Gort did not have direct authority over Park but could make his life miserable by firing off frequent letters of complaint to Park's actual boss, Arthur Tedder in Middle East Command in Cairo, and Tedder's boss, Charles Portal in London, and, indeed, to anyone else who would listen. And therefore Eleanor dreaded these weekly meetings—*weekly confrontations* was a better description.

There was just time for a cigarette before leaving for the meeting. She climbed the stairs to the surface and the sudden blast of the heat of a Mediterranean summer and saw Jenkins, Dobson, and Miller in conversation in the shade of a sandbag revetment.

"We were just coming to see you, ma'am," Jenkins said. "We think we know why the Wing Commander and Squadron Leader Digby went down."

"Why?"

"Squadron Leader Digby solved the problem of your husband's crash, or thought he probably had. The wing modifications caused the controls to malfunction. He said it was, er—"

"Aeroelasticity," Dobson offered. "Abnormal warping of the wings changing the way the controls work."

"Then why didn't—"

"He said this morning's raid was coming up so there was no time to make changes."

"But—"

"He said the raid was too important to postpone, ma'am," Miller said. "He said we'd conduct some tests to confirm his theory."

"But surely—"

"So now he's down, like your husband was, except he hasn't come back."

So Diggers had known the risk and flown anyway. She had asked him to fly in an unsafe aircraft, and he had done so. She really had killed him, she thought; it was not just hyperbole.

* * *

Eleanor and Park drove to the governor's mansion, the Grandmaster's Palace, in the center of Valletta, in Park's bright-red MG sports car; an exotic vehicle in complete contrast to Park's retiring character. Everybody recognized it instantly, and Eleanor realized that this was the point: Park wanted everyone to know that he was here and on the job. It was a window into Park's style, along with his obsolete white flying overalls and his decision to move his headquarters to Luqa, the most-bombed place in Malta. The shy, retiring, private Park had created the deliberately flamboyant public Park. Johnnie was climbing through the ranks, she reflected, and she knew his men adored him. Would he become more flamboyant, too, if he rose to be a senior officer?

The palace was an unadorned building on the outside—Eleanor couldn't decide if it was boring or ugly or, perhaps, both at once—and gaudily ornate on the inside, with grand murals and extravagant tapestries covering the walls. This was where the Grand Masters of the Knights of St. John had ruled Malta for centuries, gradually fading into the shadows of legend until Napoleon had finally dispatched them in his own pursuit of glory.

"Force K is relieving the Podium Task Force as we speak, sir," Eleanor told Gort. Calling two old destroyers and a couple of corvettes "Force K" was a bit generous, but the navy was deploying everything they had available. "There are four merchantmen due this afternoon and a fifth trying to reach us sometime overnight."

Gort grunted.

"We have a squadron of Hurricanes over Force K and another doing picket duty towards Sicily. We have three additional Spitfire squadrons waiting at readiness for the Regia Aeronautica."

"I'm glad to see you're finally listening to my advice, Park," Gort said. "We must focus on defense, first, last, and always. Everything else is a wasteful distraction."

She could see a pulse throbbing in Park's neck and knew that he was seething.

"If you'd done so from the first, we wouldn't be in such a pickle," Gort added.

She hurried on with her report, lest Gort provoke Park into a response both men would regret.

"If Podium's ships can dock and be unloaded without further losses, we should be able to be able to last until November on our new and existing rations, sir, or October, if civilian rations are increased. Almost the entire cargoes of two of the ships consist of food and civilian staples, and there are forty-gallon drums of kerosene on *Avery*, which will allow the civilian people to cook hot meals."

"I will decide whether or not to increase rations, thank you," Gort said, as if she had questioned his authority.

"Of course, sir."

The meeting did not last long. Park and Gort were both clearly anxious to escape each other's company as soon as possible. Eleanor knew that Park was here only because Portal had asked Park to extend an olive branch to Gort and keep it extended regardless of provocations. The meeting hobbled on for another five minutes while Gort suggested that he should control all supplies, including Park's vital aircraft fuel and spare parts inventory, until an aide entered and silently handed Gort a note.

"You'll have to excuse me," Gort said.

Eleanor bet herself that this was a prearranged interruption to end the meeting. Park, usually so polite and considerate, almost ran from the room, jumped in his red MG, and sped off with an uncharacteristic clashing of gears, leaving Eleanor to fend for herself.

* * *

Penelope sat staring at the operational report from *Nonsuch*. She was surprised at her own lack of emotion. Peter Lingard was dead, killed on *Nonsuch*'s flight deck when a Martlet had crash-landed. She wasn't sad to have lost him, nor glad he was gone; he'd simply moved from the list of the living to the list of the dead.

She'd run into Mrs. Lingard, Jimmy's and Peter's mother, the other day, and had a weirdly stilted conversation. They'd said nothing of any significance, just platitudes about the bombing and the rationing, but Penelope was certain that Mrs. Lingard's eyes had conveyed another message: How dare she be alive while her boy Jimmy was dead? Penelope often wondered if Mrs. Lingard knew that she and Jimmy had not waited until they were married, or that Peter had subsequently claimed his brother's place in her bed, suggesting he had a biblical obligation to do so.

It shouldn't matter in the least, and it was none of Mrs. Lingard's business, but, looking into Mrs. Lingard's eyes, perhaps it did matter, at least to Mrs. Lingard. Penelope felt a pang of guilt. Perhaps Mrs. Lingard knew. Perhaps Mrs. Lingard was thinking "like mother, like daughter." First Penelope's mother runs off with a Neapolitan opera singer, for God's sake, and then Penelope's allures rob her sons of their innocence. Mrs. Lingard was on the board of the opera house and would know all the lurid details about her mother's fall from grace, and if she didn't know them, she could always make them up.

Now Penelope knew another thing that Mrs. Lingard did not: both Mrs. Lingard's sons were dead. Now she faced the same problem that Eleanor had faced: Should she tell Mrs. Lingard or let the news grind its way through official channels?

TWENTY-THREE

Eleanor emerged into the sunlight and lit a cigarette. Thank God the meeting with Gort was over for another week. She glanced upwards, looking for aircraft, and reflected with some surprise that she had picked up the habit from Johnnie, and it had now become engrained. She wondered if the ginger runt would consider this a sign of psychosis, that Johnnie was now living, at least subconsciously, in perpetual fear of enemy aircraft, under unending existential threat from the skies above, just as Yeats's poem suggested. And he had passed the infection on to her. The Greek god Zeus had hurled thunderbolts from the heavens to destroy his enemies, as had the Nordic god Thor, and mere mortals walked in fear. She and Johnnie now glanced up at the skies just like their ancient ancestors, fearing the wrath of—

"Why so gloomy, Mrs. Shaux?"

Bert Dryden stood before her, smiling his gaunt smile.

"Oh, Doctor. Sorry. I was miles away."

Perhaps she could somehow get him and Johnnie together, and then she could ask Dryden if Johnnie was going off the rails—or, in fact, whether she was going off the rails herself.

"I understand your husband is with Podium. Let us pray they all get here safely without any more of these horrible losses."

They both glanced towards the harbor, which was visible through gaps torn by bombs in the buildings surrounding the Grandmaster's Palace.

"Let's walk down to St. Barbara Bastion and see if we can see them come in," Eleanor suggested. "They should be due at any moment." She could use the opportunity to invite him to dinner so he could spend time with Johnnie.

"Too bad about *Avery*," he said as they set off.

"What do you mean?"

"Oh, you didn't hear? The news came through about fifteen minutes ago. She was torpedoed while she was under tow, and the destroyer pulling her too. They both went down together. There's a corvette looking for the U-boat."

So just four merchant ships out of Podium's original ten would complete the journey, and there was still a danger that they'd be bombed before they could be unloaded. A sixty percent loss ratio was, tragically, pretty much par for the course.

The little girl with her hungry teddy bear would be eating cold *minestra* soup for a while longer.

"*Avery* had all the kerosene," she said.

"Yes, and the tinned sardines, and the soap," he said. "The number of new bronchitis cases I'm seeing is really alarming. What do you expect when the children aren't getting their vitamins?"

The little girl with the bear would go on coughing, Eleanor thought.

They fell into a discussion of rations and supplies as they walked, and Eleanor was again struck by his comprehensive knowledge of the situation and his understanding of the need to balance resources between military and civilian priorities. If he was in charge of distribution, instead of Gort's bureaucrats, she thought, things would be much smoother.

"Even without *Avery*, we can feed the population until November," he said. "Things may not get better, but they won't get worse. If your boss, Keith Park, can keep the bombers away, we have a chance of surviving."

"Indeed so, Doctor. Not losing is fundamental to winning."

Out of the corner of her eye, she saw him look at her sharply, as if she had surprised him. He opened his mouth to comment but closed it again and walked on in silence.

"Incidentally, my niece speaks very highly of you, Mrs. Shaux," he said, as they reached the bastion overlooking the harbor.

"Oh no. I'm sure it isn't deserved. She's doing a good job and seems to enjoy her transfer to us in Luqa."

"She had a difficult time—both parents and her fiancé—but I promise you she's a capable young woman if you give her a chance."

"I'm sure she is," Eleanor said, looking up the harbor in hope of Podium but seeing only the smoldering carcass of *Grand*. She reflected that walking to the harbor, where the chances of a bombing raid on the convoy were very high, was not, perhaps, the wisest thing that she had ever done.

"Penny's not just a pretty face, I assure you," Dryden said. "She doesn't have your depth of experience, of course, but she has a good degree from the Imperial College London."

It occurred to Eleanor that he was speaking to her as if she were considerably older than Penelope. She never spent much time staring at her reflection in search of wrinkles or other signs of aging, but perhaps she should look more closely in the mirror. It was true that, at twenty-four, she was no longer young, but neither was she old.

She expected the war to drag on for several more years, regardless of which side won; how old would she be when it ended? Her "depth of experience" consisted, in essence, of devising ways of killing the enemy. What kind of experience was that, and what would it qualify her for in peacetime?

Something was moving in the distance by the harbor entrance, by Fort Ricasoli, but it was obscured by the smoke from *Grand*. Perhaps whatever-it-might-be was painted in the navy's wartime dazzle camouflage, but it was hard to tell in the murk.

"That's very impressive. How old is she, Doctor?"

"Twenty-four."

Could that really be the first ship from Podium at long, long last?

"When's her birthday?"

A couple of tugs were coming up the harbor, directly across from her, passing Fort St. Angelo. If Podium's merchantmen were really here, the tugs would be going to shepherd them in.

"March."

"Oh, then she's older than me. Mine's in May. Look there, Doctor, through the smoke. I think they're finally here. Thank God!"

The tugs started tooting, short little excited toots, as if to welcome Podium's survivors.

* * *

Penelope and Miller had fallen into the habit of meeting near the entrance to the Luqa underground HQ, where there were always a few people smoking and taking in the evening air. The senior members of the ground crews and the Ops Room staff would mingle and trade news and gossip. Eleanor had once commented to her that the senior officers might be in charge, but these were the people that made everything work.

Although they had almost nothing else in common, Penelope and Miller found a mutual interest in high-speed motorboats. Miller was supposed to be on an MTB and she, of course, should have been designing high-speed launches. But their common interests in launches and engines were not, she acknowledged, fully sufficient reasons for them to keep turning up.

The soft Mediterranean evenings seemed to exaggerate loneliness. Peter Lingard had not been a perfect lover, or even, to be honest, a particularly adequate lover, but at least he had been a warm body to share her bed, a reason not to feel utterly forsaken by the rest of humanity. The prospect of an endless succession of empty nights stretching out into the distant future was profoundly depressing.

Miller had given her no clues to his emotions, but he, like her, kept turning up.

"Are you married?" Penelope finally blurted out.

"Spoken for, not wed. And you?"

"He's dead."

Jimmy was long dead. Peter hadn't been the same. Jimmy had always been able to make her laugh, even in their most passionate moments. He had made love to her for fun, for the sheer joy of being alive, while Peter took her as if it was his obligation to replace his brother, rather than his desire. He was religious and said something about the Old Testament, but she hadn't paid attention.

Jimmy was an ice-cream sundae on a hot day; Peter was yesterday's leftovers reheated. Leftovers are not a gourmet meal or a special treat;

you eat them because you're hungry and they're quick and easy. When Peter was posted to *Nonsuch*, she was glad he was going and felt guilty as a consequence. Now he was dead and she felt nothing at all.

Miller—she didn't even know his first name—seemed to be neither an ice-cream sundae nor leftovers. He seemed, well, she wasn't sure, but he would be, she was certain, better than Peter.

Miller wasn't sure what to do. He and Maisie were a couple, settled for life, or so he'd always thought. But that was before the war had interrupted everything and brought all assumptions into question.

Suppose Maisie met someone she fancied, perhaps a Yank, and suppose she was feeling that she really needed it and the Yank was there and available, while Miller existed only as a handful of letters and a couple of grainy snapshots. You can't take a snapshot to bed and get what you need, so what then? Suppose the Yank was one of those smooth talkers, with money to burn and perfect teeth and one of those thin mustaches, like you saw at the cinema, like that Clark Gable. Would Maisie refuse Clark Gable because she had an understanding with a snapshot taken on the North Pier in Blackpool years before? She'd always fancied Clark Gable, and she was even friskier than usual after they went to the cinema and saw one of his films.

Would Maisie look a gift horse in the mouth? Maisie needed what she needed. Would Maisie expect him to look a gift horse in the mouth? What's sauce for the goose is sauce for the gander, or so they said.

"Where can we go?" he asked. Either Penelope was a gift horse, or she was not; he might as well find out one way or the other.

"I have a house," she answered without hesitation.

* * *

Eleanor waited on the dock in Kalafrana, just along the southern coast from Hal Far, for the RAF rescue launch bringing Johnnie home. How would he seem? He'd been at sea for several days; she knew he secretly feared the sea but wouldn't admit it. His aversion to all things maritime would have been amplified by sailing through some of the most dangerous waters in the world with ships being torpedoed all around him, or so it must have seemed. In the air he'd been flying Martlets—doubtlessly good aircraft but simply not his beloved Spitfires—against enemy aircraft that heavily outnumbered him. On top of all of that, he'd had to absorb the news of Diggers's death. She wondered if Park had been correct in giving him the news so baldly rather than somehow softening the blow, though she knew that this blow could not possibly be softened.

While he was enduring all this, she, on the other hand, had simply shuffled paperwork in the safety of the Luqa bomb shelters. Her worst danger had been the risk of getting grime in her hair.

What would she think when she caught sight of him? Would she think, "Thank God he's back" or would she think, "Who is this stranger?" She had lived without him for a week, with just Charlie for company. It had seemed a bit empty at first, but she'd come to enjoy the self-indulgence of doing everything just for herself.

Things needed to change. She loved Park, but her job was simply not enough. Her brain was atrophying. There were times earlier in the war when she'd worked late into the night—sometimes all night—driven by the intellectual challenges she faced, exhilarated by the consequences of her decisions and recommendations. Now all she had to look forward to each day were the minutiae of paperwork and the stultifying idiosyncrasies of RAF bureaucracy. Then she had been fighting Hitler; now she was fighting Air Ministry pen-pushers and poohbahs. It was as if she had been playing in the Cup Final at Wembley Stadium and now she had been relegated to the Third Division North.[5]

She had sensed that Harry Hopkins wanted to ask her to return to her former role but didn't want to put Park in an awkward spot by suggesting it. Here, her horizons were the shores of the Mediterranean. If she went back, she would have no horizons, no limits to the challenges she would face.

Malta was facing an existential threat, it was true, and this was a battle just as important as the Battle of Britain. The fate of Africa and southern Europe was hanging in the balance, with immeasurable consequences for the outcome of the war and the future of the world. She could help oil the cogs and grease the bearings of Malta's defenses,

---

5. A lower-level league that ended in 1958.

but she could make no significant contribution to the fight; it was up to Park and Johnnie to win or lose.

She'd lost her innocence. She remembered—it seemed as if it was a thousand years ago—her intellectual excitement when she had first started to work on zero-sum game theory. She remembered the unadulterated joy of completing the final line of her proof for her first mathematical model. "But, as has been shown, theta is *not* the inverse of epsilon." She had written that with the Waterman fountain pen her uncle Eddie had given her as a graduation present, using green ink, an affectation she had picked up from George Rand. She had been giddy with delight and shocked that she had produced something of such magnitude. Professor Harry Pound, England's leading mathematician, had called her work seminal. She had been twenty-two and a glorious future awaited her.

In a similar fever, she had battered down the gates of Johnnie's heretofore impenetrable stoicism and compelled him to believe he could be happy. Turtles copulate in spite of their thick shells, she had reasoned, and she had been right.

Since then, two years of exposure to the endless barbarity of violence in the sky had been draining his humanity, slowly but surely. He was exactly the same on the outside, seemingly untouched, but who knew what was left on the inside, if anything?

He was turning into stone, and she was going crazy. Perhaps they were not husband and wife, companions for life, even though they were married; perhaps they were just lovers distracting themselves, he from his petrification and she from her mania.

Charlie started barking, seeing Johnnie on the RAF rescue launch long before she did; Johnnie had always had the trick of being inconspicuous, lost in a crowd. Ah, there he was, waiting on the little after-deck as the launch fussed and wriggled its way into the dock, its engines emitting irritated spluttering sounds and pungent exhaust fumes. He saw her and waved. The launch bumped against the jetty, and he scrambled ashore. Someone threw him his kit bag, and he waved a thank-you to the captain. He was smiling but obviously exhausted, lines of strain spreading out from the corners of his eyes like spiderwebs. He looked as if he hadn't slept in a week, and perhaps he hadn't.

And how did she look to him? Did he see her as Dr. Dryden did—not yet old, exactly, but with lots of depths of experience?

Charlie bounded to greet him, lifting up on his hind legs with his paws on Johnnie's chest, almost knocking him over. Either Charlie was bigger than she always assumed, or Johnnie was shorter. She thought she should embrace Johnnie, but neither of them believed in public displays of affection, and the launch crew and half the Kalafrana waterfront was watching. She smiled apologetically, telegraphing that they would greet each other properly later on, and he smiled his understanding. Between the three of us, she thought, only Charlie is brave enough to be honest.

A flight of Spitfires howled overhead at low altitude, one of many guarding what was left of Podium.

Ah yes, she thought, my lover has returned.

TWENTY-FOUR

Eleanor sat at dinner with Park and Johnnie in Park's private quarters overlooking the harbor. Park had also invited Freddie, perhaps to avoid them all staring at the empty chair upon which Digby would have sat. The room was lit dimly by candles so that they could leave the windows unshaded. Somewhere out there in the dusk, men and machines were unloading Podium's survivors as fast as they could, and, invisible in the skies above, sentinel Beaufighter night fighters were searching for intruders. Radar crews were scanning their cathode ray tubes in AMES RDF stations from Qawra Point to Giordan, searching for the elusive blips that would herald the arrival of the Regia Aeronautica. More Beaufighter crews were sitting in their cockpits, waiting for the signal to go.

Eleanor wished the evening was already over. The pall of Digby's death hung over them, and Johnnie was obviously exhausted. In one sense it was kind of Park, she thought, to entertain them here rather than make them face the officers' mess. The pilots there would be deliberately loud and boisterous, as was RAF custom, determined to drown the reality of Digby's death in a sea of beer. Here, at least, they didn't have to pretend to be happy.

An orderly entered and handed Park a note.

"Well, that's unusual," Park said. "Here's a message from the captain of *Nonsuch* to HMS St. Angelo, with a copy to me. It's about you, Shaux."

Unusual was not the right word, Shaux thought, brushing away the cobwebs in his brain. He knew Lancaster didn't like him—that frosty exchange on *Nonsuch*'s bridge about what Lancaster had described as his "fly-by" was the last they'd spoken, but he didn't think he deserved a formal complaint to the navy's higher powers. *Unwarranted* was a fairer word than *unusual*. Under normal circumstances, he wouldn't have cared what Lancaster thought of him, one way or the other, but Shaux felt he had been something of Park's ambassador, as it were, and it was very important not to have let Park down.

"Well, sir, I don't want to sound defensive, but I had no choice."

Park looked at him quizzically, but Shaux plowed on.

"I know Captain Lancaster and I didn't see eye to eye, to put it mildly, but I was trying to make sure they were receiving my messages and understanding them."

"Well—" Park began.

"Time was of the essence, sir. I—"

"So it would seem," Park said. "Let me interrupt you and read the message: 'This officer moved decisively when time was of the essence. His prompt and spirited action prevented *Nonsuch* from being torpedoed and probably sunk. Additional exemplary contributions to air defenses throughout the operation. Citation to follow.' It appears he's recommended you for a medal."

"Congratulations, old chap," Freddie said.

"Oh, surely not, sir," Shaux said.

Eleanor groaned inwardly. "Oh, surely not" was Johnnie's equivalent to stamping his foot like a petulant child yelling, "I don't want a bloody medal" and running round the room, shrieking. He hated having to wear his medal ribbons because he hated the attention they drew. He seemed more or less his usual self, playing down Diggers's death with empty platitudes she knew he didn't mean. He had focused on the cause of Diggers's death, his theory about aeroelasticity rather than the effect of Diggers's death itself. He'd devoted his energies to calculating the effect of Diggers's idea of keeping the outermost tanks dry. It was a typical Johnnie stratagem to avoid facing a truth.

He was like a sleeping volcano, quiescent for long periods of time but with pressures building inexorably deep inside himself, and she was more convinced than ever that he was having nightmares—he'd taken a nap this afternoon but tossed and turned with his fists tightly clenched.

She shook her head impatiently. This afternoon she had thought he was turning into stone; now she thought he was a volcano. Why could she not understand him? Why could she only search through metaphors that were always inadequate? She imagined herself introducing him to friends at a sherry party: "Oh, I don't think you've met my metaphor, Johnnie."

"Yes, indeed," Park said, breaking into her thoughts. "Incidentally, on that note, I'm recommending Digby for a DSO. It will have to be posthum—"

He stopped abruptly, evidently unable to complete the word *posthumously*, and Eleanor felt the sudden stab of imminent tears and tried—almost successfully—to blink them away.

"Oh, I meant to show you this newspaper, sir," Freddie said to Park. Eleanor guessed he was jumping in to cover the moment. "It reports that chap Otto Borman was shot down, the Luftwaffe chap with over a hundred victories to his name. The Germans announced it."

"Borman? Luftwaffe pilot?" Park said. "I seem to remember that name from 1940. He was a 109 pilot who started out in Galland's JD 26 wing and then went on to become a star in his own right, if memory serves. What does it say, Freddie?"

"Well, I'm quoting the *Telegraph* quoting the German *Völkischer Beobachter*, so it's a bit thirdhand, sir. But anyway: 'Oberstleutnant Otto Borman gave his life for the Reich in the Mediterranean Theater. Borman, the son of the Deputy Reich Minister for the Luftwaffe, sunk two Royal Navy warships and was awarded the addition of swords to his Iron Cross with oak leaves.'"

"Good Lord," Park said. "I thought all their top chaps were in Russia. Kesselring must really be putting an emphasis on Malta. Perhaps he's getting desperate, if he's transferring his best chaps from Russia."

Shaux looked at Eleanor and saw her looking back at him. Her face was expressionless, but her eyes were full of pain. She was the only person he had ever told about Otto, the Luftwaffe pilot who had saved his life.

"So it would seem, sir," Freddie said. "Where was I? Ah, yes: 'Borman was serving on temporary secondment to the Regia Aeronautica. He was held in high regard and affection by his Italian allies and colleagues, who nicknamed him The Shark because of his great fighting skills and painted his Ju 87 Stuka aircraft to match.'"

Time stopped. The stars and the sun and the moon stopped. Everything stopped.

This, Shaux thought, was far, far worse than even Diggers's death—indescribably worse. This, now, was the worst moment of his life, and time has stopped and so this moment will never end.

When Shaux had been a POW in France, Otto had saved him from German military intelligence, the Abwehr. He owed his life to Otto: it was that simple. Otto had befriended him and, at incredible personal risk, helped him escape. Now Shaux had killed him—and not just killed him but killed him with a sneer, thinking him to be an arrogant show-off. Shaux had shot down *il pescecane*, the man who had befriended him in his hour of need.

Eleanor, he thought, didn't know the half of it. She was sympathizing with him for losing his friend Otto, the man who had saved his life. She didn't know that he was the one who had killed Otto.

What was the worst crime ever? Was it Cain killing his brother Abel? This was at least as bad—no, it was worse.

It was as if Shaux was that certain man who fell among thieves on the road to Jericho, as the bible told it, and had been left half dead, and Otto, the Good Samaritan, had found him and bound up his wounds and cared for him and taken him to an inn to rest and recover. And when the Good Samaritan returned to settle the innkeeper's bill, the certain man, now fully recovered, shot and killed the Good Samaritan with a three-second burst of 50-caliber machine-gun fire at close range, firing over a hundred semi-armor-piercing rounds that ripped the Good Samaritan to shreds, sneering as he did so.

The silent crowd in his recurring dream would now include a familiar face. Would Otto also stay silent or greet him in his usual boisterous manner: "Ha, the famous Johnnie Shaux! You got me good.

I must admit it!" If so, should Shaux reply, in their old, bantering manner: "Piece of cake, old chap!" Or should he not? In either case, whether he replied or not, would the old man on the hill take up his quill and make a silent note of it?

Otto had taught him the German words for "piece of cake."

"Stück Kuchen," he murmured.

"What? What did you say, Shaux?" Park asked.

"Oh, nothing, sir. Just thinking aloud."

PART THREE

Pickpocket

TWENTY-FIVE

Eleanor stared at her reflection intently. She had come to the mirror to inspect herself during the nighttime rituals of cleaning her teeth and washing her face and could see no noticeable lines on her face, nor did she appear to have a single gray hair. Dr. Dryden had thought she was older than his niece, but it must be because of something other than her physical features, surely?

It was, of course, a face she knew in intimate detail, but sometimes, as now, she seemed to see a stranger staring back. Tonight there was something in her reflection's eyes, something appraising. The Eleanor in the mirror was assessing the Eleanor looking into the mirror, and the assessment did not seem to be going well.

She had her father's features, which probably explained why her mother disliked her so profoundly. She had spent the first twenty years of her life seeking her mother's approval while rejecting her mother's values, opinions, and wishes. Her swiftness of thought, so widely admired by her teachers and fellow students, meant, in her mother's eyes, that she was "Little Miss Know-It-All." Her three sisters had been married at eighteen, pregnant at nineteen, and mothers at twenty. Eleanor, by contrast, had taken herself off to Oxford but failed to find a husband by the time she graduated, thus completely wasting three very important years. On the day she graduated with First Class Honors and invitations from Princeton in America and Cambridge University to study for a PhD, her mother had told her that, at the advanced age of twenty-one, she'd have to lower her sights and grab whomever she could from the rapidly shrinking pool of eligible bachelors.

There was a fleeting moment when Rawley, an heir to a peerage, reached down from the Olympian heights—or so it seemed to her mother's ecstatic delight—and in an act of droit du seigneur, deigned to take her as his mistress. Eventually she had rejected him, and her mother, incandescent with fury, had barely spoken to her since.

That was two years ago, although it seemed like two hundred.

Then everything had changed. The Battle of Britain exploded over southern England. Perhaps it was catharsis, perhaps it was an epiphany—it didn't really matter—she had suddenly seen, in her mind's eye, a completely new version of von Neumann's zero-sum game theory, a new way of analyzing the war, a mathematical model made up of interlocking derivatives that accurately assessed the present balance of the battle and predicted its most probable future direction. She had written it all down in a sort of intellectual frenzy.

Park had seized upon her model as a valuable input to his tactical planning. In the space of three short weeks, she had metamorphosed from a drone-like role deep in the bowels of Air Ministry bureaucracy into a crucial role at Park's side at 11 Group Headquarters. Her success was admired in the highest quarters; even Churchill acknowledged her achievement and elevated her to lofty heights in Whitehall.

The appraising eyes seemed to be saying, "Were you really that good, or just lucky?" She had no immediate response, but, looking back, *lucky* seemed quite likely.

And in those same few weeks she had found Johnnie, an old friend from Oxford, now a Spitfire pilot in the midst of the battle, the antithesis of Rawley. Even now, even after living with Johnnie for two years, she found him more tightly sealed, more difficult to break into, than the vaults beneath the Bank of England.

The war was an excuse for making no plans, no commitments. As long as the war lasted, she could be a cog in the machine, with very little responsibility for her own destiny, carried along by forces far greater than she, or anyone, could control. She was a mere ant, a drone, toiling in a greater cause, like an Egyptian slave heaving stones up a pyramid, one in countless thousands of other slaves.

The day peace was declared, all that would change. Her success or failure, her happiness or misery, would suddenly sit squarely on her own shoulders.

She pondered a deeply disturbing thought: Did she *not* want the war to end? When peace came, the sun would come out and she should blossom. But supposing she couldn't blossom? Suppose she needed the stresses and anxieties of war to function, and the lack of personal responsibility to justify an existence in which nothing was her fault. Suppose, once the pressure was off, she'd just eat ice-cream sundaes and lemon curd and become enormous.

Suppose Johnnie couldn't blossom either. Suppose Johnnie was capable only of stoicism, regardless of time and place. Was she destined to live with a clam for fifty years? If they knew he would live until tomorrow night, and the night after that, would they still make love tonight? Why tonight if tomorrow night was just as convenient? Would he still make love to her if she was enormous?

As often as she wanted to crack open Johnnie's shell, she feared doing so. Suppose the act of cracking his shell, of revealing the hidden Johnnie, would kill him, like the act of opening Schrödinger's cat's box? Or suppose the shell was all there was, and he was hollow inside? Could she make love to a hollow man?

In the grand scheme of things, she was fiddling around, marking time in Malta, in a job that required persistence but not the kind of creativity that had conceived Red Tape. Johnnie, too, was fiddling around in his own way. He was nominally commanding a fighter wing, but that was almost a sinecure; instead he kept inventing excuses to fly as often as possible, as if he needed to fly as often as possible . . . Perhaps they were both past their peaks, slipping slowly downhill into mediocrity.

Her image in the mirror shook its head to clear it, and Eleanor did the same.

She made herself stop.

"Go away!" she said to her image in the mirror. "Leave me alone."

"What?" Johnnie asked, appearing round the bathroom door.

"Not you—I was just thinking about something out loud."

"Are you sure?"

She pulled off her nightdress and tossed it aside. "Definitely."

* * *

"One of Podium's freighters had a couple of Whalebacks on board as deck cargo," Park said, looking up from one of the many reports and memoranda that littered his desk. "That's a very welcome surprise. I asked for them some time ago, but I didn't know they were coming."

"I'm afraid I have never heard of a Whaleback, sir," Eleanor said. "What kind of aircraft is that?"

"Oh no. It's not an aircraft; it's a rescue launch. It's a high-speed launch, an HSL, made by the British Power Boat Company."

"Oh, I see. Then I must have seen one when they brought Johnnie back from Podium."

"Those rescue chaps are first class," Park said. "Their motto is 'The sea shall not have them,' and they've saved dozens of crews—on both sides."

But not Diggers, Eleanor thought, although that was certainly not the air-sea rescue crews' fault.

"Now we'll be able to reinforce our chaps at St. Paul's Bay and Kalafrana," Park said. "Well, I should say, to be accurate, we'll be able to reinforce them if we can find crews for them. We'll have to ask St. Angelo if they can spare anyone."

"I'll ask Penelope Dryden to do it. I'm sure she'll know the right people to ask."

* * *

"Yes, ma'am," Penelope said. "As a matter of fact, there are some small-boat crews that were supposed to man MTBs, ma'am, Fairmile Dog Boats, but their boats were lost in one of the earlier convoys, so they were mustered out to the flak barges. They're quartered in *Silkworm*, or were. They came in to Malta recently. They're fully trained for small-boat operations, so they'd be very suitable."

"Excellent!" Eleanor said. "Who do we ask in HMS St. Angelo? I hope it's not Commander Thompson."

"No, ma'am, I'm glad to say. We should ask the dockyard super-intendent's duty office. I know those people, so I could ask them if—"

"Please do so. You can say it's a request from the AOC."

"Yes, ma'am."

"There's also the matter of getting the launches fitted out, if that's the right expression, and ready for sea. We'll have to ask for their help on that as well."

Penelope felt her heart rise to her throat. Dare she? Why not?

"Oh, the Malta Boat Company yard would be perfect for that, ma'am."

"Do you know anyone there?"

She'll throw me out for some horrible breach of regulations for pursuing my own interests, some sort of self-promotion, Penelope thought, or she wouldn't. In any case, it was already too late to turn back.

"It was my father's yard until he was killed last year, ma'am, and I suppose it's mine now, although it's requisitioned and run by the navy until the war finishes."

"Really? You own a boat-building company?"

Eleanor seemed interested rather than angry.

"Well, I suppose so, legally, but not until the war's over, ma'am. I have nothing to do with it now. They use it for cargo lighters and the flak platforms and barges and things like that, but the shipwrights who work in the yard are small-boat and launch craftsmen."

"Excellent! I'm putting you in charge. Ask the navy to let us share the yard to get the launches ready. Let me know how you're getting on and if you need anything."

"Well, there is one thing, ma'am. Petty Officer Miller, ma'am, who's working here on loan with the ground crews, was the senior rating for the MTBs. He could be put back in charge of the crews."

"Good idea. He's yours."

Penelope looked at Eleanor, wondering if that was a not-so-subtle double entendre, and if rumors were flying about Miller and her, but Eleanor didn't seem to mean it that way. She was already speaking on the telephone on some other matter.

My goodness, Penelope thought, drawing a deep breath, that all happened really quickly!

Well, Eleanor thought, as Penelope left her office, her uncle made a point of saying she was more than just a pretty face; now we'll find out.

* * *

"Now we've got some fuel, thanks to the chaps in Podium. I want to make a maximum effort to cut off Rommel's supply lines," Park said. "What's your analysis, Eleanor?"

"Well, sir, I think Rommel will want to move quickly," Eleanor said. "It's not in his nature to sit and wait for things to happen; he likes to dictate his own terms of engagement."

She recalled an early profile of Rommel they'd developed for Red Tape when he was first posted to North Africa. She wondered if she should light a cigarette but resisted the temptation.

"He'll move the moment he gets supplies. He's very short of fuel, he's short of ammunition, and he's short of tanks. Montgomery, on the other hand, will hold the Eighth Army back, building up his reserves until he's got a decisive advantage. Now that the Americans are in the game, Montgomery's starting to get Sherman tanks, and he's gradually getting more aircraft for the Desert Air Force."

She remembered she hadn't liked Montgomery, now the new commanding general of the Eighth Army, when she met him; he reminded her a little of a snake waiting to strike. Damn! She had hated her former job running Red Tape. Yet it felt completely natural to be analyzing strategic options like this. She felt . . . at home in a place where she didn't want to be. She had to acknowledge she was very good at doing something she didn't want to do. She drew on her cigarette and realized she was smoking after all.

"It's a race, sir. If Rommel can get enough fuel and supplies, he'll move before Montgomery can overwhelm him, perhaps with a lightning raid through Montgomery's forward lines, perhaps a flanking movement around El Alamein. He raced around the French army in 1940 to reach the English Channel, and perhaps he'll try something similar in Egypt."

"El Alamein?"

"It's the Eighth Army's forward position, sir, about sixty miles west of Alexandria. It's just a railway halt, nothing else, but it's vital from a supply point of view. If Rommel can get two weeks' supply of fuel for his tanks, say, he can be in Alex in a week and Cairo in two."

"Can Montgomery hold him?"

"Rommel's style is all movement, speed, and surprise. Montgomery has never fought a major battle, and Rommel's fought, and won, several. Montgomery might win, but I would suggest his best chance is to wait until he has overwhelming numbers and hope Rommel can't get the fuel he needs to attack. Rommel's tactics are brilliant, but they use a lot of fuel."

"How long will it take them to resupply Rommel, do you think?"

"A month, sir, perhaps six weeks. It all depends on whether we can stop the convoys from Italy and Greece bringing his fuel supplies. But he won't wait forever; he'll try to break through to reach the Suez Canal. He has no choice. But if we can deny him his fuel, he can't win."

"Then that's our objective," Park said. "Our objective is to sink every single ship trying to reach Rommel. We have enough Spitfire Vs in Malta now, with enough fuel, to protect our airfields and the harbor. That means we can fly our Beauforts, and the navy's Tenth Submarine Flotilla at Bishop's Island, HMS Talbot, can sail their subs."

"Yes, sir," Eleanor said. "And, given Podium's arrival, they can suspend their Magic Carpet runs and focus everything on Rommel's convoys."

"We're going on the offensive," Park said. "We're going all out! We want Rommel to get nothing. Nothing! I want to pick his pockets and leave him nothing! In fact, that would be a good name for this operation: nothing!"

"With due respect, sir, you can't ask men to fight for nothing," Shaux said, speaking for the first time. He had sat back and watched Eleanor. She was really, really good at this stuff, and it obviously excited her, even though she claimed to hate it. At some point she would go back to it; she just wouldn't be able to stay away. She'd spread her wings and fly away, and there'd be nothing that Park or he could do about it—nor should they.

"Well, that's true, Shaux," Park said. "Let's see: 'No passageway'? 'They shall not pass'?"

"You said you wanted to pick his pockets, sir. How about Operation Pickpocket?"

"Excellent."

* * *

The superintendent's duty officer stared at Penelope's chest. Some things never change, she thought.

"Very well," she said. "These are the ratings' names; there are twenty in all."

She had found the original orders transferring the MTB crews to ack-ack duties and went over the list with Miller, who'd selected the men he thought were best. An HSL had a crew of seven, plus a medical orderly and a captain. She thought it wise to take a few extra men just to be on the safe side.

"I'll look into it," the DO said, his eyes still glued to her chest.

"Here's the transfer order. You just need to sign at the bottom."

"I'll look into it."

Could that be some horrid double entendre?

She wondered if it was best to use an enticement or a threat to get his signature. She decided to try a threat first, before demeaning herself with an enticement.

"Look, if you have any concerns, I'm sure you're right," she said. "Let's just go up to Thompson's office, and you can explain to him why you haven't signed the order."

Commander Thompson knew nothing of any of this, but she had discovered in the past that junior officers would do almost anything to avoid direct contact with Thompson. She handed a pen to the DO, who removed his eyes from her chest just long enough to find the signature line on the form.

"Thank you. Here's your carbon copy."

"There's a dance tonight at the—" the DO began, before realizing he was speaking to her back as she departed.

TWENTY-SIX

"Oh my! Oh, my giddy aunt!" Miller exclaimed. "Now, that is a thing of beauty!"

To Penelope it was just a large, complicated, ugly piece of machinery, but Miller touched the engine almost as if he was caressing it, almost as he caressed her.

"I've never seen anything like it! Three banks of four cylinders; double overhead cams, I'll be bound. I think it's called a 'broad arrow' design. My giddy aunt!"

"No. It's called a Napier Sea Lion," Penelope said. "Each launch has three, and there are two spares in packing cases."

"My giddy aunt!"

"It's only an engine, Miller."

"There's no such thing as 'only an engine,' ma'am."

It struck her as comforting that she still called him 'Miller,' and he still called her 'ma'am,' even in their most intimate moments. It implied a certain distance between them, a welcome distinction between a strictly physical relationship without any other consequences and a far more complicated emotional relationship. It was, however, somewhat belittling to see him almost aroused by a mere hunk of metal. She wondered which he would choose to get his hands on, her or the engine, if he could only have one; the answer was far from obvious.

* * *

Shaux flew a reconnaissance patrol searching for supply ships, a long, lazy route along the coast of Libya between Tripoli and Benghazi and back, zigzagging as if he were a sailing ship tacking into the wind. As always, the challenge in flying a Spitfire was staying alert: not letting the steady roar of the Merlin make your eyelids heavier, not letting the endless uniformity of the wrinkled sea below and the hazy sky above convince you there was nothing to see, not letting boredom or complacency dull your senses.

It was all Eleanor's idea. The very, very secret Ultra program, the interception and decryption of what the Germans thought were their unbreakable codes, had to be kept super-secret. Ultra intercepts produced invaluable information about the supply ships attempting to reach Rommel, but the RAF and the navy couldn't just appear at the right time at the right spot every time without the Germans realizing their codes had been broken. Therefore Eleanor had devised an elaborate system of patrols, whether there were supply ships or not, to create the impression that the supply ships were being "discovered" by the reconnaissance patrols.

In this particular case, there was no Ultra intelligence to indicate that there might be a convoy in this area, but Ultra didn't catch every single convoy. He resettled himself in his seat. Yellow Two, his wing man, was a hundred yards behind him and a little to his left, just as he was supposed to be. This, once again, was a duty for which Diggers was eminently better qualified. He forced himself to search the sky around them diligently. There were no aircraft in the Mediterranean that could match a Spitfire Mark IX, but there were plenty of aircraft that could jump a pilot who wasn't paying attention, no matter how good his aircraft was.

Benghazi would be in sight in ten minutes . . . He thought of himself, as he often did, as simply part of the Spitfire. The Merlin had servomechanisms to control the fuel supply, the oil pressure, and a dozen other functions. The dynamic flexing of the Spitfire's control surfaces allowed the aircraft to swim smoothly through the turbulences and vortexes in the air flowing around them; he, the eyes of the aircraft, was simply another mechanism among many.

He remembered the first time he had flown; he had been giddy with pleasure. One minute they were on the ground and the next they were airborne, climbing above the trees and the college buildings at Cranwell. The officer cadets, far below, looked like blue ants. The instructor rolled the aircraft and suddenly the world was upside down and only his straps were preventing him from falling out. His stomach was in his throat—it seemed literally so—but he trusted the aircraft and in due course the world righted itself.

He was not an instinctive pilot. He studied the physics of flight, envisioning the aircraft as a machine, and the pilot as part of the machine. Everything in the aircraft could be, in Shaux's mind, expressed as a mathematical equation, such as the amount of power generated by the engine to keep the aircraft in level flight—thrust in relation to the drag of air resistance, lift generated by the wings versus gravity, and so on.

He envisioned the pilot's movements on the controls as mechanical and the pilot as part of the mechanism. Natural pilots, like natural drivers, just commanded their aircraft, it seemed to Shaux, and the aircraft obeyed. Shaux, on the other hand, had to make conscious adjustments to the control surfaces or the engine knobs and levers in order to achieve the desired mechanical effect.

As a result he flew in an erratic fashion caused by a series of discrete actions, much to the displeasure of his instructor.

"Herky-jerky will no workie!" his instructor had said, moving in stiff, abrupt movements like an animated automaton. He developed a parody of Shaux drinking a glass of beer in the same jerky manner as Shaux flew. The climax had come, much to the amusement of the officers' mess, when he raised his glass in staccato starts and stops and then jerked it back towards his mouth and splashed beer all over his face.

Over time Shaux's movements smoothed out and became unconscious, as all professional pilots' do—a servomechanism among all the other servomechanisms and feedback loops within the aircraft.

In due course his instructor had passed him as fully qualified to fly, and he was awarded the coveted pilot's wings badge to wear on his uniform. Pretty girls could see the badge and give him appraising glances on the Underground, but Shaux always remembered the instructor's single-word assessment of his flying when he signed the official certificate: "Mediocre."

Yet, in spite of all of that, there was something far, far beyond physics and mechanics. There was something visceral, primitive, that set his hair on end and sent quivers down his spine. His Gipsy Moth had lifted him from the two-dimensional earth into the three-dimensional sky, a sky in which he could soar as an eagle—even mediocre eagles can soar—and plunge like a stone, and swoop and slide, pitch and yaw, roll and glide, as if his prosaic, tired, and rattling old beaten-up Gipsy Moth trainer was a chariot of fire, as the bible said, and had lifted him up into heaven by a whirlwind.

Benghazi appeared on the horizon, and Shaux swung round on the reciprocal course.

* * *

"It's a bit on the tight side," Miller said, staring down through the engine room hatch. It seemed amazing that three Napier engines could fit into so small a place. It must be extremely noisy at full power. There was just enough room for an engine room rating to squeeze between the engines, and it looked almost impossible to do any serious repair work on them while they were at sea. Still, noise and tight spaces were par for the course on boats, and who cared anyway? Those engines delivered 500 horsepower each, and that much power allowed the Whaleback to maintain a steady thirty knots when needed. Now, where were the batteries?

He'd leave the rest of the launch, particularly the wheelhouse, until last, after he felt confident he could manage all the machinery. He'd never commanded anything except for that pathetic ack-ack barge for half a day, and he was bit apprehensive, to tell the truth. He knew nothing of radios, but radios were machines and therefore comprehensible. Charts and navigation were a bit beyond his experience; he'd have to find some reference books and someone sympathetic to explain them. He did not doubt he could command an HSL—he just wasn't sure if he could command it well.

The HSL was rocking gently against the jetty at Penelope's father's boatyard in French Creek; its sister HSL was moored just aft. The mighty fortifications of the Città Invicta—the Invincible City—rose behind the yard. Malta had survived the Great Siege of 1565 thanks to those ramparts and battlements, when the Knights Hospitaller fought off the invading Ottomans, but it was still very uncertain whether Malta would survive this modern siege.

The yard had been bombed again since she'd last been here, she saw. When the war was over—if the war was ever over—she'd be pretty much starting again from scratch. It was probably beyond her. Eleanor, on the other hand, would doubtless have the yard up and running as a thriving business in no time, but Penelope wasn't Eleanor. She knew she wasn't a natural leader—contact with the AOC as well as Eleanor had made that blindingly obvious; perhaps she was just one of nature's followers, like almost everyone else.

She shook all that off and turned her attention to the HSL. She cast an approving professional eye along the launch's lines. It was very clean and uncluttered, built for speed, with all the crew positions inside the Whaleback cabin to protect them from the elements. It would be interesting to put the HSL in slings and haul it out of the water to study the design of the hull, particularly the exact contours of the hard chine keel at the point of plane.

The only jarring notes were the gun platforms. There was a machine-gun position on each side of the tiny cockpit and another inside a little glassed-in turret on top of the cabin. They all seemed to have been added as an afterthought.

"Look at all these guns," Penelope said. "You'll be well protected."

"That's just daft," Miller said. "Peashooters—bloody useless. We'll get rid of all those and get a couple of 20-millimeter Oerlikons."

She had learned not to disagree with him on such matters. He seldom gave his opinion, but when he did it was always on a subject well within his breadth of knowledge. On everything else he deferred to her; it was one of his appealing characteristics. Perhaps she couldn't resurrect the yard on her own, but she and Miller had complementary skills, and between them they might make a good team, although he wasn't in her class, of course . . . Still, she'd asked Eleanor to arrange the paperwork to get his temporary rank of petty officer made permanent, just to be certain that he'd be senior enough in the eyes of the powers that be to captain one of the launches. It was his birthday next week, and she planned to surprise him.

* * *

Charlie picked his way cautiously over the mounds of rubble that con-
stituted all that remained of the hospital annex. His head was down,
and his ears were erect. When he paused Eleanor could see that he was
quivering, concentrating his entire being into his senses of hearing and
smell. He could keep this up for an hour or more. When he came off
duty, he'd be utterly exhausted, panting as if he'd run five miles. She
wished he could wear slippers or some sort of protection for his paws.
The rubble was full of sharp shards of broken glass and wooden splin-
ters like daggers, and he sometimes came home limping. Once he'd
been badly scorched when he stepped on a smoldering beam.

Charlie had saved lives, but, alas, too many of the people he'd
found were already dead.

His Royal Engineer handler, Sapper Jones, clambered across the
debris after him. Jones struck Eleanor as totally unsuited to the hor-
rors of war. He had been a chorister at Kings College, Cambridge, and
he was destined to become a minister in the Church of England. It
seemed to Eleanor that he was made of the finest, thinnest, most delicate porcelain and would faint away at the slightest sight of blood.

But, like Charlie, he was devoted to the service of mankind. When,
a couple of days ago, Charlie had found two children in the ruins of
what had been their house—a little boy about five years old and a little
girl a year or two younger, buried but still alive—Jones had dug down
through the smoking rubble with his bare hands until he reached them
and pulled them out and then dug down more until he found the boy's
other leg.

Eleanor had watched in helpless horror as the children were borne
away on a stretcher.

"How is this possible?" she asked Jones.

He was kneeling on one knee, catching his breath. He was filthy.
His hands were torn and bleeding, and he was panting from exhaus-
tion. Yet his face, when he looked up at her, was calm.

"God moves in a mysterious way, ma'am," he said, shaking his head.

Oh no, she thought. That's not a good enough answer. God had no
right to hide behind a veil of incomprehension.

"Too damned mysterious, Jones, if you ask me. Too mysterious by half!"

She had walked away before he could reply, and Charlie had limped after her.

Now Charlie and Sapper Jones were at it again, searching another pile of rubble for more survivors, another example of God's little mysteries.

TWENTY-SEVEN

Shaux yawned and resettled himself in a deck chair outside the dispersal hut, content to waste the morning while the paperwork mounted inexorably on his desk. Marine patrols were always tiring, but marine patrols when absolutely nothing happened, like yesterday's, seemed completely exhausting; perhaps it was just the frustration of all that wasted time and effort. But no patrol could ever be as exhausting as a pile of RAF bumph.[6]

A Beaufort and a Beaufighter thundered down the runway and rose ponderously into the air, turning southeast. They were now the stars of Malta's air resources. Under Operation Pickpocket, everything was focused on finding and destroying Rommel's supply ships. That was a job for which the Beaufort torpedo bombers were well suited, with their close cousins, the Beaufighters, at their shoulders to protect them.

Having sunk almost no enemy supply ships in the months before Podium, Malta was now on the offensive; the simultaneous arrival of Park, dozens of Spitfires, and plenty of aviation fuel had completely changed the balance of the battle. Park was a man who knew how to win, who had the clarity of mind to cut through the "fog of war," as Clausewitz had put it, and Spitfires were winners in a way that no other aircraft in Europe were.

---

6. A slang term for official forms.

Was Park a great air commander, Shaux wondered, or just lucky to have arrived in Malta as Spitfires and fuel became available? Who cared—let the historians fight that out in future years, he thought. In the meantime, he'd take being lucky over being good any day of the week.

The move from defensive to offensive operations was a similar story for the navy's submarines; having been almost immobilized, hiding from Axis bombers, they were now out in force. Many of Rommel's convoys were attacked both by Beaus and subs; Shaux had heard of a couple of occasions when the Beaus slowed down an enemy supply ship and a sub finished it off. Just the other day, a Beau from 39 Squadron had torpedoed the big Italian cruiser *Trento* and a U-class submarine, Shaux thought its name might have been *Umbra*, had sunk her.

Rommel's supply convoys were heavily defended and the Beaus were taking heavy losses. He recalled Diggers saying that it took nerve to fly a Spit into enemy fire, but it took true bravery to fly a bomber into heavy ack-ack. He lifted his arm in salute as the Beaus turned southward; bomber "bus drivers" were the true heroes, not Spit pilots like him.

Speaking of heroes, he thought, the chaps in the subs were in a class of their own. He'd been to the Tenth Submarine Flotilla depot at HMS Talbot, over at Fort Manoel, and had been invited into one of their U-class submarines. An air raid warning had sounded as he was being given a guided tour by the captain, and the submarine had promptly submerged. He'd spent the day sitting on the harbor bed, wondering if he would ever see the sun again and desperately trying not to stare at the hull walls in search of leaks, while the crew worked nonchalantly around him. The chief petty officer coxswain, a grizzled veteran with the ribbon of the Conspicuous Gallantry Medal on his chest, told Shaux he was terrified of heights and suffered badly from airsickness.

"I could never do what you do, sir," the coxswain had said. "I simply don't have the balls."

Shaux had sat at their tiny wardroom table, squeezed between the captain and the first lieutenant, learning all he could about submarine tactics. Submarines, he'd discovered, were usually slower than the convoys they attacked, sometimes much slower, so they had to position themselves ahead and wait for the convoys to come to them.

"Actually we're not really submarines in a true sense," the captain had explained. "We're submersibles; we spend most of our time on the surface, diving only when we have to."

Ultra's code intercepts had given the navy a huge advantage: if the submarines knew where Rommel's convoys were going, they had time to get ahead of them, rather than chasing round the Mediterranean, hoping to get lucky.

When Shaux was aboard *Nonsuch*, he'd thought of the U-boats as implacable killers, wolves of the seas. Now, sitting in thirty feet of water off HMS Talbot, he felt he was in a frail little tube skulking in the shadows, vulnerable to even the slightest blow.

The captain seemed to guess his train of thought.

"We're perfectly safe, old chap, I assure you. Subs are very strong unless they're hit—I expect it's the same with Spitfires. The trick, of course, is to avoid being hit."

"Exactly so," Shaux said. "If I may, I've been meaning to ask you how submarines defend themselves against aircraft."

"We simply don't," the captain said. "We dive as fast as we can and hope the aircraft, whatever it is, isn't carrying depth charges. You chaps have all the advantages—speed and firepower and maneuverability. We have no way of firing back, and all we can do is disappear. Even that's a bit dodgy in the Med; the water's very clear. That's why we prefer these small U-class boats."

Shaux recalled the U-boat he'd seen firing at *Nonsuch* and how quickly it had dived when he attacked it.

"How long does it take to dive?" he asked the captain.

"If we're attacked by an aircraft, less than a minute, old chap. It's a bit tricky, because you have to do several things in the right sequence very quickly. We practice, of course, 'crash-diving' as we call it; the fastest we've managed is thirty-three seconds."

"I had no idea! You can get this entire boat underwater in thirty-three seconds, from first warning to fully immersed?"

"Fear is a great motivator, my dear fellow. My advice to you, if you spot a U-boat, is to hit him as fast as you can."

* * *

"What do you mean, Miller? Of course I'm going too," Penelope said.

"No, you're bloody well not," Miller countered.

"This is as much my boat as yours, Miller. If we're going to take her out for a sea trial, I want to be there. You might know more about the engines, but you have no idea of how she handles or why. I do."

"Girls don't belong on boats—leastways, not at sea."

"I've been in boats at sea since I could walk."

"Not in wartime you haven't."

He turned and walked away. He didn't like arguments, and this one was pointless. He would have no part in somehow smuggling a female officer out on a trip outside the harbor. He'd be the first to admit she'd done an excellent job of fitting out the launches, of selecting and training the crews, of even browbeating the dockyard superintendent's office into giving them their own dedicated fuel reserve so that they didn't have to keep begging, and of overcoming the endless paperwork that getting supplies always entailed. She'd spent several hours learning the basics of the Napier Sea Lion engines, and she'd found, God alone knew where, all kinds of useful spare parts. Yes, they wouldn't be ready without her; but no, she would not go out with them. Yes, she was technically in charge—well, actually in charge—but that didn't mean she could do whatever she wanted. So, no, she would bloody well stay ashore so the whole venture wouldn't turn into a scandal and he, Miller, as the senior rating, would get the blame.

He walked to the end of Senglea Point, just to give her a chance to calm down and realize he was right. He lit a cigarette and looked out over the harbor. It seemed like only yesterday he'd been swamped on that stupid ack-ack barge, just over there by Fort St. Angelo, under the command of that wanker Sublieutenant Whatever-his-name-was . . .

An HSL rumbled past, shrouded in exhaust fumes, low and gleaming in the filthy water. Blast! She was taking the boat out without him! He couldn't see who was in the wheelhouse, but he'd bet anything she was there. She'd simply waited until he walked away and then told Anderson, the coxswain, to start up. Anderson was too young and too stupid to know any better and obeyed her. He couldn't jump in and swim after them; he couldn't see another boat that he could somehow commandeer . . . Blast!

* * *

"I understand your husband disobeyed my orders, Mrs. Shaux."

The young redheaded doctor stood in her office doorway, a picture of agitation. He was wearing his white coat as if to reinforce his authority.

"I beg your pardon?"

"I've just been informed that he flew to Gibraltar and participated in a convoy. He flew. I had instructed him to remain on the ground for eight weeks."

This was silly, she thought. She'd almost forgotten all about the doctor; so much had happened and it all seemed long ago.

"His arm is healed, Doctor. Thank you. He has returned to flying duties."

"Then he has returned without my permission." He almost took a step into her office but seemed undecided. "I shall lodge a formal complaint with the AHQ senior medical officer."

She felt her patience ebbing. "Do as you will, Doctor." Harry Planter, the SMO, wouldn't put up with this idiot's nonsense.

"Your husband is not well, Mrs. Shaux. He is a danger to himself and others. He should not be flying."

"He has recovered."

"One does not recover from acute trauma, Mrs. Shaux. Not for a long time, perhaps never."

He took a step forward. "You cannot ignore this, Mrs. Shaux. It's time to face reality, however much you would prefer not to. The human mind, the psyche, is frail."

"I don't think that—"

"You don't think? Mrs. Shaux, with due respect, in these circumstances only my opinion counts."

Eleanor heard a tiny, low pitched-noise, deeper than the deepest bass note, like the distant rumbling of thunder far, far away on the edge of the horizon.

"Please step slowly backwards, Doctor, into the corridor. And please keep your hands hanging loosely by your sides."

"What do you mean? Why should I do so?"

"Because my dog thinks you may be threatening me."

"But I'm not."

"In these circumstances, my dog's opinion is the only one that counts."

Charlie, who had been lying beside her desk, stood up. He had the trick of becoming much larger than he really was. The doctor seemed to be estimating the probable size of Charlie's jaws in comparison to his own hand and did not like the result.

He stepped backward, turned on his heel, and was gone. Charlie yawned, stretched, and puttered off in search of a snack.

Eleanor almost made a rude gesture in the doctor's direction but stopped before she did so. Assuming there was a ninety-eight percent chance the doctor was wrong, ridiculously wrong, there was still a two percent chance he was right.

* * *

"We went up to St. Paul's Bay and docked," Penelope said. "I wanted the crew to be familiar with the docks and all the equipment up there. Then we came back down and around to Kalafrana at speed to get the cobwebs out, docked again, and then came back here. There's a bit of a chop and a bit of a breeze but nothing to speak of. We opened her up and let her run."

She looked excited, Miller thought, like she looked when—

"She rides nicely, except the starboard screw is cavitating more than I'd like, and the middle engine's running rough. You look at that engine, and then we'll put her in slings and check the angle of star-board shaft."

Perhaps he had been wrong, Miller thought. Perhaps he should—

"It was so much fun to be out there, Miller! Just to be out there! I've missed it so much!"

She laughed up at him. The wind had managed to get into her hair, and her cheeks were a fresh, rosy color, making her look as if she was eighteen at the most.

Yes, he thought, I was wrong. I might as well admit it.

"What does 'cavitating' mean?"

* * *

"Rommel is unwell, according to these reports," Park said. "He's gone back to Germany to recuperate."

"What's the matter with him?" Eleanor asked.

"No one seems to know for certain. Some stomach thing or other; anyway, enough to send him home. A chap named Stumme is replacing him, transferring from Russia."

"Stumme? Georg Stumme? I thought he was in prison! He's a complete nobody." She discovered she was smoking as she stared up at the map. "This changes everything; Montgomery has a good chance now. He outnumbers the Afrika Korps and is no longer facing the best battlefield general in the world."

"Montgomery says he's almost ready, I understand. He'll attack before the month is over."

"Excellent. Let's just keep those convoys from getting through, sir. Let's just keep picking the Afrika Korps's pockets."

* * *

Thank God that's over, Eleanor thought, as the latest bout between Gort and Park drew to a close, and Park drove off, once more, in high dudgeon.

"Tea, Doctor?" Eleanor asked Dr. Dryden as they emerged from Gort's palatial headquarters. Dryden had been there to discuss—plead—the case for more civilian medical supplies.

"An excellent idea."

A rudimentary officers' mess was housed in a side entrance to the Grandmaster's Palace, with a tiny, shaded tea garden beside it.

"I'd say that on this occasion, Park won by a TKO, Doctor."

"A technical knockout?" Dryden chuckled. "Yes, that's fair. I have to thank you, Mrs. Shaux, for taking my side on the medical supplies question. It's true Podium came in, thank God, or enough of them did, but that doesn't mean we're out of the woods. The medical state of the civilian population is pitiful."

"I merely asked Lord Gort if he had contingency plans to cover the possibility of the civilian population rebelling against British rule if they were not better supplied."

"The look he gave you!" Dryden grinned.

"Actually, I wanted to speak to you about something else. I need your professional advice, off the record, if that's all right, Doctor?"

"Of course!"

"I'm worried about my husband."

"Why? Is he ill? What are his sym—"

"Look, I don't know how to put this delicately, but do you think my husband is going off the rails? Mentally, I mean?"

"Goodness me! Well, I only see Johnnie once or twice a week, of course, but when we had dinner—"

"The RAF doctor thinks he's got shell shock, or something of that sort; excessive stress, a nervous breakdown, that kind of thing."

"Who? Harry Planter?"

"No, the new one, the ginger runt."

Dryden choked on his tea. "I must say, that's very unkind," he gasped. "But also very true."

"Sorry. I shouldn't have said that, true or not."

"Well, you did!" Dryden chuckled, wiping his chin with his handkerchief. "And what do you think? You know Johnnie better than anyone else."

"I don't know," Eleanor said. "He's always been very reserved, ever since we met at Oxford. He's, well, I sometimes think of him as a turtle with a protective shell. On the outside all is calm and placid, but inside, who knows?"

"Have you noticed any changes in him? Has anything new happened to him since he was dumped in the Mediterranean?"

"He's lost two very close friends. In fact, at this point he's lost all his friends. I'm all he's got. Well, and Charlie, of course."

"Oh yes, Digby. Such a good man, such a pity."

An orderly brought fresh tea.

"Is he showing reluctance to fly or any disturbing behavior?" Dryden asked. "Is he eating normally? Drinking excessively? Smoking excessively? Anything out of the ordinary?"

"He can't give up smoking, but who can? Apart from that, he's completely normal."

Dryden pondered for a moment. "I don't wish to be indelicate, but since you asked my professional opinion, is everything well between you? Often a decline or loss of libido is a warning sign."

"Quite to the contrary, as a matter of fact."

She felt herself reddening. She had no right, regardless of her good intentions, to discuss Johnnie's libido with anyone, even a doctor, let alone his libido's trajectory, and she felt as if she had betrayed him.

"Does he sleep well?" Dryden continued, comfortingly professional. "Does he dream?"

She hesitated. "He sleeps on his back. Do you know Leonardo's drawing of a man in a circle? You do? Well, he looks like that."

"That doesn't seem alarming. That's an open, confident, relaxed posture."

"Leonardo's man has open palms, Doctor. Johnnie's fists are tightly clenched."

TWENTY-EIGHT

Shaux had not seen an enemy aircraft in several days, but that didn't mean he could become complacent. Up here, in the blinding haze, an enemy could appear at any moment.

While Malta's Spitfire Mark Vs were defending the island, standing constant daylight patrols between Malta and Sicily, with radar-equipped Beaufighters taking over at night, the few Mark IXs were flying long, lonely antishipping patrols along the coast of Libya, taking advantage of their extra fuel capacity. Park had considered, based on Diggers's theory of aeroelasticity, whether they should remove the wing tanks or the rocket rails, but there had been no further accidents, so Diggers's idea of keeping just the outer tanks dry had proven correct. Besides, the long-range, heavily armed Mark IXs were just too useful to be refitted. The Mark IXs were only in Malta at all because they'd originally been shipped from England to Gibraltar by mistake, and it had been less expensive for the Air Ministry to send them on to Malta than send them back to England.

What a hostile place Libya must be, Shaux thought, looking down, as dry and barren and inhospitable as the surface of the moon, boiling hot by day and frigid at night. It must be difficult to live down there in the best of times, in the heat and dust, let alone fight a battle locked up in armor-plated ovens under the broiling sun. Park had told him there was a secret group of chaps, the Long Range Desert Group, or some such name, that drove American trucks deep behind enemy lines to sabotage Afrika Korps positions. Shaux could only begin to imagine how tough they must be. All he had to do, in comparison, was to sit still up here for two or three hours and suffer a numb bum.

In twelve more minutes, he'd turn onto the reciprocal course, back as far as Tripoli, and then turn for home. Eleanor thought it was important that he be spotted by the enemy to reinforce the impression that all the convoys were being found by patrols and not discovered by Ultra decrypts. Way up here, the Axis had nothing that could endanger him, unless he did something really stupid.

It was only a question of time before they put Eleanor back into Intelligence, he thought. She was just too good at it to be, in the scheme of things, wasting her time in Malta, even though Malta was a critically important battlefield; one of two battlefields, along with Stalingrad, where she said the future of the war in Europe was being decided. Perhaps that American chap Harry Hopkins would ask for her, and she'd go, and then he'd just have Charlie's prodigious snoring to keep him company at night. Charlie could actually out-snore Lingard—Charlie was the best at everything he did.

He'd killed Otto! He hadn't known it was Otto, but that was no excuse. He'd killed Otto, and he had therefore forfeited any right to happiness. If Germany was ever to be rescued from the Nazis, a different kind of German would have to step forward, a cadre of new leaders who could reshape the country within the standards of common human decency. Otto would have been one of those future leaders, Shaux thought, if he hadn't murdered him. Otto was only fighting because his father was a friend of Göring, and he couldn't put his father at risk by refusing to fight. Otto had loved a Jewish girl. If Shaux hadn't slaughtered him, he could have married her and proved that human decency is more powerful than racist hatreds. But he had sent *il pesce-cane* to the bottom of the Mediterranean, and the store of human decency was the lesser for it.

That raised an important question: What would he say to Otto when they met by the river? He had a feeling that the old man with the quill pen would be paying very close attention. Would Otto be accompanied by the ethereal children he'd never had, the children Shaux had denied him?

In the meantime, Shaux would just go on flying until someone shot him down . . . He had, in effect, been doing this for over two years, and it was, frankly, getting a bit tedious. What was that poem? "Something, something, my life is dreary, something, something . . . I am aweary, I wish that I was dead."

Would the old man in his nightmare take "dreary" as an answer when he asked Shaux to evaluate his life? Probably not; it was a bit too flattering.

"Hastings," he said, using Freddie's code word for the end of this leg of the patrol.

"Hastings," Freddie's voice replied as Shaux began to turn.

* * *

"Just look at these children," Dr. Dryden said. "They're underweight and malnourished. They're getting weaker and increasingly vulnerable to illness." He became more heated as he continued. "Just look at that little girl, the one with the teddy bear. Just look at her posture. Just look at the way she moves. That's a case of rickets, a lack of vitamin D. She needs cod-liver oil, and all the cod-liver oil went down on *Avery*."

Charlie had sauntered over to greet the crowd—well, almost sauntered; Eleanor saw he was limping again, just enough to be noticeable. Perhaps she should tell Sapper Jones he couldn't have Charlie anymore, but of course she'd never do that. His work was far too important, and he was becoming known among the Maltese people as a sort of unofficial ambassador from the RAF, a sort of totem. He was working his way down the line of women and children waiting for the Victory Kitchen to open, pausing to meet each person, as if he were a visiting dignitary. He reached the little girl. She wrapped her arms tightly around his mighty head as if to draw strength from him.

"We all have to just hang on as best we can—the children too," Eleanor said. "There's nothing else we can do. This will end, sooner or later."

"Whether it's sooner or later, Eleanor, it's already too late for that child. She'll suffer the consequences of this siege for the rest of her life. Come back in twenty years and tell her there was nothing we could do."

Eleanor felt as if he had struck her. He hadn't meant his comment as a criticism of her personally, of course, but it could have been. She was accomplishing nothing, helping no one, in Malta, and that little girl was suffering because she and Park and Gort and the navy and everyone else had been unable to end the siege and get her the cod-liver oil she needed. The little girl should be running or jumping or climbing trees, bursting with energy, growing stronger and taller every day, not clinging to Charlie for strength and then shuffling through the door into the Victory Kitchen for her tiny share of vitamin-deficient gruel. Charlie's instinctive empathy had done more for the little girl in a minute than Eleanor had done for her in a month.

* * *

"I'm going to ask for more emergency medical flights," Eleanor said. "We have to do more for the children. Perhaps we could do a Magic Carpet run just with things like cod-liver oil and orange juice. It's horrible to see how deprived they are."

"That's a good idea, El," Shaux said, and yawned; those long patrols exhausted him, she knew.

"Tomorrow morning Miller's giving me a tour of his HSL," he said, yawning again. "I'm looking forward to it."

"They've done a very good job, Penelope and Miller, I must say."

She cradled his head in her arms, just as the little girl had cradled Charlie's. At times like this, he was just a tired little orphan boy in need of comfort, open and trusting, rather than an armored turtle with an impenetrable shell. She kissed the top of his head vaguely, wondering if the Americans might help . . . they had an infinite supply of everything . . . she'd get in contact with Harry Hopkins. This was right up his alley . . .

Shaux's breathing grew deeper, and she kissed the top of his head again. Soon he would fall asleep. His brow would be unfurrowed, but, alas, his fists would be tightly clenched.

* * *

"Did you change that frayed wiring in the radio compartment, Miller?"

"Yes, ma'am."

"What about the port engine?"

"We drained the sump and changed both oil filters again. It seems to be running fine again."

This is ridiculous, she thought. We can't go on sharing a bed like this. She finally, finally, had found a way to make a contribution to the defense of Malta, her way of pushing back against Mussolini's destruction of everything she valued, but this had to end. She'd joined the navy, in part, to meet available young officers with the right social standing; she couldn't risk throwing all her hard work away on a cheap scandal with a petty officer from Manchester. "Like mother, like daughter," all the respectable ladies would say, tittering over their afternoon tea. St. Angelo would have no mercy when they found out; she'd be stripped of this wonderful opportunity and sent back to Thompson's tender mercies.

"Are you tired, ma'am?" Miller asked, leaning over her.

"Not really, no."

* * *

"Calling ASRS Kalafrana One," the dockside loudspeakers announced. "Blenheim crew Mayday Orange Sixer. Blenheim crew Mayday Orange Sixer."

It was strange to hear Freddie's voice coming from such an unexpected source. Shaux was more used to Freddie's voice emanating from a flying helmet, where it could assume the sounds of a variety of insects. Hearing Freddie blaring from the loudspeakers in stentorian tones reinforced his impression of Freddie as the omniscient voice of AHQ Malta, the source of all knowledge and instruction. Perhaps, in previous lives, Freddie had made pronouncements for the Oracle of Delphi, or even promulgated the Ten Commandments on God's behalf on Mount Sinai: "Thou shalt-er not covet thy neighbor's wifer . . ."

Miller had just finished showing Shaux over the newly commissioned HSL. He was clearly delighted in and very proud of his new assignment, and Shaux was certain he would do an excellent job.

"Blast!" Miller said. "Brown's away over at St. Paul's Bay. I'll have to go without a navigator. Damn!"

"I'll go," Shaux said instantly, forgetting his intense dislike of the sea. "It's far too dangerous for you to go without a navigator. I can read a chart and a compass."

"Are you sure, sir?" Miller asked. But he did not wait for an answer, bellowing out instructions to his crew. This would be Miller's first true solo search-and-rescue mission, Shaux realized, and he wouldn't stop just because he was shorthanded. Perhaps Shaux shouldn't leave, in case something came up and Park needed him, but there wasn't time to spare, and the bus drivers' lives were at risk.

Shaux scrambled back on board. Someone handed him a lifejacket, and he put it on with a sudden qualm as he realized to what he had committed himself, but it was already too late for second thoughts. Three big engines started one after the other in the stern, coughing and spluttering before settling into an angry grumble, pumping clouds of exhaust fumes into every nook and cranny of the HSL. Two deck hands, fore and aft, loosened the lines. There was a sudden clunk as Miller let in the clutch of the starboard engine, and the bow swung away from the jetty. The deck hands expertly flicked the lines loose from the bollards on the jetty and began to tidy them away. There were two more clunks as Miller let in the other clutches, and the engines rose from a grumble to a rumble as the HSL turned towards the mouth of the Kalafrana inlet.

They were passing the massive ramparts of Fort Delimara on their left—their port, Shaux corrected himself—already, and Il-Kalanka lighthouse was coming up beyond it. The entire island of Malta really was just one entire ancient fortress, he thought, and—

Shaux reminded himself that he was not on a sightseeing cruise but was supposed to be Kalafrana One's navigator, and ducked into the cabin. He rummaged through the maps strewn on the chart table until he found one showing Malta at the top—at the north—and the coast of Libya at the bottom. Let's see: Tripoli was almost directly below them, perhaps sou-sou-west, and Benghazi, in the bottom right-hand corner of the chart, was about southeast. Someone had drawn a grid over the sea; the square marked Orange Six was approximately north of Misrata, one hundred miles from Malta.

He fumbled with the navigating instruments until he remembered how to work them and made the necessary measurements. He stuck his head into the tiny wheelhouse where Miller and the coxswain sat.

"Bearing 175 degrees," he said loudly. The HSL was incredibly noisy—as noisy as a Spitfire! "Target is three hours at 30 knots."

Miller pointed at his helmet. Shaux belatedly realized they were wearing helmets like pilots, with intercoms built into them. He retreated into the chart area and retrieved a headset dangling from a hook. He shrugged it on—its owner, Brown, must have a really, really big head, he thought—and heard Freddie in his ears.

"What is your position, Kalafrana One?" To the extent that Freddie's urbane voice was capable of expressing irritation, it was. The wires from Shaux's headset led to a toggle switch in a panel full of radio equipment. The toggle switch was marked AHQ and Int. He turned it to AHQ.

"Er, sorry, Freddie. Just passing Il-Kalanka. Setting course for Orange Six. ETA three hours."

"Location Kalanka, en route Orange Sixer, Kalafrana One," Freddie's voice replied in an impeccable imitation of Freddie at his pedantic best. "Winds at target location gusting easterly."

"Winds gusting easterly," Shaux acknowledged.

"I'm not even going to ask, Kalafrana One," Freddie's voice said, and the connection went dead.

The HSL opened up and climbed steeply onto its bow wave in an exhilarating burst of power. Strangely—and thankfully—the engines were much quieter now as the slipstream blew their noise away sternward. The launch was almost skipping from wave to wave. Thank God the seas were calm! Almost half the launch was out of the water, all the way back to the cabin, riding on its bow wave so that they almost seemed to be flying. He'd have to get a book on the geometry of speedboat hulls; perhaps Penelope Dryden had one she could lend him.

Shaux hurriedly made a note of the time. The only way they'd know they were in Orange Sixer was that they'd been heading there for three hours.

There wasn't much to do for the next three hours; in fact, all the unoccupied crew members had already gone to sleep. Shaux did not. There was something about the thought of several hundred feet of water below the flying keel that kept him wide awake.

Eventually the crew began to stir, and someone handed him a cup of tea.

"Wheelhouse, navigator," he said, having no idea of communications conventions. "We are entering Orange Sixer."

"Righty-ho, sir," Miller responded. Clearly his version of the conventions was far less formal. "Speed for 12 knots and everyone out and looking."

Their speed fell away immediately, and the HSL sank down off its plane, becoming a conventional motorboat once more.

"AHQ, Kalafrana One is searching Orange Sixer," Shaux reported.

"Searching Orange Sixer," Freddie acknowledged. "Stand by for air support."

Sometime in the last half hour or so, a Spit had taken off from Malta and ambled down to the search area at ten times the speed of Kalafrana One. It was yet another way in which Podium's fuel supplies were allowing Park to flex his muscles and multiply the effectiveness of his resources; the Spit could search a hundred times the area that the HSL could. Indeed, within ten minutes, the Spit found the HSL, roaring dramatically over them, and then found the Blenheim crew just ten minutes later.

Shaux watched the crew rig scrambling nets over the starboard side as the HSL sidled up to the life raft. Three men were huddled in the raft, soaked in salt seawater and already burning from the sun and breeze. One of them waved his arm feebly, and Shaux recalled exactly how he had felt when he had been rescued, exhausted and delirious. One of the deckhands climbed down into the raft to help them climb up. One of the men remained motionless; the medical orderly jumped down and knelt over him, and then shook his head.

They turned for home. Two of the Blenheim crew lay propped against the cabin walls, wrapped in blankets, sipping tea and sucking eagerly on cigarettes, while the third lay silently beneath a blanket.

Shaux speculated how much it might have cost to rescue these two men: the care and upkeep of the HSL and all its dockside services, all the needs of the crew of nine, the scores of gallons of fuel for the HSL, the costs of maintaining the Spit and the needs of its pilot, and all the other resources necessary to run a search-and-rescue operation, ad infinitum, all just to bring back two exhausted men. Was it worth all that? Of course it's worth it, he thought: that's the whole point of having a motto that says "The sea shall not have them."

TWENTY-NINE

The waves rolled on in endless unbroken lines, one after another. They were topped by flying spume, heading northwest from horizon to horizon, glinting in the glare of the sun and making it almost impossible to see if anything was down there but water.

The admiral commanding St. Angelo had decided that it would be a splendid idea to hold a ceremonial parade in St. George's Square at which he would pin Shaux's new Distinguished Service Cross on his breast in public recognition of Shaux's service during Operation Podium. Worse yet, the admiral had arranged for Pathé News to film the event, causing Lord Gort to decide that he would also attend the parade, leaving Park with no choice but to attend also. Shaux hadn't heard if the Archbishop of Canterbury was flying in, but he wouldn't be surprised.

Shaux would rather walk across hot coals, but Park had told him he had to do it for the sake of interservice amity. Within weeks images of Shaux would flicker across cinema screens around the world, doubtlessly accompanied by stirring music and a commentator's rousing, sycophantic description of "fearless fighters of the skies" or some such nonsense, and little children would be encouraged thereby to think of Shaux as someone admirable, someone to be emulated, rather than as an airman with a penchant for killing his fellow pilots.

Shaux's one chance was that there'd be a Stuka raid and the thing would be cancelled at the last moment. Perhaps Otto's old *squadriglia* would return to avenge *il pescecane*'s death.

Shaux turned and turned again. What was it he had read in school? Something about an eagle looking down, something like "the wrinkled sea beneath him crawls." How could Tennyson have known that? He'd died many years before the Wright brothers first flew. He must have looked down from a cliff, or—

What was that? There! Could be wreckage. Could be the kind of trick that bored, tired eyes play. No, nothing, but let's go round again just to be sure. Where was Diggers when you needed him? No, must have been an illusion . . . Wait! Yes, there was a rubber dinghy in the water, wallowing in the waves. He turned tightly again and dropped down to be sure. Yes! He couldn't tell how many men were in it, or whether they were alive, although Diggers would have been able to give a detailed description.

"Calpurnia located, Delta Five," he said.

"Cal-purn-ia located, Delta Five," Freddie's unmistakable voice sounded in his earphones.

Freddie would relay that information to the RAF rescue launch. In the meantime, he had enough fuel to circle for, let's see, forty-five minutes, hoping the launch would be able to spot him and find the Blenheim crew. He hadn't really expected to find them, to tell the truth, one tiny dinghy in a wilderness of water . . . Why had Freddie chosen *Calpurnia* as the code word for the dinghy? Wasn't that the name of one of Caesar's wives? And trust Freddie to find every possible syllable in her name!

Shaux began a lazy circle at two thousand feet, judging that to be the best height for the launch to spot him and for him to keep an eye on the dinghy. The crew would be immensely comforted; a circling Spitfire had to mean that help was on the way. He was very vulnerable down here, an easy target for any 202s that might wander by, but that was a chance he had to take. Perhaps the launch would have Miller on board. Miller was a really good chap, and he was finally back where he belonged: in a high-speed powerboat.

It hadn't been that many weeks since he'd been in the water himself, without even a raft, coming to grips with the idea that he would die in the next few hours, until Diggers had found him just as he had now found the dinghy. Shaux checked his watch; half an hour had passed.

Still no 202s, thank God, but no rescue launch, either. A major battle was about to begin in Egypt, Eleanor expected, which would explain the absence of 202s. They'd be waiting to attack the Eighth Army. He hoped this new chap Montgomery was a bit more successful than his predecessors. Eleanor said he was a strange combination of arrogance and caution; perhaps arrogance and caution were what it took to beat the Afrika Korps.

"You are in sight," Freddie announced. The launch had spotted him and told Freddie. This was, in Shaux's opinion, another example of communications being too centralized. Why couldn't the launch be given the same R/T as his Spitfire so that they could speak directly? He'd have to remember to give Freddie a ribbing for not having a code word for this situation—"you are in sight" was far too explicit. He should use something suitable like *flowerpot* or *lace curtains*.

He turned to his left to find the launch to lead it in. He didn't dare go too far for fear of losing the tiny dinghy again. He found the launch within a minute. It was bounding across the waves, wreathed in white spray with a long white wake behind it. He turned to overfly it on the bearing to the dinghy to lead the launch in that direction. The "Whaleback" nickname was very apt for its long, sloping cabin. He couldn't tell if it was Miller's launch or not. It must have been pretty uncomfortable down there, rising and swooping over the waves; he was amazed he'd managed it when he'd done it. He overflew the dinghy and turned back yet again. The launch and the dinghy were now less than half a mile apart and should be able to see each other at any moment.

As he overflew the launch a second time, he saw another following it. Freddie had said nothing about a second rescue mission. This one must have been searching in a different area but turned when he'd told Freddie the dinghy was in square Delta Five. This new launch was much larger, as much as twice the size. It must be one of the new Fairmile Dog Boats that RAF Middle East Command had been promising. He didn't know they'd arrived in Malta. Good lord, it was big! It was—wait! The bridge house was semicircular, and those were torpedo tubes. That was a long-barreled gun behind the bridge. This was no RAF rescue launch. This was a full-fledged E-boat! The curving, rounded bridge house was unmistakable. It would catch the Whaleback as soon as it slowed down.

Very well: nothing to decide. He was a mile away—twelve seconds. Line up. Safety off. A two-second burst of cannon fire would deliver eighty shells, each of which would go straight through the E-boat's unarmored hull and out the other side, unless it hit something—or someone—on the way. The engines and fuel tanks would be behind the bridge, below that machine-gun platform. All lined up. Half a mile— six seconds: open fire. He was close enough to see lines of spray as his cannon shells walked their way up to, through, and beyond the E-boat's afterdeck. Cease firing.

He flashed over the E-boat and began to turn. Out of the corner of his eye, he saw something else in the water a mile or so behind the E-boat, low and dark, like the upturned hull of a small steamer. What the hell was that?

* * *

An apathetic line of civilians waited their turns outside the Victory Kitchen. The women carried empty shopping bags, and the children sat listlessly in the gravel road. One of them, Eleanor saw, was the little girl with the one-eyed teddy bear.

Eleanor stopped her car to let more stragglers cross the road to join the queue. She was giving Penelope a ride back to the ASRS station at St. Paul's Bay; it would be interesting to see the new Whalebacks in the water. Johnnie had been full of praise. Perhaps the excitement of high-speed launches could overcome his fear of the sea.

She climbed out to let Charlie stretch his legs a little.

"Kelby!" the little girl called to Charlie. "Kelby!"

"Charlie, stay," Eleanor said. She didn't want to be mean, but it would take at least fifteen minutes to let all the children pet him. Charlie sat down with a thump, obviously disagreeing with her decision.

"Miller's HSL had another successful operation, I'm told," Eleanor said.

"Yes, a Wellington crew, ma'am; all five men saved. He's doing really well. He's out again now, after a Blenheim crew."

Penelope seemed to have grown five years in a week, Eleanor thought. Her uncle had assured Eleanor that Penelope was not just a pretty face, and he was clearly right. Everyone is really good at something, Eleanor thought. It's just a question of finding the right something.

"You've done an excellent job."

She was flourishing in her new responsibilities; perhaps she could take on more . . .

"I have to thank you, ma'am, for all you've done," Penelope said.

"Kelby!" the girl called again. Charlie looked up at Eleanor but did not move.

Air raid sirens burst into life, and she could hear the thunder of approaching aircraft. The line of women and children filled her with guilt. She *must* convince Gort to mount a Magic Carpet submarine run consisting only of food and medicines and supplements for children. Or would it be better to fly in a nighttime delivery by a Blenheim or a Beaufighter? Why hadn't she done all this before, weeks ago?

"Nonsense—enough of that. I did nothing," Eleanor said. "Now, I wanted to talk to you about—"

"Down!" someone shouted. The sound of aircraft was now a deafening roar, and above it shrieked the unmistakable sound of falling bombs.

Eleanor threw herself down in the gravel, dragging Charlie down under her, and covered her head with her hands. There was a very loud, flat sort of sound, a crump rather than a bang, followed by a whoosh as the Victory Kitchen burst into its individual bricks. The ground shook, and something very hard struck her on her arm.

The quiet that followed was almost as shocking as the crump. Eleanor wondered if her eardrums had burst, but in a second or two, new sounds rushed in to fill the vacuum of silence: screams of pain, voices shouting for help, children wailing, and the drone of departing bombers.

She rose unsteadily to her hands and knees. Her right sleeve was torn from the shoulder to the elbow, and blood was oozing through the tatters. The scorched and limbless torso of a teddy bear with one eye lay in the gravel just in front of her, but it wasn't quite in focus. The little girl must have dropped it; Eleanor picked it up to give it back.

She struggled to her feet and wondered if she was concussed; everything seemed very difficult and wobbly. The building where the Victory Kitchen had been had disappeared completely; only its basement remained, half filled with broken bricks and masonry and shattered glass.

Charlie bounded forward unbidden and jumped down into the wreckage. Eleanor clambered after him. He began searching and then stopped and barked to fetch her. The little girl lay half-buried in the rumble. Charlie bent over her, and she lifted one hand to fondle his head, staring into his eyes. Her breathing was shallow and painful, as if she was trying to gather her breath to cough but lacked the strength to do so. Charlie licked her cheek, just once; her arm dropped and the sound of her labored breathing ceased.

Charlie looked at Eleanor. They say dogs don't cry, Eleanor thought, but they're wrong, completely wrong. Dogs cry on the inside.

"Don't cry, little one," she whispered. "Don't cry."

Charlie was covered in gray grime, almost as if he was in a black-and-white snapshot. Oh God, if she'd let him go to greet the children, he'd be dead. It was the merest chance that had kept him alive.

Her arm hurt like hell, she noticed, but it wasn't broken; perhaps it had been struck by a flying brick. Charlie began to inspect it.

She eased her jacket off as carefully as her arm permitted and laid it over the little girl. She and Charlie clambered back up out of the rubble. Where was Penelope?

"Charlie, where is she? Charlie: find."

Charlie adopted his working posture, taut and purposeful, and began a careful search pattern. It took him only a minute or so to find Penelope, or, to be more precise, what had once been Penelope, amid the debris that had killed her. It took Eleanor a moment to accept that that . . . that really had been Penelope, but the tatters of her WRNS uniform were unmistakable.

The world seemed curiously unreachable, as if Eleanor were looking at it through a window—no, not a window but a sheet of ice. It was very, very cold.

That's enough, she thought. That's enough! People are dying, and I have done nothing to prevent it. The little girl should be growing up

strong and healthy, and Penelope Dryden should be building more rescue launches—that was what she was about to tell her.

She had nothing left to cover . . . well, it was still Penelope, even if
almost torn in two, and she couldn't leave her like this. She would stand
guard until someone came. Besides, you can't move if you're encased
in ice. The sound of the bombers faded away; the cries of the wounded
and the shouts of the rescuers remained. Perhaps she was concussed a
little. Malta seemed shaky.

She had failed to protect the little girl, and she had failed to protect
Penelope. She had sent Diggers to his death, and now she had almost
killed Charlie.

Penelope had always seemed concerned about her appearance,
Eleanor thought, and she'd been very pretty, almost like a film star. It
was a particularly cruel twist of fate—another of Sapper Jones's God's
mysterious ways—that she should end her life looking like . . . like that.

Park knows exactly what to do to hold Malta and frustrate Rommel,
she thought. He doesn't need my help. The Axis starved Malta for two
years; now it's our turn to starve the Afrika Korps. It doesn't take a
strategist to work that out.

Raids on Malta were declining steeply, thanks to Counterpunch,
and attacks on enemy supply ships were becoming more and more
effective, thanks to Pickpocket. The Beauforts had succeeded in
severely damaging Tobruk, and it was reported that the Afrika Korps
was down to only three days' fuel supplies.

Park was keeping his promise to Hopkins. Malta would hold. Park
didn't need her.

Montgomery had amassed over a thousand tanks and was finally,
finally ready to attack the Afrika Korps at El Alamein. Rommel was still
sick in a sanatorium in Germany, and that idiot Stumme was in command. Now it was time to roll the dice; it was all up to Montgomery.

She looked around for something to cover Penelope but could find
nothing. Suddenly it was remarkably hot instead of icy cold. Perhaps
she should sit down, but that seemed like too much effort and there
was too much to consider.

She hoped someone was thinking about the bigger picture. If the
German Sixth Army took Stalingrad, they could race south through
Georgia, through the Caucasus Mountains, and potentially turn the

British flank in Iraq or Iran . . . Perhaps the key to the Afrika Korps' survival does not lie in Egypt but in Russia . . .

Red Tape would be ideal for this sort of situation; it was built to evaluate complex alternatives and measure probabilities. Her team could have an analysis within a week. Well, they could if she was there to give them direction . . . Of course, Park would have to agree to let her go, and Churchill would have to agree to take her back, but she doubted either man would stand in her way . . .

Park didn't need her because he didn't make mistakes. The powers that be in Whitehall and Washington, on the other hand, made mistakes constantly, endlessly, and needed to be—

"Are you all right, miss?" someone asked Eleanor. "You'd better sit down in the shade for a minute." He had a blanket to cover Penelope.

"Oh, I'm fine. Thank you. I have to get back to London as soon as possible."

"Of course you do, but it's best to sit down, miss. What was your friend's name and address?"

"Oh, she wasn't a friend. Wait—no, I didn't mean it like that; she was . . . Penelope Dryden, Dr. Dryden's niece."

"You need to get your arm taken care of."

"I'll have someone look at it at Luqa."

"Luqa?"

"I just need someone to drive my car to Luqa. That's all. I can't manage it."

"But Luqa is RAF only, miss."

"I know. So am I—I'm AHQ Malta. I can't crank the engine with one arm, and I can't change gears. Please, please, just drive me there, and my dog."

"Well, I—"

"Please!"

"Are you sure, miss?"

Today is Tuesday, she thought. If there's a transport to Gibraltar tonight, I could be in London tomorrow evening.

"I'm certain."

It might be better to take Charlie to London because it would be terrible when Johnnie went missing and left Charlie alone in Malta as a de facto orphan. No—she meant *if* Johnnie went missing, of course.

Sapper Jones would not be the right person to take on Charlie. Warrant Officer Jenkins would spoil him, and Charlie would look terrible if he grew a little pudgy.

Of course she couldn't take Charlie. He was Johnnie's link to Froggie Potter; he still wore the tattered remnants of Froggie's scarf. If she took Charlie away, she'd be taking Froggie away too, and Johnnie had just lost Diggers and Otto.

She needed to see Park and send a telegram to Churchill's office—to Edward Bridges, the cabinet secretary.

She'd tell Johnnie this afternoon, as soon as he landed. She had a sense he was expecting it . . . Perhaps, if they were separated for a while, it might be good for them . . . Perhaps, when they met again, he would finally let her inside his armor-plated soul.

She found she was still holding the ragged remainder of the teddy bear and pushed it into her pocket. It would remind her of why she was doing all this and that war is not just a mathematically measurable clash of kinetic forces or a construct of the mind but an evil that first starves children and then kills them.

THIRTY

That menacing shape in the water, black and shiny, low enough for the swell to be breaking over it, could that really be a U-boat? There was a long-barreled deck gun of some sort on a bandstand behind the conning tower, facing aft. There were no Royal Navy submarines with that configuration in the Mediterranean, Shaux was certain, and HMS St. Angelo had said there were no British submarines currently in this area. He'd studied the recognition profiles the navy issued, and this looked exactly like a Kriegsmarine Type VII. Very well. He had to attack immediately before the U-boat could dive to safety.

The last time he'd encountered a U-boat, he had been flying a Martlet armed only with machine guns. Now he was flying a Spitfire armed with machine guns, cannons, and rockets.

A couple of crew members were visible on the upperworks, staring up at him in shock as he flashed over their heads. He imagined alarm bells ringing and loudspeakers blasting out orders, hands hastily turning valve wheels to flood the buoyancy tanks or whatever it took to make the submarine descend.

This would be a race. The chaps at HMS Talbot had warned him he'd have less than a minute.

He turned hard left. Spitfires had many superb characteristics, but Shaux had always felt that the best of them all was their ability to turn. R. J. Reynolds, their designer, had given them wings with the very unusual quality of stalling from the roots outward, rather than from the wingtips inward like almost all other aircraft. This characteristic, called *washout*, meant that he could turn tighter and tighter until he could feel the turbulence of the air from the stalling wing roots banging against the tail. That feeling told him exactly how tightly he could turn before the aircraft fell out of the sky; that feeling was probably why he had survived the bloodbaths of aerial warfare for so long.

Where should he hit the U-boat? There wasn't much to hit. The humped bow was the highest point, but that already seemed lower, and the hull was lower yet. It would have to be the conning tower, although he didn't know if the conning tower was part of the pressure hull. If he knocked a hole in the tower, would the U-boat sink or survive? There wasn't any time to debate the issue. He was around and lining up. Safety catches off. The hull was now completely awash, and the tower was a target no more than twelve feet high and thirty feet wide, sliding forward and downwards into the rollers. The crew was all inside; they'd be waiting in agonizing suspense to see whether they'd escape him or not. He was really, really low, so low that the surface of the sea was no longer flat, and he could see white spume flying off the bumpy wave tops. No time to check for 109s or 202s, and no need to do so. No one could follow him at this level.

How close to go? Who knew? Now! The rockets jumped off the rails like wild beasts leaping at their prey, propelled by torrents of fire and streaking ahead of his Spitfire as if it were stationary. The conning tower disintegrated as if it was made of tissue paper instead of steel, and the side of the hull broke the surface as it heeled far over with the force of the impact.

He flashed over the U-boat, almost brushing the wreckage of the conning tower, and pulled the Spitfire into a climbing turn, throttle wide open, with the sound of the Merlin rising to a scream. He ignored whatever might be going on below him as he searched the skies for enemy aircraft but could see none. It was at times like this that Diggers's loss cut most deeply. Diggers would have surveyed the sky in a single all-seeing sweep of his eyes, far better than the latest version of a flying radar set, whereas Shaux had to make himself slow down and do it twice, just to be fairly confident at best.

There was nothing to see of the U-boat when he finally looked down, just a patch of white amid the green-black waves. As he passed

over it, he realized he was looking down the top of a volcano of air bub-
bling up from below. Somewhere beneath the waves, forty or so sailors
were dying or were already dead. Perhaps the hull had cracked open
when he hit the conning tower and the Mediterranean had rushed in,
or maybe he'd just jarred the welded joints and split some seams or
snapped some rivets and the boat was dying a slower death, with little jets of water spraying unstoppably from hairline fractures in the
pressure hull as the crew grasped the reality of their dreadful fate as
the jets of water became stronger as the boat sank and outside water
pressure rose. Their home was turning into a steel coffin.

It didn't matter that this crew had sent other crews to their deaths
in the last day or so. Each life is still a life, and these lives were on
Shaux's account.

"Bananas," he said into the R/T. Why did Freddie pick such silly
code words? What kind of a valediction was that?

* * *

Eleanor winced as Harry Planter, the SMO, bandaged her arm. Thank
God he'd been at Luqa when she arrived, bloody and disheveled; otherwise she'd have been at the mercy of the ginger runt. Her thoughts
were in chaos, as if the bomb that had killed Penelope and the little girl
had jumbled up her brain.

Johnnie had his favorite poem, she thought, the one by Yeats that
began *I know that I will meet my fate somewhere above the clouds
above*, the poem upon which he had built his governing philosophy:
his life didn't matter and therefore his inevitable death wouldn't either.
The nihilist Friedrich Nietzsche would have admired Johnnie's suc-
cinct analysis. It was a logical idea, she conceded, and a necessary one,
because he needed his impenetrable stoicism to get himself through
each day. It was a remarkable thing to deliberately fly towards a well-
armed enemy, as Diggers had always said. Johnnie's stoicism had sustained him yesterday and the day before and the day before that; it was
doubtless sustaining him now.

It had sustained him through the hammer blows of his life—
Froggie Potter's death, Diggers's death, and now Otto's death—and it
would sustain him until the end. It had cushioned him through his

own brushes with death until even the most harrowing experiences were just mishaps along the way. Shot down over Dunkirk? One of those things! Shot down in the Battle of Britain? Goes with the territory! Bailed out of a burning aircraft over occupied France? Just a day at the office! Crashed into the Mediterranean upside down? Piece of cake!

Johnnie's philosophy had, however, two problems. One was that dream, whatever it was—the dream he had every night, the dream he denied having, the dream he couldn't dare to acknowledge, the dream he clenched his fists to resist but couldn't. That dream was inside his Yeatsian armor, an enemy within his gates, a worm in his apple, a cancer in his soul eating away at him inexorably.

The other problem was that there was no room for her inside his Yeatsian world, which permitted no hope, no future, no chance of redemption, and no happiness. He needed a mistress but not a wife, just as, in truth, she had to admit, finally admit, she needed a lover, not a husband.

What would her father say? "Lean on it, Ellie!" He'd have had her back in Allied Headquarters, working with Hopkins and Eisenhower and Churchill. "God gave you a brain, Ellie, for a purpose," her father had told her. "I don't know what purpose, but he knows. Don't waste it! Carpe diem!"

Should her brain be used on calculating how much food it took to keep a Maltese child alive or how to defeat Hitler?

If she gave up Johnnie, she would never forgive herself. If, on the other hand, she simply waited until he was killed, she'd have a clean conscience. That, of course, was sophistry, although it was true. She imagined a future in which, every time he landed safely, she'd say, "Oh no. He's home again. I'll have to keep waiting."

No, she had to go. She had to take a Blenheim tonight, and she had to take Charlie with her. Carpe diem. It was objectively true that Red Tape was a valuable Allied asset. Her father needed her; she had to protect him from her mother. She might have failed as a wife, but she still had a chance to succeed as a daughter.

And, to be fair, she thought, she'd been a damned good mistress; she thought Johnnie would agree.

She walked through the tunnels to Park's office before she could change her mind. Charlie padded behind her.

* * *

There was the E-boat. Unlike the U-boat crew, the E-boat crewmen were clearly visible, driven on deck by the imminent danger that their boat would sink. He could see their white faces staring up in fear and loathing as he flashed over them. Someone on the tiny bridge was firing a light machine gun at him in futile defiance. Four men were hard at work at manual bilge pumps, the kind with long handles that two men have to pump up and down with two arms, trying to keep their boat afloat. Two more were wrestling with inflatable life rafts, preparing for the inevitable. Three men were clustered round their Flak 37 gun. This was a fearsome long-barreled weapon he had seen attached to Stukas on underwing pylons, a Panzerknacker, as they called it, a gun designed to kill tanks as well as aircraft. As he completed his turn, he could see that the 37-millimeter crew had loaded a clip and were turning the gun to face him.

This was almost like the climax to an American Western film, he thought, a dramatic confrontation between a RP3 rocket-armed Spitfire IX and a Panzerknacker-armed Schnellboot.

He had still had four rockets, each with a hardened steel projectile inside an explosive shell. His Spitfire was travelling at more than 300 miles per hour; the rockets travelled more than five times faster. The 37-millimeter cannon probably had a similar shell, and the crew would be able to fire a full clip of six shells at him in less than a second as he approached them. Each shell could crack open an armored tank; each shell would punch a hole through a Spitfire the size of an armchair.

The E-boat was a large, stationary target. His Spitfire, seen head-on, would seem far smaller as he approached them at more than four hundred feet every second, but he would be easier and easier to hit as he approached, until he'd be huge in the sky, half as wide as the E-boat was long, and the 37-millimeter cannon was much more accurate than the rockets.

Any one of his four rockets would smash the E-boat's hull and sink it. Any one of the 37-millimeter's six shells would knock him out of the air.

He tucked down near the wave tops, at fifty feet or less, lining up to hit the E-boat at the water line. An automatic glance upwards and behind for 109s or 202s; there were none.

Rocket safety catch off. Probably the most humiliating mistake a pilot could make was to line up and press the firing button at the exactly right moment only to have nothing happen because the safety was still on. Now, when he pressed the button, he'd complete the electrical circuits out to the triggers in each rocket's tail, igniting their cordite propellant.

Apply the minutest amount of rudder to offset the extra drag on the right wing caused by the remaining rockets.

Everything seemed much faster down here, skimming over the whitecaps, and his Merlin seemed louder, although that was absurd.

Five seconds, he decided, before firing.

He'd always felt comfortable in a Spitfire. There was no room to move, of course, and his knees were practically touching the instrument panel. If he stretched out his arms, he'd hit the canopy, and his backside had gone to sleep. The ground crew practically had to use a shoehorn to cram the pilot in, but it felt safe, like home—not that he'd ever had a home beyond a boarding school dormitory, or an RAF barracks, or the room he shared with Eleanor in the commandeered *pensione* in Valletta. The cockpit of a Spitfire was his place, a place he understood. His place was with Eleanor too, of course, but not in the same way; he didn't understand Eleanor like he understood a Spitfire. All he could do was adore her without comprehension, and that was not the same thing at all. She was beyond understanding. Her judgments were unsearchable and her ways past understanding, as the bible said, or something like that.

His Spitfire had never failed him—well, he'd been dumped into the Med, but that was due to aeroelasticity, and therefore not the Spitfire's fault. Eleanor had never failed him either, but he knew, just *knew*, she would, in the sense that one day she'd be gone, just like that. She was a racehorse, and he was a cart horse; it simply wasn't fair to harness her to him. He was a moth, and she was a flame. It wasn't the flame's fault when the moth got burned.

The thundering Merlin pulled him forward; the air swept over and under the elegant elliptical wings. The Spitfire was silky-smooth and quivering with power at the same time, as only a Spitfire could be.

The long barrel of the 37-millimeter Panzerknacker had foreshortened and disappeared as the crew aimed at him; he was looking straight into the muzzle. Panzerknacker—that was a really good name for a gun, he thought.

The E-boat had grown large and unmissable. Time to fire.

It occurred to him that, if he didn't fire his remaining rockets, the E-boat would probably sink anyway, but its crew might take to those life rafts and survive. The E-boat was no longer a threat to Miller's Whaleback or the Blenheim crew . . .

The silent crowd in his dream was already swollen by the U-boat crew and all their unborn children. Surely it didn't need to get bigger yet, with another dozen or so drowned sailors and their never-to-be offspring. It would take ages to pass through the crowd to reach the old man waiting at his desk, and he still had no idea what he'd do about greeting Otto, or how he'd answer the old man.

The 37-millimeter gunner had a pretty fair chance of hitting him as he closed in—fifty-fifty, perhaps better, Shaux estimated—particularly if the gunner had steady nerves and took the rolling of the swell into consideration and waited until the last moment.

What would he say to the old man on the hill when he asked Shaux to summarize his life? "Killer"? That wasn't entirely fair; he had some redeeming characteristics, and Otto's death had been a ghastly mistake. "Piece of cake"? Too glib. "Executioner"? Closer to the truth.

"Mediocre," Shaux decided—it really was the best, most honest answer. It summed him up perfectly; his flying instructor at Cranwell had been right. He wondered if Eleanor thought he was only a mediocre lover but was too polite to say. He hoped not, but there wasn't anything he could do about it now.

He flicked the rocket safety catch back on and stared down the barrel of the Panzerknacker, making a mental note to ask Diggers, when he saw him, the Latin word for "mediocre."

* * *

Pity about Penelope, Miller thought. Still, given a choice between Penelope and Maisie, he'd chosen Maisie, on balance, and what Maisie didn't know wouldn't hurt her. Well, to be fair, sauce for the goose— what he didn't know about Maisie wouldn't hurt him, either.

He'd write to Maisie this evening. She'd be tickled pink he was going to be a confirmed petty officer. She could tick it off on her diagram of badges, and she'd know exactly how to make the most of it.

* * *

"Have you heard from Johnnie, Freddie?"

"Not since he reported 'Bananas.' Can you believe it? 'Bananas'!"

"'Bananas'? He radioed 'Bananas'?"

"He did; he really did."

Oh God! Johnnie had sunk a U-boat. They'd give him another medal, poor man. They'd parade him at Buckingham Palace and give him afternoon tea with the queen and the little princesses. They'd send him off to Canada and Australia and America to wow the factory girls, and he would hate every single second of it.

The Blenheim for Gibraltar was leaving in just forty-five minutes. Churchill had sent her a personal cable of approval: "Once more unto the breach!" Now that was interesting, she thought. Churchill understands that Whitehall is an even deadlier battlefield than Malta.

So now she had to go, but she couldn't just leave Johnnie, could she, just like that? She could write a letter, but there was no time. Charlie was looking at her, sensing her indecision. Could she really take Charlie with her as well, without saying goodbye? How would she manage her travel bag with her arm in a sling?

Her father needed her. She had to protect him from her mother. Charlie needed her to protect him from Johnnie's inevitable death.

Stalingrad was closer to Egypt than Casablanca was—had anyone thought through the implications of . . .

Her father was helpless. Johnnie, on the other hand, could take care of himself . . . well, not really.

She had to make a choice. She had to go. Perhaps she should go and leave Charlie to comfort Johnnie, but what would happen to Charlie in the future? She had to take him with her; she'd been through this a thousand times. Who would Charlie choose if he was given a choice?

Johnnie would understand—wouldn't he? Of course not! He'd blame himself when it wasn't his fault.

She gestured to Charlie, and he picked up her bag by the handle so that it dangled from his jaws.

Stay or go? Take Charlie or leave him?

Charlie was staring, his head on one side, sensing imminent action but not knowing what it would be.

"Nothing since that, Freddie? Nothing since he radioed 'Bananas'? Nothing at all?"

"No, nothing," Freddie said. "Nothing at all."

AUTHOR'S NOTES

The Siege of Malta was one of the greatest British victories in World War II, arguably of as great a significance as the Battle of Britain. Malta was under siege for two brutal years but survived and was able to choke off Axis supply lines in the vital weeks leading to the Second Battle of El Alamein in October 1942, the battle in which Montgomery's Eighth Army defeated Rommel's Afrika Korps. In the following months, Malta supplied much of the air power necessary to crush the Axis powers in Africa, leading to the surrender of the Afrika Korps in May 1943 and the subsequent invasion of Sicily in July 1943.

The distinguished historian Hugh Trevor-Roper once commented, "History is not merely what happened; it is what happened in the context of what might have happened. Therefore it must incorporate the might-have-beens."

If Malta had fallen in mid-1942, a fully supplied Afrika Korps would almost certainly have defeated the Eighth Army. The Axis powers would then have gained control of the Suez Canal and the Arabian oil fields, and the Kriegsmarine would have roamed the Indian Ocean. Rommel would also have been able to race back across northern Africa and defeat the Anglo-American forces landing in Morocco in Operation Torch, in November 1942, if that landing had still been attempted.

Or, intriguingly, Cairo is closer to Stalingrad (now Volgograd) than to Morocco: perhaps, had he won, Rommel might have gone north, as Eleanor speculated he might, and helped defeat the Soviet forces defending Stalingrad.

In either case, with access to the Indian Ocean and the Far East, and with unlimited oil supplies, Hitler would have been able to focus all his forces on defeating Russia in 1943 and would have been in a much better position to resist any invasion of France.

Churchill said, in 1940, "What a slender thread the greatest of things can hang by." He said it in reference to the Battle of Britain, and I took it as my title as it applies equally well to the Siege of Malta. One is also reminded of Churchill's refusal not to use prepositions to end sentences: "This is the sort of nonsense up with which I will not put."

Malta really was close to surrender in August 1942; that part of my story is not fictional hyperbole. It really was saved by a convoy—Pedestal in real life, Podium in my story.

Needless to say, the specific events and people I portray are all fictitious, with the exception of certain wartime leaders, to whom I have given dialogue that, I hope, respects their memories and reflects their real views. There was no 505, no MI6-3b, and no Red Tape. I tried to use the names of military operations and Royal Navy ship's names that were not used in World War II; if I have erred, I apologize.

MALTA, 1940 TO 1942

Malta is a small archipelago of islands southeast of Sicily in the Mediterranean Sea. The vast majority of the population lives in and around the capital city of Valletta, a splendid natural harbor on the eastern side of the main island.

The main island is approximately seventeen miles long and nine miles wide. The entire country is about the size of the Isle of Wight and less than half the size of New York City.

Malta has been continuously lived on since 6000 BCE and has some of the oldest known Neolithic sites in Europe, with stone buildings, assumed to be temples, dating back to almost 3500 BCE (a thousand years older than Stonehenge). Malta has its own unique language derived from Arabic, from the era of the Fatimid Caliphate, and from Latin languages (French and Italian) from the subsequent Norman era. The British population during World War II was a relatively thin veneer of colonial, commercial, and naval/military ex-patriates.

As a small but strategically desirable island, Malta's long history was, until recently, a series of occupations by more powerful nations, including the Phoenicians and Carthaginians, the Romans and Greeks, Arab Caliphates, the Normans, the Aragonese, the Knights Templar of St. John, the French, and the British. The British acquired Malta from France in 1807, during the Napoleonic wars, and it remained a British crown colony until gaining its independence in 1964. Malta is now a member of the European Union.

Located between Sicily and Libya, Malta was one of the two or three most important strategic locations in World War II. Like Stalingrad and Iwo Jima, for example, its survival or loss was pivotal to the outcome of the war.

Malta lay at the crossroads of two vital supply routes—the east-west British supply route from Gibraltar to Egypt, and the north-south Axis supply route from Italy to Libya. Whichever side held Malta controlled these supply routes, upon which the future of Africa and the Middle East depended.

The population of Malta in 1942 was approximately two hundred and fifty thousand; it is now approximately five hundred thousand. The year in which *A Slender Thread* is set, 1942, is the only year in recorded history that the number of deaths exceeded the number of births.

Siege of Malta

As soon as Italy entered World War II as a belligerent in June 1940, Mussolini set out to capture Malta. He planned to accomplish this by:

- Siege: starving the garrison and population of food and supplies with the aim of forcing them to surrender.
- Destroying Malta as an air and naval base by an intense bombing campaign so that forces based in Malta could

neither defend British supply convoys nor attack those of
the Axis powers.
- If Malta could be sufficiently beaten down, the island
  would be finished off in a combined air/sea invasion, code
  named Herkules.

Over the two years that the siege lasted, the Axis powers conducted more than three thousand air raids and dropped almost seven
thousand tons of bombs on Valletta alone, making it one of the most-
bombed cities in the world.

However, the island never quite ran out of supplies—although it
came perilously close to doing so—and Malta-based naval and air units
carried out numerous successful attacks on Axis bases and convoys.

Such was the bravery and determination of the people of Malta in
the face of this onslaught that in 1942 King George VI awarded them
Britain's highest civilian award for bravery, the George Cross, a unique
distinction:

> To honour her brave people I award the George Cross
> to the Island Fortress of Malta to bear witness to a her-
> oism and devotion that will long be famous in history.
>   George R.I.
>   15th April 1942

(Although the people of Malta subsequently demanded and
received full independence from the United Kingdom, they chose to
retain this award as part of their flag.)

British defensive operations consisted of defending relief convoys
from Axis attacks and defending Maltese airspace. The balance of
forces shifted back and forth, partly because of diversions of resources
to other fronts. For example, Axis air resources were diverted to the
Russian Front when Hitler launched Barbarossa in June 1941 and to
support the Axis invasions of Greece and Crete.

Although the bulk of the attacks against Malta and the convoys were conducted by the Italians, the absence or presence of the
Luftwaffe seems to have tipped the balances heavily.

The Siege of Malta finally ended at the close of 1942, with the British victory at El Alamein at one end of the Mediterranean and Operation Torch, the Anglo-American invasion of Morocco, at the other.

Malta Convoys

Supply convoys were run to Malta from both Alexandria in Egypt and from Gibraltar. Three main strategies were attempted:

- Convoys of merchant shipping with extensive naval escorts. These included not only military supplies but also food and innumerable other supplies for the civilian population, which became less and less capable of feeding itself as the siege continued and destroyed the island's economy.
- "Club Runs" consisting of high-speed dashes by aircraft carriers to fly off Hurricanes and Spitfires. In 1940, air defenses were almost nonexistent, and it was not until mid-1942, under Park, that the RAF was fully able to defend Malta.
- "Magic Carpet" operations by individual British submarines bringing high-priority supplies, such as aviation fuel.

The Axis powers used four main strategies against the convoys:

- Italian Regia Marina surface warships, including destroyers, cruisers, and battleships (they had no aircraft carriers). Four battleships were badly damaged in a brilliant attack by Royal Navy FAA Swordfish torpedo bombers in the Battle of Taranto in November 1940, much reducing the Italians' ability to interdict British convoys or defend their own.
- Regia Marina MAS (motoscafo armato silurante) boats. These small, high-speed motor torpedo boats achieved remarkable successes, including the sinking of three merchantmen in the Pedestal convoy in August 1942.

- Kriegsmarine U-boats. The German navy deployed a total of sixty U-boats in the Mediterranean in 1941 and 1942. They sunk ninety-five merchant ships and twenty-four naval ships, but all sixty U-boats were lost.
- Italian and German aircraft, primarily bombers supported by fighters. Bombing attacks using conventional, torpedo, and dive-bombers proved to be very effective. Pedestal, for example, was bombed seven times in thirty-six hours.

For long periods between June 1940 and August 1942, the Axis powers were successful in operations against the convoys. Of the thirty-five major convoys over this period, eight failed to deliver any supplies at all, and only two arrived in Malta without losses.

The most famous of these convoys sailed in August 1942 under the code name Pedestal. (I named my fictitious Podium in honor of the men of Pedestal.) Pedestal consisted of seventy-one warships escorting fourteen merchantmen. The Royal Navy had four ships sunk (including an aircraft carrier) and three damaged (including another aircraft carrier). Of the fourteen merchantmen, nine were sunk and three were damaged. The navy had 102 aircraft, of which thirty-four were destroyed. Approximately 550 men died.

Axis forces included twenty-one U-boats, twenty-three MAS boats, and approximately six hundred aircraft.

This convoy included the tanker SS *Ohio*, which was carrying ten thousand tons of fuel. *Ohio*, nicknamed "the ship that wouldn't die," was bombed repeatedly and reached Malta under tow, awash to her gunnels and strapped between two destroyers to hold her up, with two crashed bombers on her decks. She sunk as soon as the vital fuel was pumped out of her. Her civilian captain was awarded the George Cross.

Because of *Ohio*, it could be argued, Park was able to keep his aircraft flying and therefore continue to attack Rommel's supply convoys, denying him the spare parts and fuel he needed and causing him to lose the Second Battle of El Alamein.

Faith, Hope, and Charity

At the very beginning to the Siege of Malta in 1940, when Italy entered the war and began bombing Malta, the only fighters in Malta were a few Gloster Sea Gladiator aircraft that had been delivered, unassembled, to Hal Far (FAA HMS Falcon). Only two or three were operational at any time. The Gladiators flew against vastly superior numbers of Italian aircraft, which were faster than they were, and achieved some successes, although the exact number of victories remains obscure. Hurricanes started to be flown in as of August but in woefully small numbers.

The Gladiators were named (after the event) *Faith, Hope,* and *Charity* and became symbolic of Malta's resistance. *Charity* was shot down in July 1940, and *Hope* was destroyed in February 1941. *Faith* survived and is on display in Malta.

Air Defenses

The air battle over Malta went through several phases as the pendulum of air superiority swung back and forth. Italian bombing efforts were relatively consistent, with hundreds of aircraft flying from bases in Sicily and the toe of Italy for two full years.

The pendulum swung heavily in favor of the Axis powers when the Luftwaffe was able to concentrate on Malta, rather than its competing priorities in Russia, Greece, and Crete. Axis control of Malta's skies reached its pinnacle in March and April of 1942, when they were able to bomb Malta's airfields continuously (dropping sixteen hundred bombs on Luqa in one day, for example) and severely damage the submarine base at Manoel Island, forcing the submarines to submerge all day.

All this neutered Malta as an offensive base for bomber and submarine attacks against Rommel's convoys. The RAF began flying in Spitfires from Club Runs, but almost all were destroyed on arrival. For several days in April, there were no operational Spitfires on Malta at all.

Albert Kesselring reported to Berlin that "there is nothing left to bomb." The determination of the Axis effort against Malta is indicated in the sorties flown. Between 20 March and 28 April 1942, the Axis flew 11,819 sorties against the island and dropped 6,557 tons of bombs (3,150 tons on Valletta).

With Malta's airfields and submarines under siege, Axis convoys were able to reach Rommel without significant losses.

The pendulum swung back when the Club Runs were finally able to deliver a significant number of Spitfires. Axis losses mounted steeply (for example, the Regia Aeronautica and Luftwaffe lost one hundred aircraft over Malta in only two days in May).

Inversely, as the Spitfires recovered control so that Malta's bombers and submarines could reopen their offensive, Rommel's supply convoys immediately suffered increasing losses.

Rommel's Supply Lines and the Second Battle of El Alamein

Most of Rommel's supplies came from Italy, being loaded primarily in Naples. The question was how to get his supplies from there to North Africa. The answer was keeping as far away from Malta, with its submarines and torpedo bombers, as possible. In the months leading up to El Alamein in October 1942, Rommel held all of Tunisia and Libya, giving him ports (from west to east) at Tunis, Tripoli, Benghazi, and Tobruk.

The safest route was from Naples north of Sicily to Tunis, but Tunis was hundreds of miles from the front lines, and all of Rommel's supplies had to be dragged by road or rail. Tripoli was closer to Rommel, but reaching Tripoli required sailing close enough to Malta to be in danger. Benghazi and Tobruk were closest to Rommel, but, to avoid Malta, convoys had to go far north, from Italy to Greece, and then approach Africa from Crete.

These routes were not only vulnerable to attacks from Malta (with Rommel losing a quarter to half of all his supplies in September and October) but also were two or three times as long as the direct routes.

The Second Battle of El Alamein began on 23 October 1942 and lasted until 11 November, resulting in a decisive British victory. It is often said (incorrectly) that before El Alamein, the British never won a battle, and after it the British never lost a battle. Montgomery's Eighth Army had almost twice as many men as Rommel's German/Italian Panzerarmee Afrika, twice as many tanks, almost twice as many artillery pieces, and several times as much fuel, all due, in large part, to RAF and naval forces based in Malta.

Signals Intelligence

Encrypted code breaking played a key role in the Siege of Malta and the Second Battle of El Alamein.

- On the Allied side, the British had managed to break the German military Enigma Code, producing the Ultra decrypted messages. This brilliant achievement was accomplished by Alan Turing and other mathematicians at Bletchley Park in England and has been memorialized in many books and films, most recently in *The Imitation Game*. Depending on the circumstances, the Allies obtained detailed information about their enemy's plans and conditions. Of particular importance in 1942 was Montgomery's access to Rommel's deployments, and the RAF and RN's detailed intelligence about Rommel's supply convoys, allowing a high interception and destruction rate that crippled Rommel's mobility in the weeks leading to El Alamein.
- On the Axis side, the Italians succeeded in breaking the American diplomatic Black Code. Bonner Fellers, the US military attaché in Cairo, used this code to send frequent detailed information to Washington covering British plans, resources, and troop movements. The Italians relayed this information to Rommel, giving him accurate information. The Americans changed their code at the end of June 1942, and Rommel lost the benefit of this source. It is not a coincidence that Rommel's brilliant anticipation of British maneuvers declined in the months

leading up to El Alamein, whereas Montgomery continued to have the benefit of Ultra.

Air-Sea Rescue Service

The RAF Air-Sea Rescue Service (ASRS), famous for the motto "The
sea shall not have them," operated search-and-rescue operations based
at Tal-Vecca, in St. Paul's Bay in northwest Malta, and Kalafrana on
the south coast, adjacent to RAF Hal Far. Between 1940 and 1943, the
air-sea rescue craft operating from Malta rescued 123 downed Allied
airmen, 34 Germans, and 212 Italian aircrew.

Their primary rescue launches were British Power Boat Company
High-Speed Launches Type 2, known as Type 2 HLS. This craft had
a distinctive curved, sloping cabin enclosure that housed the wheelhouse, radio and map rooms, sick bay, and crew's quarters, giving the
Type 2 HLS its nickname, Whaleback. The Whaleback was sixty-three
feet long, had a crew of nine, and was powered by three Napier Lion
W12 engines producing a total of 1,500 horsepower for a top speed of
36 knots. They had "hard chine" planing hulls made of mahogany.

A variety of armaments were used at various stages of the war, ranging from Lewis guns to 20-millimeter Oerlikons. Some Whalebacks
had anti-shrapnel padding on the cabin roof and armor plating for the
crew stations.

Radar Defenses

Like other aspects of its defenses, Malta's radar capabilities evolved
rapidly from 1940 to 1942. By 1942, there were four AM.13/14 units at
Qawra Point at the southern end of St. Paul's Bay, Ghar Lapsi on the
southwest coast near the Ghar Lapsi airfield, and Giordan Lighthouse
in the north of Gozo. The stations looked north towards the main
threats of Sicily and Italy, south and west towards Tunisia and Libya,
and west towards Greece and Crete.

By 1942 Beaufighters had been equipped with airborne AI Mark
VIII radar and were able to provide effective night defenses.

Royal Engineers (Sappers)

The Royal Engineers had their own Maltese militia section, the Malta Fortress Squadron, as well as regular RE units posted to Malta. All RE personnel were known as sappers. One of their most important and dangerous responsibilities was unexploded bomb disposal and search-and-rescue in bomb-damaged buildings. In the two years of the Siege of Malta, these extraordinarily brave men disposed of 7,300 unexploded bombs.

Royal Navy Organization

During World War II, the Royal Navy in Malta was split into two parts.

- Fighting ships were commanded by the flag officer, Malta, who was the admiral in command of HMS St. Angelo. They attacked Axis shipping and convoys. Malta had a powerful surface task force consisting of light cruisers and destroyers, Force K, until the end of 1941, when intense bombing forced it to withdraw, leaving the Tenth Submarine Flotilla as the primary offensive formation. The last cruiser to leave Malta in 1942 was HMS *Penelope*. She was so holed by bomb fragments and shrapnel that she was known as HMS *Pepperpot*. She was sunk by a U-boat in 1944. (I named my WRNS officer Penelope in honor of her crew.)
- Naval installations were commanded by the admiral-superintendent, Malta Dockyard. The navy's docks, wharves, dry docks, and repair facilities were all so severely damaged that they were only partially operational.

Royal Navy U-class Submarines

These British submarines, not to be confused with German U-boats, were "small" two-hundred-foot submarines with a crew of approximately thirty men that formed the core of Malta's Tenth Submarine Flotilla based at HMS Talbot. They carried up to ten torpedoes and had a speed of 10 knots and a range of 4,500 miles.

They provided pivotal defenses for the British convoys attempting to reach Malta, including Pedestal, and pivotal offense against Rommel's supply lines later in 1942. In the years 1941 and 1942, the Tenth Flotilla, which had up to twelve submarines at any one time, sunk more than four hundred thousand tons of Axis shipping.

Women's Services

During World War II, British uniformed women's services were separate from, subservient to, and less well-paid than the regular armed forces. After 1941, service in one of the branches became compulsory for unmarried women in their twenties.

- The Women's Royal Naval Service, WRNS, was a voluntary service fulfilling many noncombatant and logistical support roles. The service expanded to seventy thousand Wrens at the height of the war. The Wrens were amalgamated into the Royal Navy in 1993. Penelope's rank was third officer (one stripe), the most junior rank of an officer.
- The Women's Auxiliary Air Force (WAAF) provided corresponding support services to the RAF and expanded to over 180,000 WAAFs during World War II. The WAAFs were incorporated into the RAF in 1994. Eleanor's rank of wing officer (three stripes) was a senior position.
- Although not featured in this book, other British uniformed women's services included the Auxiliary Territorial Service (ATS), Women's Transport Service (WTS), Women's Voluntary Service (WVS), and the

Women's Land Army, as well as the nursing services. Queen Elizabeth II served in the ATS.

REGIA AERONAUTICA AIRCRAFT

Italian military aircraft from World War II tend to be considered second-rate but were considerably better than their reputations would suggest.

Several aircraft were fundamentally comparable with their German and British equivalents but were plagued with recurring technical issues that were never quite ironed out, perhaps because Italy invested less in its aircraft and had more limited resources. All aircraft have teething problems that take years to overcome. By the time the other major combatants were perfecting their aircraft in 1943 and beyond—the later model Yaks, P51s, Spitfires, and Zeros, etc.—Italy was already out of the war.

The Regia Aeronautica fought in all of Italy's campaigns—even the Battle of Britain. It had some limited successes but was never able to dominate any airspace, perhaps because its resources were spread too thin across too many missions in too many theaters.

The Regia Aeronautica made significant contributions to Axis operations against Malta relief convoys, working in conjunction with the Luftwaffe and the Axis navies—a campaign the Axis came close to winning.

The Regia Aeronautica's longest and most sustained campaign, the Siege of Malta, ended in failure. Malta was bombed thousands of times from June 1940 until October 1942 but was able to defend itself and continue to act as a base of offensive operations. It is reported that the Italian aircrew came to call the Malta run the *rotta della morte*, the "route of death."

CANT Z.1007 Alcione (Kingfisher)

The Z.1007bis was a tri-engine bomber. It had a slim, aerodynamically superior design and was built from laminated wood, resulting in a remarkably fast bomber. This design was derived from earlier flying boats built by CANT. (Like Supermarine, the company that developed the Spitfire, CANT was a seaplane manufacturer.) Unfortunately the Alcione's wooden fabric was easily damaged by weather, and it was significantly underpowered. The 1007 used three engines to develop approximately 2,000 horsepower, whereas the RAF's comparable Beaufort required only two engines to generate the same power. The extra weight of the 1007's third engine was one thousand five hundred pounds.

Fiat CR.42 Falco (Falcon)

The CR.42 was a single-seat sesquiplane fighter—a biplane in which the lower wing was about half the size of the upper—a "one-and-a-half plane." It was compact, robust, and highly maneuverable and could hold its own against Gladiators, Blenheims, and even Hurricanes in the early years of the war. Unfortunately Falchi were dogged by the typical Regia Aeronautica weaknesses of inadequate armament and terrible radios and were gradually switched to ground attack missions.

Almost two thousand of them were built. (These aircraft had also been purchased by Belgium before the war and performed remarkably against the Luftwaffe during the invasion of Belgium in 1940. In the few hours before Belgium collapsed, Falchi managed to shoot down not only Dornier 17 bombers but Me 109s as well.)

My canine protagonist Charlie's first owner was a Belgian pilot who flew a CR.42 in this campaign. His Falco was destroyed, but he managed to escape to England in a tiny Renard R.31 with Charlie sitting on his lap.

Macchi C.202 Folgore (Thunderbolt)

The C.202 was a single-seat fighter somewhat resembling the German Fw 190. It used a version of the DB 601 engine (which powered the Me 109) built by Alfa Romeo. Its performance was superior to the Hurricane IIs and P-40 Tomahawks it encountered, and it could have been competitive with Spitfire Mark Vs had it been able to overcome its enduring vulnerabilities, particularly its lack of firepower (it was never equipped with cannons) and its abysmal radio, which meant that C.202 pilots often flew and fought without any communications.

Savoia-Marchetti SM.79 Sparviero (Sparrowhawk)

The SM.79 was Italy's primary medium bomber, sharing the trimotor design and wooden structures that were common features of Italian aircraft of that time. This aircraft had a distinctive humpbacked profile and was known to its crews as *il gobbo maledetto* (damned hunchback). The SM.79 was used in all Italian theaters as a conventional bomber; it also proved to be effective as a torpedo bomber against Allied shipping.

Junkers Ju 87 B-1 (Stuka)

The Junkers Ju 87 Sturzkampfflugzeug "Stuka" dive-bomber was one of the definitive weapons of World War II, capable of delivering a bomb weighing five hundred pounds with remarkable accuracy while diving at more than 350 miles per hour at an angle greater than 60 degrees. The design had to resist extreme stresses, and the "pull out" maneuver was automated because the pilot might lose consciousness.

The Stukas were greatly feared, and their terror factor was heightened by wailing wind-blown sirens attached to their wings known as *Jericho-Trompetes* (Jericho trumpets), a name taken from the biblical story of Joshua blowing down the walls of Jericho with his trumpet.

Approximately one hundred Stukas were delivered to the Regia Aeronautica in 1940. Italian pilots were trained in Austria and formed 96° Gruppo Bombardamento a Tuffo.

RAF AND FAA AIRCRAFT

The Air Ministry had a tendency to keep the best and most advanced versions of RAF aircraft in England, sending older aircraft to the

Mediterranean and Egypt as hand-me-downs. Given the strategic situation in 1941 and 1942, it would probably have been best to send the very best to the Mediterranean theater of operations (MTO.)

Spitfires, for example, were not strategically vital over Western Europe at that time, because Hitler had sent all his daylight bombers to the Eastern Front, and the western European war was evolving into a campaign of night bombers versus night fighters. In the MTO, by contrast, with its heavy accent on daylight operations, Spitfires were vital.

Unlike the RAF, the Royal Navy's Fleet Air Arm entered the war with no modern monoplane aircraft. Its mainstays were the Gloster Sea Gladiator fighter and the Fairey Swordfish torpedo bomber, both of which performed very well against superior opposition—for example, the famous Swordfish attack on the German battleship *Bismarck* and their brilliant success at Taranto.

In 1942 the FAA had been unable to develop fully successful carrier-based versions of the Hurricane and Spitfire and turned to the Grumman F4F Wildcat, renamed the Martlet, an extraordinarily successful American aircraft that flew in all theaters of war.

Bristol Blenheim

The Blenheim was the predecessor to the Beaufort and Beaufighter. Like many aircraft built in the midthirties, it could not survive contact with the new generation of monoplane fighters such as the Me 109 and the Fw 190. It was, however, robust and reliable, and it was widely used in the Mediterranean until the end of 1942. It was extensively redesigned into the successful Beaufort and Beaufighter, which fought until the end of the war.

Bristol Beaufort

The Beaufort was a two-engine aircraft that proved to be an effective night fighter and torpedo bomber. During the run-up to the Battle of El Alamein, the Beauforts of 39 Squadron, based at Luqa under the command of Patrick Gibbs, sank several key supply ships, including four large tankers. In addition to torpedoes, some Beauforts were also equipped with RP3 rockets, an idea I borrowed for Shaux's Spitfire Mark IXs.

Bristol Beaufighter

The Beaufighter was a heavy fighter derivative of the Beaufort and assumed many of the Beaufort's roles. The Beaufighter was used to escort Beauforts in their attacks on Rommel's convoys and was also used very successfully by the Desert Air Force to support Eighth Army operations.

Consolidated PBY Catalina

The Catalina flying boat was a highly successful multipurpose aircraft built in the United States and obtained by the RAF through the Lend-Lease Act. It had a high wing above the fuselage/hull and was powered by two Twin Wasp engines. The "Cat" had blister observation stations on each side that could also serve as gun platforms.

Fairey Swordfish

The Swordfish was a two-seater biplane torpedo bomber introduced in 1935. Although made obsolete by monoplanes, the Swordfish had spectacular successes, including the sinking of three Italian battle-ships at Taranto in 1940 and damaging the *Bismarck* in 1941.

Gloster Gladiator

The Sea Gladiator was a single-seat fighter. Like the Swordfish and the Fiat CR.42 *Falco* (Falcon), the Gladiator had the disadvantage of being an obsolescent biplane just when monoplanes were taking over. Swordfish and Falcons fought on equal terms over the desert in 1941.

(See also the notes on *Faith*, *Hope*, and *Charity*, above.)

Grumman F4F Martlet (Wildcat)

The Martlet was the Fleet Air Arm version of the Grumman F4F Wildcat. It was fully equipped for carrier operations, and its Sto-Wing folding wing design meant that it could be carried in large numbers and fit on small elevators and was effective as a convoy defense aircraft in the Mediterranean in 1942 when the naval versions of the Spitfire and the Hurricane were encountering difficulties. The Sto-Wing was designed by Leroy Grumman himself. It is said that he used paper clips stuck into a soap eraser to discover the exact pivot point that made the Sto-Wing possible. (He also invented retractable undercarriages in 1932.)

Wildcats were very successful in US navy operations in the Pacific, even though Zeros were faster and more maneuverable.

Hawker Hurricane Mark IIB

The Hurricane suffers from being in the shade of the iconic Spitfire, but it was a highly successful aircraft that shot down far more aircraft than the Spitfire did during the Battle of Britain. It was the principal fighter over Malta until mid-1942 and is therefore the primary reason that Malta was able to survive during that period. It was also the mainstay of the Desert Air Force and the primary reason that Rommel was never able to enjoy air superiority. Some DAF Hurricanes were equipped with early versions of rockets.

Supermarine Spitfire Mark V

The iconic Spitfire was developed continuously throughout the war. The final version was the Mark XXIV (Mark 24), and there were numerous additional specialized variations.

The primary fighters in the Mediterranean in 1942 were Spitfire Mark Vc/Trop (Mark 5) and Hurricane Mark IIB/Trop. ("Trop" for "Tropical" were versions modified for hot weather conditions.)

Supermarine Spitfire Mark IX

There were no Mark IX (Mark 9) Spitfires in Malta in 1942. In this fictional story, a shipment of Mark IXs was sent to Gibraltar in error instead of Mark V Trops. (All the other aircraft I describe really were there at the time in 1942.) I chose to include this aircraft for the following reasons:

- It was a highly successful aircraft that could compete with the Luftwaffe Fw 190.
- The Air Ministry tended to keep its most advanced aircraft in England, sending soon-to-be obsolete Spitfire Mark Vs and Hurricane Mark IIs to the Mediterranean. (It similarly short-changed RAF units in Asia.) One can argue that, in 1942, the Air Ministry should have put its best aircraft in the most critical theaters. The Desert Air Force, although successful, was a ragtag collection of whatever was available with, for example, slow bombers acting as fighter escorts.
- Spitfires were never developed as long-range fighters like the American P-51s that escorted B-17s to Germany. This was, in some ways, a curious omission. There is an interesting exploration of the Spitfire's long-range potential by Paul Stoddart written for the Royal Aeronautical Society.
- The control reversal effect I describe really existed in a number of well-known aircraft, starting with the Wright brothers. In real life, the effect occurred in Spitfires at

the very high speed of 580 miles per hour. An interesting contemporary aeroelasticity challenge is found in the blades of very large wind turbines.

- Spitfires were never fitted with rockets, although contemporary Hurricanes were. Park did, however, install bomb racks on some Spitfire Vs.

Aero Engines

One of the most important subtexts of the war was the dramatic advancement and improvement of aero engines and the extraordinary range of the applications to which the most successful were put. Those mentioned in this story include:

- **Napier Lion W12:** This venerable and versatile engine dated from 1917 and powered many successful aircraft, powerboats, and racing cars. It had twelve cylinders arranged in three separate banks of four cylinders driving a single common crankshaft, termed a "W," although better envisioned as an "broad arrow," as my Miller said. The Lion powered 160 types of aircraft, several world speed record racing cars, and several successful powerboats, including the British Power Boat Company Type Two 63 ft. HSL—the Whaleback.
- **Pratt and Whitney R 1830 Twin Wasp:** The Twin Wasp was the most-produced aero engine in history, with more than one hundred and seventy thousand built. It was a fourteen-cylinder air-cooled radial engine with two banks of seven cylinders. It powered many of the most successful aircraft in World War II, including the Grumman F4F, the Douglas DC3 and C47, the Consolidated PBY Catalina, and the Boeing B24 Liberator.
- **Rolls-Royce Mercury V12:** Perhaps the most famous of all liquid-cooled engines, one hundred and fifty thousand Mercuries were built, including fifty thousand built by Packard in Detroit under license from Rolls-Royce.

Mercuries powered several iconic aircraft, including the British Lancasters, Mosquitos, Hurricanes, and Spitfires, and the US P51 Mustang. The first prototype developed 700 horsepower; the late-production model Merlin 131/132 developed over 2,000 horsepower.

HISTORICAL FIGURES

Lord Gort

John Vereker, Sixth Viscount Gort, was a distinguished British soldier. In World War I, he was awarded the Victoria Cross for his gallantry in the trenches and was also awarded the Distinguished Service Order three times. During the interwar years, he rose to be chief of the Imperial General Staff, the professional head of the army.

He took command of the British Expeditionary Force at the outbreak of war in 1939 and was therefore in charge during the collapse of the army and the evacuation at Dunkirk and the subsequent surrender of France. This tarnished his career, and for the remainder of the war, he was given administrative positions in outposts: first Gibraltar, then Malta, and finally the Palestinian Mandate.

He was a popular governor of Malta during very difficult circumstances. However, he believed that he had been let down by the RAF in 1940 (by Dowding and Park), and in Malta he opposed Park's use of RAF resources for anything other than defense. In fact, it was Park's switch to aggressive tactics that cleared the skies above Malta and starved Rommel of the supplies he needed.

Harry Hopkins

Harry Hopkins was President Roosevelt's closest aide and advisor during the Depression and World War II—so close an aide that he actually moved into the White House and lived there during the war. He was also Roosevelt's emissary to Churchill, with whom he enjoyed

a very strong relationship. Hopkins suffered from stomach cancer and
was sick for much of the war; he died in 1946.

Keith Park

Keith Park, a New Zealander, was a successful fighter pilot in World
War I and was appointed to 11 Group, Fighter Command, shortly
before the beginning of the Battle of Britain in 1940. Following that
brilliant success, he fell out of political favor and was sidelined until
1942, when he was appointed first to the defense of the Nile Delta and
then to AHQ Malta.

It is true that he benefitted from the arrival of supplies of Spitfires
to replace outmatched Hurricanes, which allowed him to establish air
superiority over Malta for the first time. But it is also true that he completely reorganized RAF resources into the dominant air power in the
mid-Mediterranean, starving Rommel of supplies and setting the stage
for his defeat in North Africa. Park's Malta subsequently became the
principal air base for the Allied invasion of Sicily in 1943.

It is often said that history repeats itself. Park's principal opponent
in the Battle of Britain was Albert Kesselring's Luftflotte II, whom he
defeated again in the Malta campaign.

Others Mentioned

- **Winston Churchill** needs no introduction. I am grateful
  to him for the quotations I borrowed in naming the three
  books in this series, as well as for saving the world from
  fascism.
- **Dwight D. Eisenhower** was Supreme Commander Allied
  Forces HQ in 1942 and led the Operation Torch landings
  in North Africa. He subsequently commanded the Allied
  invasions of Sicily, Italy, and Normandy. He became the
  first commander of NATO and the thirty-fourth president of the United States in 1953.

- Generalfeldmarschall **Albert Kesselring** was the commander of all German forces in the Mediterranean region, as Oberbefehlshaber Süd—Commander-in-Chief South. Until mid-1942, he led a successful siege against Malta and provided his subordinate Rommel with adequate supply lines from Italy to the Afrika Korps. In mid-1942, however, the arrival in Malta of Keith Park and a steadily increasing number of Spitfires changed the balance of forces over the island. Kesselring lost any chance of air superiority over the Mediterranean, resulting in the survival of Malta and a severe reduction in the supplies reaching Rommel. It is important to note that Kesselring had been Park's principal opponent during the Battle of Britain, and it is therefore fair to say that Park beat him twice.
- **General George C. Marshall** was the US Army chief of staff during World War II. Following the war, he was secretary of state. He authored the Marshall Plan, for which he was awarded the Nobel Peace Prize. He opposed the Plan for Operation Torch, like my fictional Eleanor, favoring a direct invasion of Europe.
- Lieutenant-General **Bernard Montgomery** took over command of the British Eighth Army in August 1942 and prepared for a battle against Rommel, which took place at El Alamein in October and November 1942 and resulted in a decisive British victory. He subsequently led, under Eisenhower's overall command, British forces in the invasions of Sicily, Italy, and Normandy. Park's Maltese squadrons played a key part in his victory by destroying much of Rommel's supplies. Indeed, the sinking of two tankers shortly before the start of the Second Battle of El Alamein left Rommel's tanks with only two or three days of fuel.
- Generalleutnant **Erwin Rommel, the "Desert Fox,"** was the commander of the Afrika Korps from February 1941 until its defeat in 1943. Generally considered to be the ablest battlefield commander in the German army, he enjoyed great success until British air attacks against his

supply convoys cut his supplies by seventy percent. In addition, he fell ill and flew home to Germany to recover and only returned to Africa after the Battle of El Alamein had actually started. In 1944 he was part of Operation Valkyrie, the conspiracy to kill Hitler, although his exact involvement is not clear. After the plot's failure, he was permitted to commit suicide rather than face charges in court.

- Air Chief Marshall **Sir Arthur Tedder** was Park's commander in 1942 as AOC-in-C Middle East Command. He subsequently became Eisenhower's deputy as deputy supreme Allied commander for the D-Day invasion of Normandy. If my fictional Eleanor had returned to her strategic planning role, she would have worked closely with him.

Notable Malta Airmen and Squadrons

I have not attempted to weave any contemporary RAF pilots or squadrons into this story, because I knew I could never do them justice, and it would require several books to even try. However, these are some names that are very worthy of investigation:

- **W/C Patrick Gibbs,** DSO, DFC and bar, 39 Squadron, Beaufort torpedo bombers
- **F/L George "Buzz" Beurling**, DSO, DFC, DFM and bar, 249 Squadron, Spitfire, credited with shooting down twenty-seven Axis aircraft in fourteen days
- **W/C Adrian "Warby" Warburton**, DSO and bar, DFC and two bars, 341 Flight, photoreconnaissance

I cannot omit two great submarine commanders:

- **L/C Malcolm Wanklyn,** VC, DSO and two bars, HMS *Upholder*
- **L/C Alastair Mars,** DSO, DSC and Bar, HMS *Unbroken*

REFERENCES

Alfred Lord Tennyson

"The Charge of the Light Brigade"
> *Cannon to right of them,*
> *Cannon to left of them,*
> *Cannon in front of them*
> *Volley'd and thunder'd;*
> *Storm'd at with shot and shell,*
> *Boldly they rode and well,*
> *Into the jaws of Death,*
> *Into the mouth of hell*
> *Rode the six hundred.*

"The Eagle"
> *He clasps the crag with crooked hands;*
> *Close to the sun in lonely lands,*
> *Ring'd with the azure world, he stands.*
>
>
> *The wrinkled sea beneath him crawls;*
> *He watches from his mountain walls,*
> *And like a thunderbolt he falls.*

"Mariana in the Moated Grange"
> *She only said, "My life is dreary,*
> *He cometh not," she said;*
> *She said, "I am aweary, aweary,*
> *I would that I were dead!"*

King James Bible

Genesis 4:8
And Cain talked with Abel his brother: and it came to pass, when they were in the field, that Cain rose up against Abel his brother, and slew him.

2 Kings 2:11
And it came to pass, as they still went on, and talked, that, behold, there appeared a chariot of fire, and horses of fire, and parted them both asunder; and Elijah went up by a whirlwind into heaven.

Joshua 6:5
And it shall come to pass, that when they make a long blast with the ram's horn, and when ye hear the sound of the trumpet, all the people shall shout with a great shout; and the wall of the city shall fall down flat . . .

Deuteronomy 25:5
If brethren dwell together, and one of them die, and have no child, the wife of the dead shall not marry without unto a stranger: her husband's brother shall go in unto her, and take her to him to wife, and perform the duty of an husband's brother unto her.

Luke 6:37
Judge not, and ye shall not be judged: condemn not, and ye shall not be condemned: forgive, and ye shall be forgiven.

Luke 10:30
And Jesus answering said, A certain man went down from Jerusalem to Jericho, and fell among thieves, which stripped him of his raiment, and wounded him, and departed, leaving him half dead.

1 Corinthians 13:13
And now abideth faith, hope, charity, these three; but the greatest of these is charity.

Romans 11:33
O the depth of the riches both of the wisdom and knowledge of God! How unsearchable are his judgments, and his ways past finding out!

William Cowper

Hymn based on Romans 11:33

> God moves in a mysterious way
> His wonders to perform;
> He plants His footsteps in the sea
> And rides upon the storm.

William Butler Yeats

"An Irish Airman Foresees his Death"

> I know that I shall meet my fate
> Somewhere among the clouds above;
> Those that I fight I do not hate,
> Those that I guard I do not love;
> My country is Kiltartan Cross,
> My countrymen Kiltartan's poor,
> No likely end could bring them loss
> Or leave them happier than before.
> Nor law, nor duty bade me fight,
> Nor public men, nor cheering crowds,
> A lonely impulse of delight
> Drove to this tumult in the clouds;
> I balanced all, brought all to mind,
> The years to come seemed waste of breath,
> A waste of breath the years behind
> In balance with this life, this death.

William Shakespeare

Henry V, Act II, Scene III

> But when the blast of war blows in our ears,
> Then imitate the action of the tiger;
> Stiffen the sinews, summon up the blood,
> Disguise fair nature with hard-favour'd rage;

Henry Wadsworth Longfellow

"Retribution"

> *"Though the mills of God grind slowly, yet they*
> *grind exceeding small;*
> *Though with patience He stands waiting, with*
> *exactness grinds He all."*

Plato

The Republic

Plato envisioned a group of people imprisoned in a cave, facing a wall. Behind them is a fire with figures in front of it. The people cannot look back. They look forward and see the shadows thrown on the wall by the people behind them. Having no other knowledge, they assume the shadows are real. Plato uses this allegory to suggest that what we perceive as real is not actual reality.

BIBLIOGRAPHY

Many books have been written about the Siege of Malta, some very good and some less so. This is not meant to be a comprehensive bibliography but just a few books my readers might choose to sample. They are all nonfiction, except for *The Ship*, a story about a convoy, written by the incomparable C. S. Forrester.

- Ian Cameron: *Red Duster, White Ensign*
- C. S. Forrester: *The Ship*
- Max Hastings: *Operation Pedestal: The Fleet That Battled to Malta, 1942*
- Alan Levine: *The War Against Rommel's Supply Lines, 1942–43*
- Alastair Mars: *Unbroken: The Story of a Submarine*
- Vincent Orange: *Park*
- Peter Smith: *Pedestal: The Malta Convoy of August 1942*
- Paul Williams: *Malta: Island Under Siege*

ABOUT THE AUTHOR

John Rhodes is the award-winning author of the Second World War Breaking Point series, and of the Thomas Ford cozy detective series. Rhodes graduated from Cambridge University with an MA in History. His focus on World War II stems from his earliest memories—he grew up in London where, he says, the shells of bombed-out buildings "served as our adventure playgrounds." He is currently working on the next book in the Breaking Point series, and he blogs regularly at johnrhodesbooks.com.

Made in the USA
Monee, IL
17 April 2022

94670934R00177